I0752737

IMAGES
of America

HAZARD
PERRY COUNTY

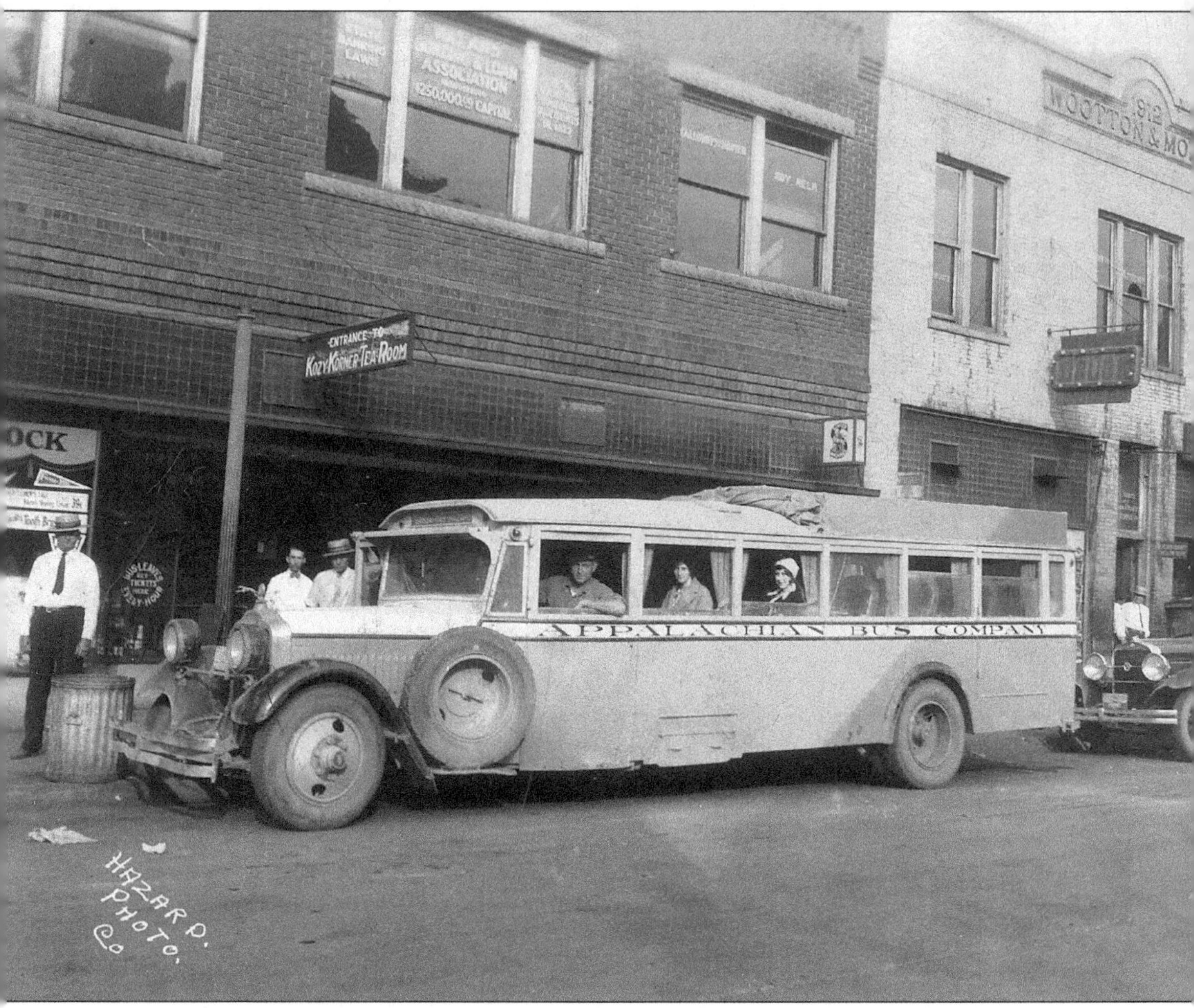

The Appalachian Bus Company carried passengers from Lexington to the Eastern Kentucky coalfields in the 1930s. Northbound buses leaving Hazard turned left on Fleet Street (now Lovern Street) and left on High Street.

Cover Photo: Walking the railroad tracks after train transportation arrived was an important part of the social scene in Hazard, indicated by these well-dressed young people. At the time this photograph was taken, it cost a penny per person to cross the river on the "Penny Bridge" stretching from Hazard to the railroad tracks.

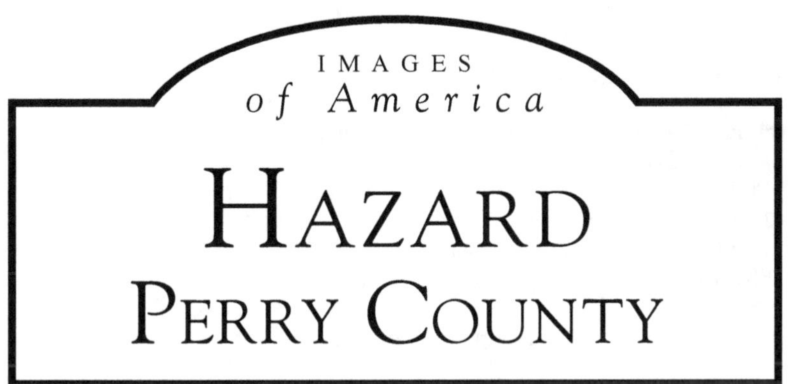

Martha Hall Quigley

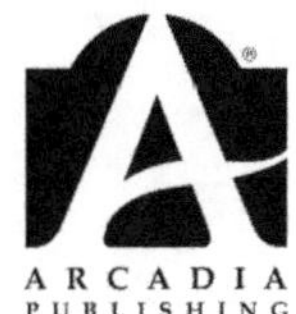

ISBN 978-1-5316-0370-0

Published by Arcadia Publishing
Charleston, South Carolina

Library of Congress Catalog Card Number: 00-103180

For all general information contact Arcadia Publishing at:
Telephone 843-853-2070
Fax 843-853-0044
E-mail: sales@arcadiapublishing.com
For customer service and orders:
Toll-Free 1-888-313-2665

Visit us on the Internet at www.arcadiapublishing.com

ACKNOWLEDGMENTS

From 1945 through 1965, Hal Cooner lived in Hazard, photographing every event and documenting the growth and development of the town. In an interview in 1995 he spoke of losing a large amount of his work in the 1957 flood, but many of his pictures had been saved by individuals in albums, trunks, closets, and drawers all over town. He died on July 5, 1998, leaving as his legacy thousands of images of Hazard and Perry County. No pictorial of Hazard would be complete without his photographs. His portraiture was exhibited in Mexico City at the Palace of Art; the International Exhibit of Photographic Art in Bath, England; the Second International Exhibition of Photographic Art in Helsinki, Finland; and seven other exhibits in the U.S. He is fondly remembered by students in the Hazard schools for the yearly class pictures and the yearbook pictures he took and his body of work is one of the town's treasures.

Contents

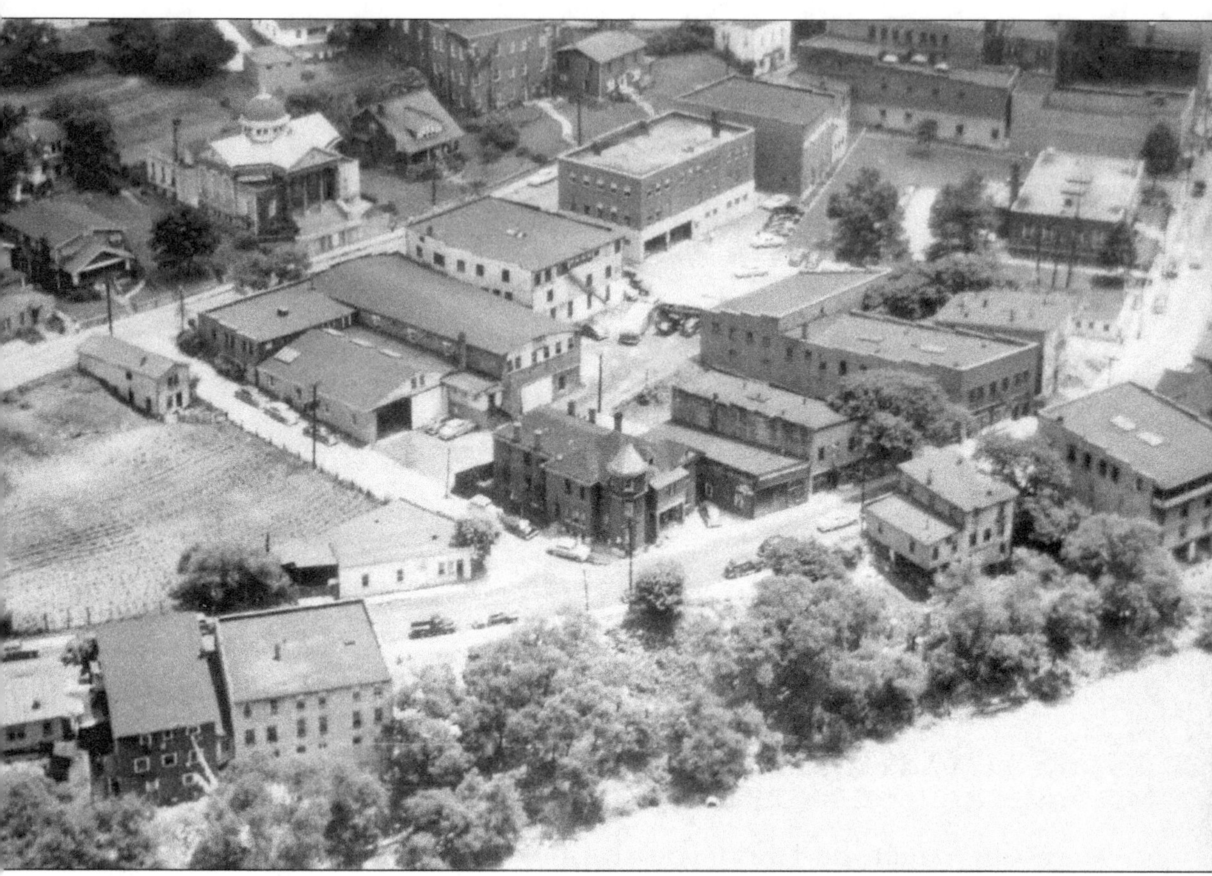

This photograph, of the north end of Main Street, shows that early in the 1950s farmland (on the left) was still being cultivated close to downtown Hazard. The small, long-frame structure on the corner adjacent to the farmland is Mary Ann Combs' Millinery Shop. The back of First Presbyterian Church is in the upper middle. Across from the Bowman Memorial Methodist Church on High Street, from left to right, are the Star Apartments, the bowling alley, Taulbee Furniture Store, and the Kentucky Power Company. The castle-like building near the center of the picture is the Perry County jail. The triangular building across from the jail is Homer Eversole's Sterling Dry Cleaners. To the right of the jail are the Rachel Tye Baker Stores and Boarding House. The post office building is visible on the right. On the river side of Main Street, the first building on the left, beside the house, is the *Hazard Plaindealer* newspaper office. Next door to the paper is Tony Hall's store. The small one-story building attached to the two-story building is Gene Fields Barber Shop. The large building by the river on the right is the Piggley Wiggley.

INTRODUCTION

The purpose of this book is to feature photographs from the collection of the Bobby Davis Museum and Park. The images do not document the whole history of Hazard, Perry County. However, the photograph collection covers a wide spectrum, particularly from the 1910s to the 1950s.

The community has shown great interest in the museum from its inception. Most amazingly, people from the community have donated photos from their family collections to demonstrate interest and support for the museum.

The family of John Kinner donated his photographs and negatives of the area to the museum in 1992. The museum published the book *1911–1913: Years of Change* containing his work, in celebration of the Kentucky Bicentennial. His images depicting the coming of the railroad are found on walls all over Hazard.

Lawrence Davis, who built Bobby Davis Park after the end of World War II, established the museum in 1983. An experienced photographer, he took hundreds of photographs in Hazard, Perry County, locations near his Florida homes, and around the world on his many travels with his wife, Hazel Eversole Davis. His photographs of Hazard and Perry County also reside in the museum.

Mr. Davis built the park in memory of his son, Robert Oren Davis, who died in Germany on July 13, 1945, while serving our country in World War II. The design of the park is contemplative, providing benches and gardens for visitors to use for relaxation while they enjoy the beauty of the mountain scenery. The local history museum is the main focus of the park. The years have taken Bobby Davis Park through many transitions, but Lawrence Davis' remarkable design still remains.

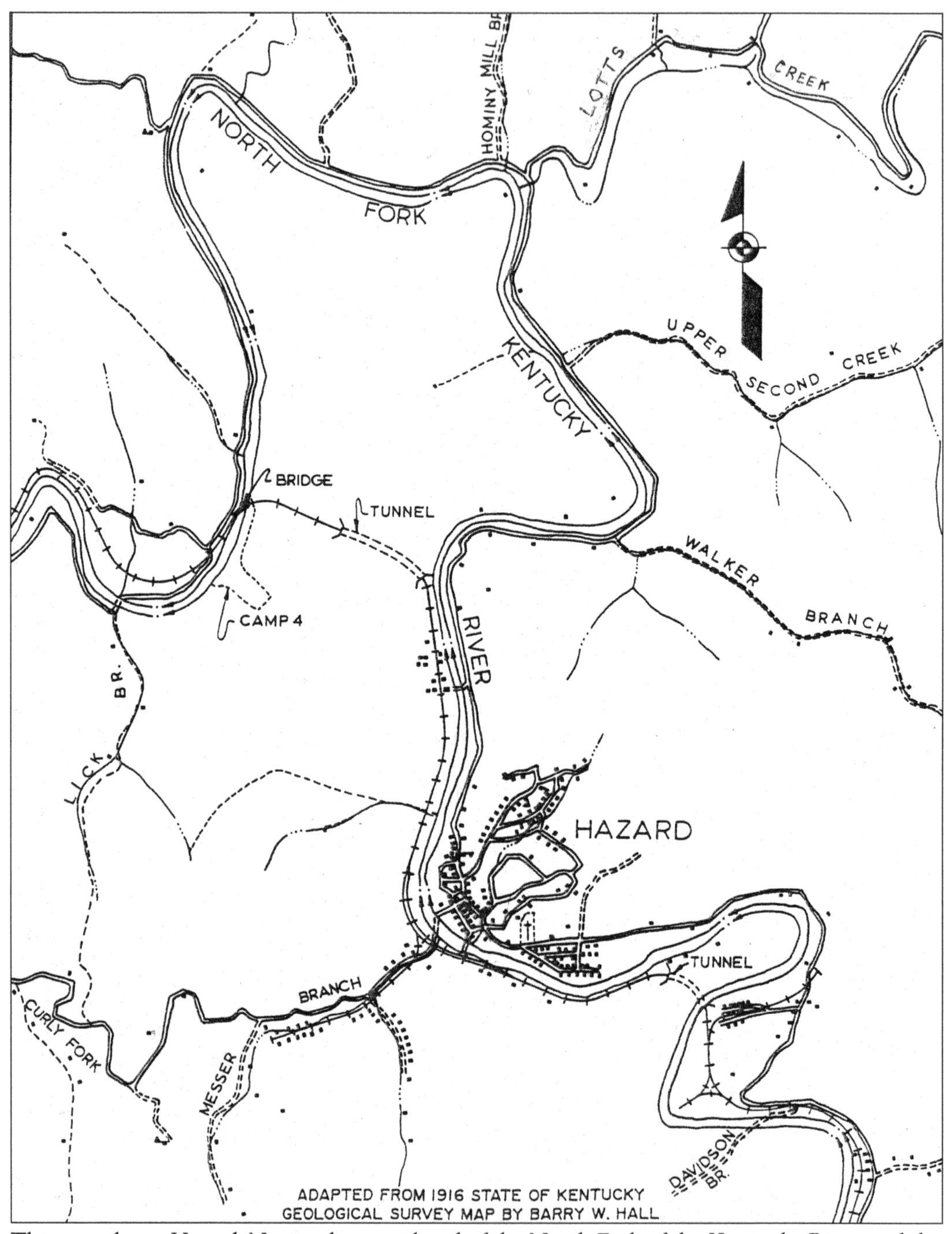

This map shows Hazard. Notice the great bend of the North Fork of the Kentucky River and the roads evident after the coming of the railroad.

One

Some Old Days in Hazard Town

In the late 1700s Elijah Combs and a slave left Virginia, on foot. They found the North Fork of the Kentucky River and followed it until they came to a small salt lick. They built an "improver's cabin" and walked back to Virginia to get Elijah's wife, Sarah. Elijah and Sarah raised their family on this location that he selected by the river. In 1821 the state established a county, named for Oliver Hazard Perry. Elijah's original homestead became the county seat.

Josiah H. Combs proclaimed the courageous and creative nature of the Perry County settlers in this portion of his poem, "The Pioneers of Perry."

No inn or tavern greets them in the wild,
They eat wild game, each father, mother, child;
No music greets their weary ears by night,
Except the lonely screech owl in its fright.
They braved the weather, tempest and the cry
Of savage Indian whom they durst defy,
And traveled ever onward in their quest
Of land and forest, and of happiness.

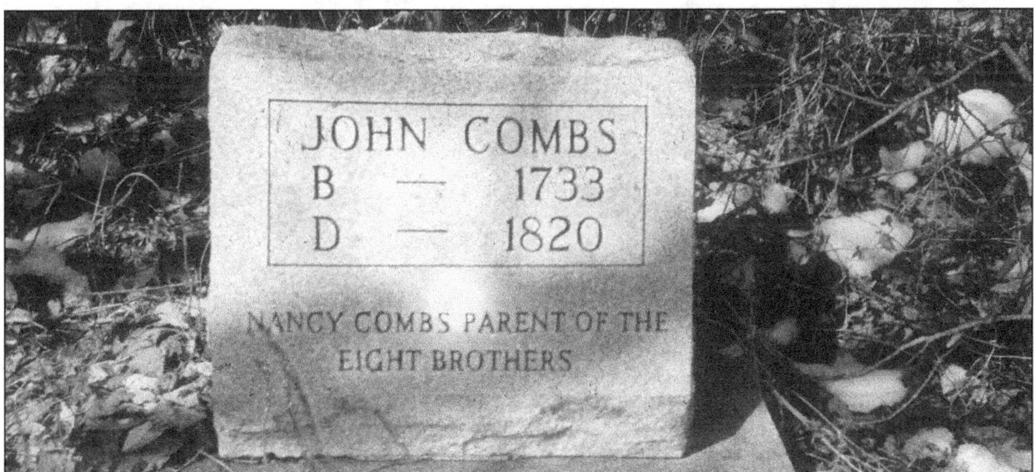

The grave of John Combs and Nancy Combs is several miles south of Hazard. They were the parents of Elijah Combs, the first settler and founder of Perry County. Elijah came to Kentucky in 1795, and his parents and seven brothers followed. Perry County is known as the "Combs capitol of the world." Families followed with the names Cornett, Eversole, Hall, Campbell, Smith, Duff, Ison, Baker, and others.

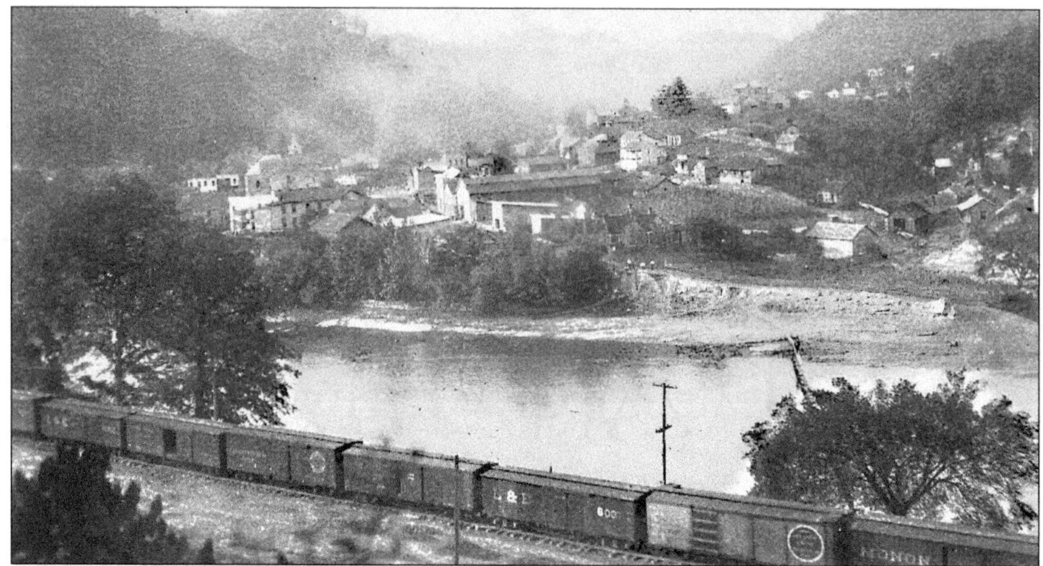

A description of Elijah Combs' "Old Log Fort" was passed down by word of mouth. He finished the two-story, 40-by-60-foot log cabin on the river around 1796. Elijah's family occupied one side of the first floor, opposite a tavern. There was an inn upstairs. The trustees of the town held court in Elijah's tavern until they built a courthouse in 1836. Elijah operated the tavern until 1850. The "Old Log Fort" stood until shortly after 1900 on the empty lot up from the end of the walking bridge in this picture, *c.* 1913. (See another photo of the walking bridge on p. 31.)

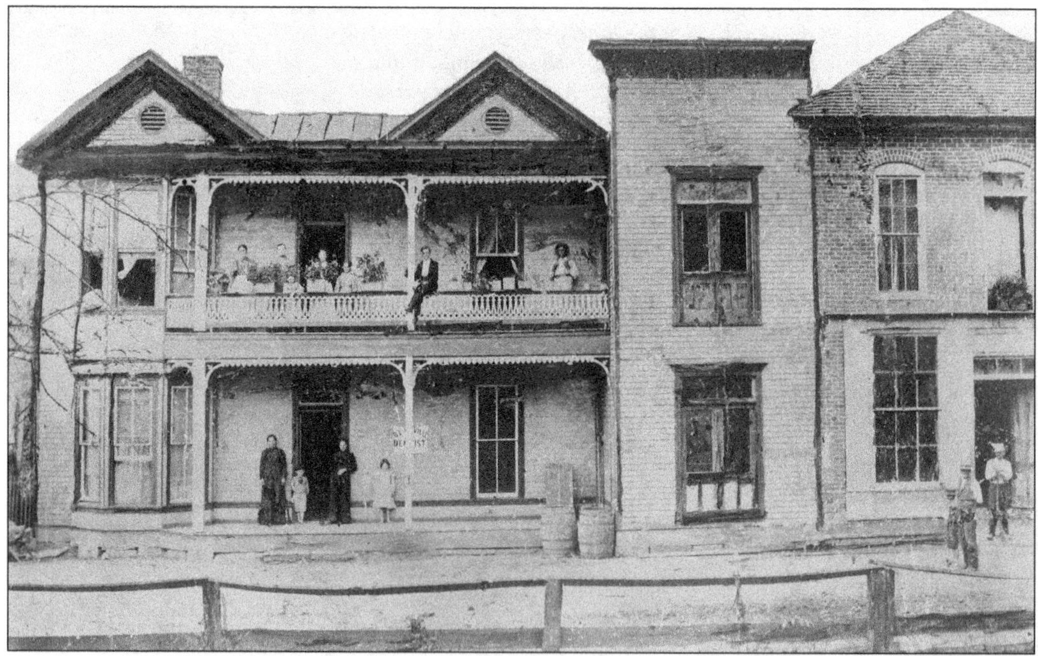

One of the early frame buildings on Main Street in the late 1800s was the Davis Hotel (on the left). Rev. A.S. Petrey was staying at this hotel when townspeople came and appealed to him to establish a Baptist church. Fulton French, the adversary of Joe Eversole in the French and Eversole Feud, stayed in the middle building during the Battle of Hazard in 1889. The entrance to the middle building is behind the barrels.

On August 27, 1898, at the request of Dr. R.R. Baker and Pearl Combs, Rev. A.S. Petrey organized the First Missionary Baptist Church of Hazard. Immediately, Reverend Petrey and others began cutting timber to build the church on land secured from Polly Ann Combs and her family. The new congregation finished their church building in 1899. Tragically, it burned in 1910.

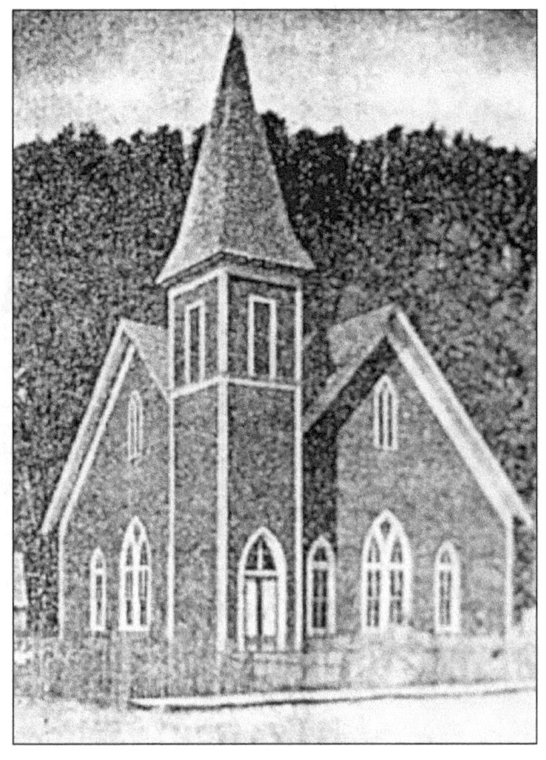

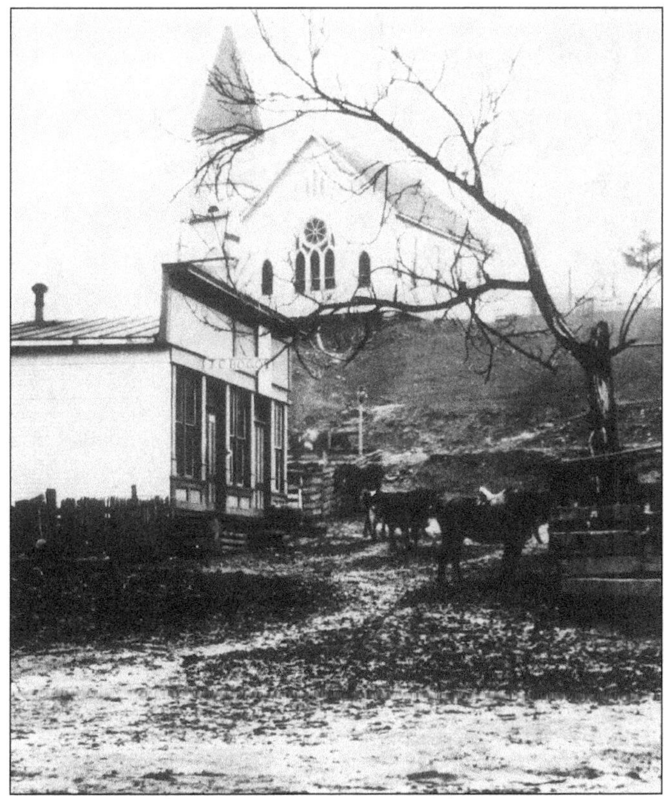

The Presbyterian congregation built the First Presbyterian Church in 1895. The church stood on the hill overlooking High Street, above J.C. Boggs' store. A big wind blew it down on March 22, 1904. Boggs' customers knew him to be the tightest man in town. He counted out one coffee bean at a time. The overturned barrel in the picture was there to trip anyone who might try to rob him and make a fast getaway. Others tripped over it too. (Courtesy of the Special Collections Library, Alice Lloyd College.)

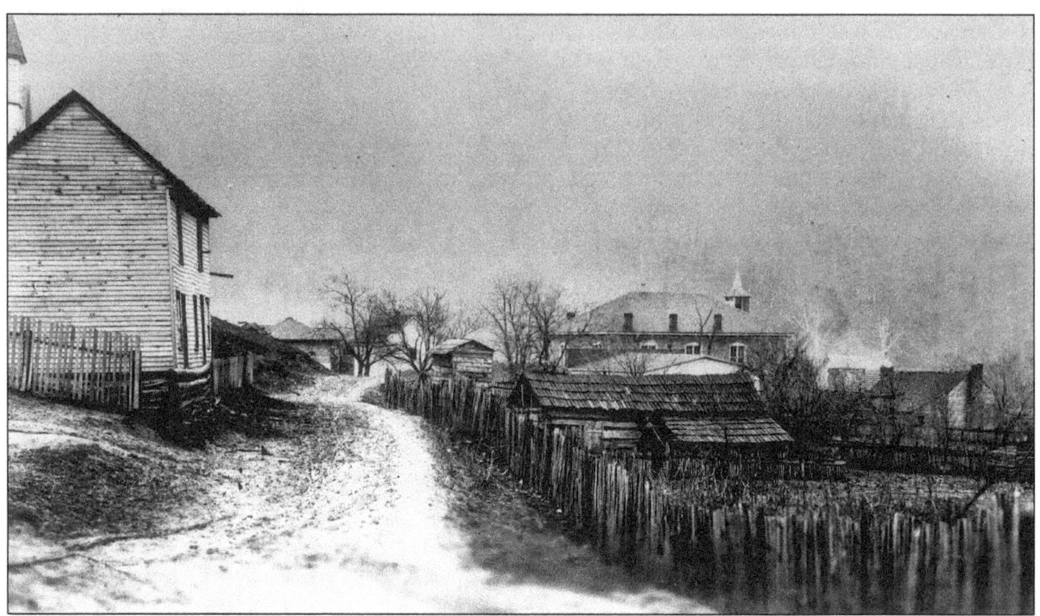
The view of this photograph is looking south on High Street. The log house on the right is the old home of Judge Josiah H. Combs. The hip-roof building with a spire is the fourth Perry County Court House, which was built in 1886. (Courtesy of the Special Collections Library, Alice Lloyd College.)

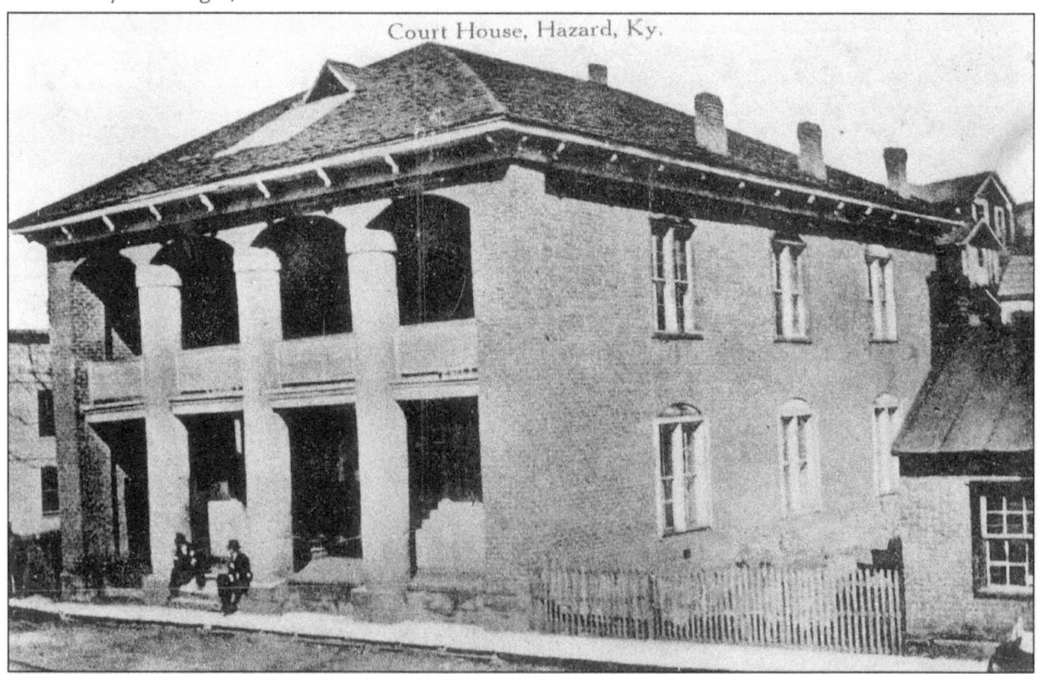

Lightning struck the spire of the Perry County Court House on August 28, 1903. It was apparently attracted to the gun on Johnny Baker's hip as he stood inside, directly under the tower. Both Baker and his dog died. County Judge Cash Eversole sat in his office writing with a metal-tipped pen. St. Elmo's fire danced across his desk. The scorched steeple was removed and the opening was covered.

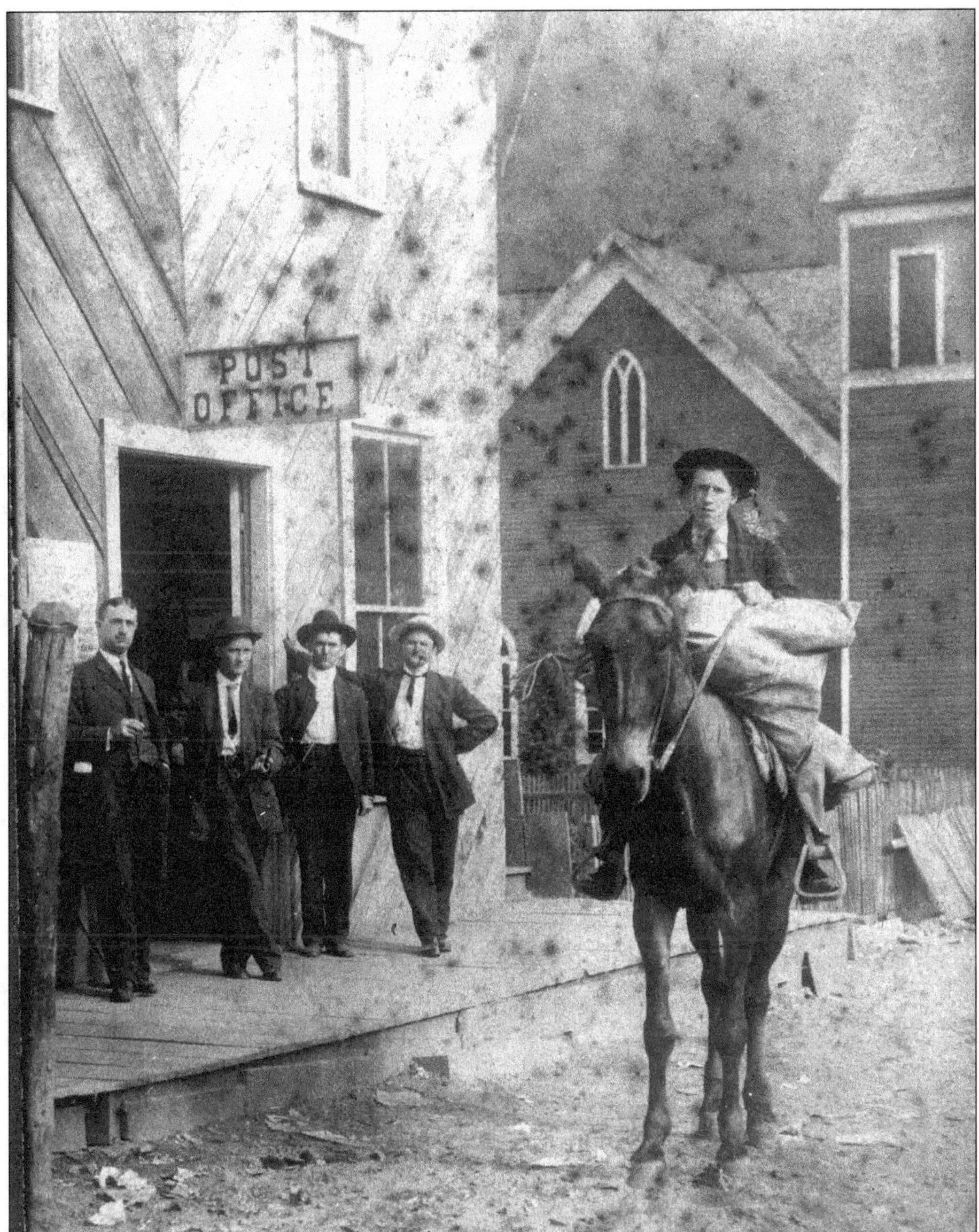

The mail carrier with his bags full stopped for the photographer in front of the Hazard Post Office and Baptist church (see p. 11). Every family in town had their own mailbox. Townspeople had to come to the post office to get their mail. When there was not enough room in the post office for outgoing mail the sacks were piled out front. The pigs that wandered on Main Street would sleep on the bags of mail. One postmaster liked to sit out front and shoot at squirrels and birds. Of course, this made it hard for people to come to the post office for their mail. (Courtesy of the Special Collections Library, Alice Lloyd College.)

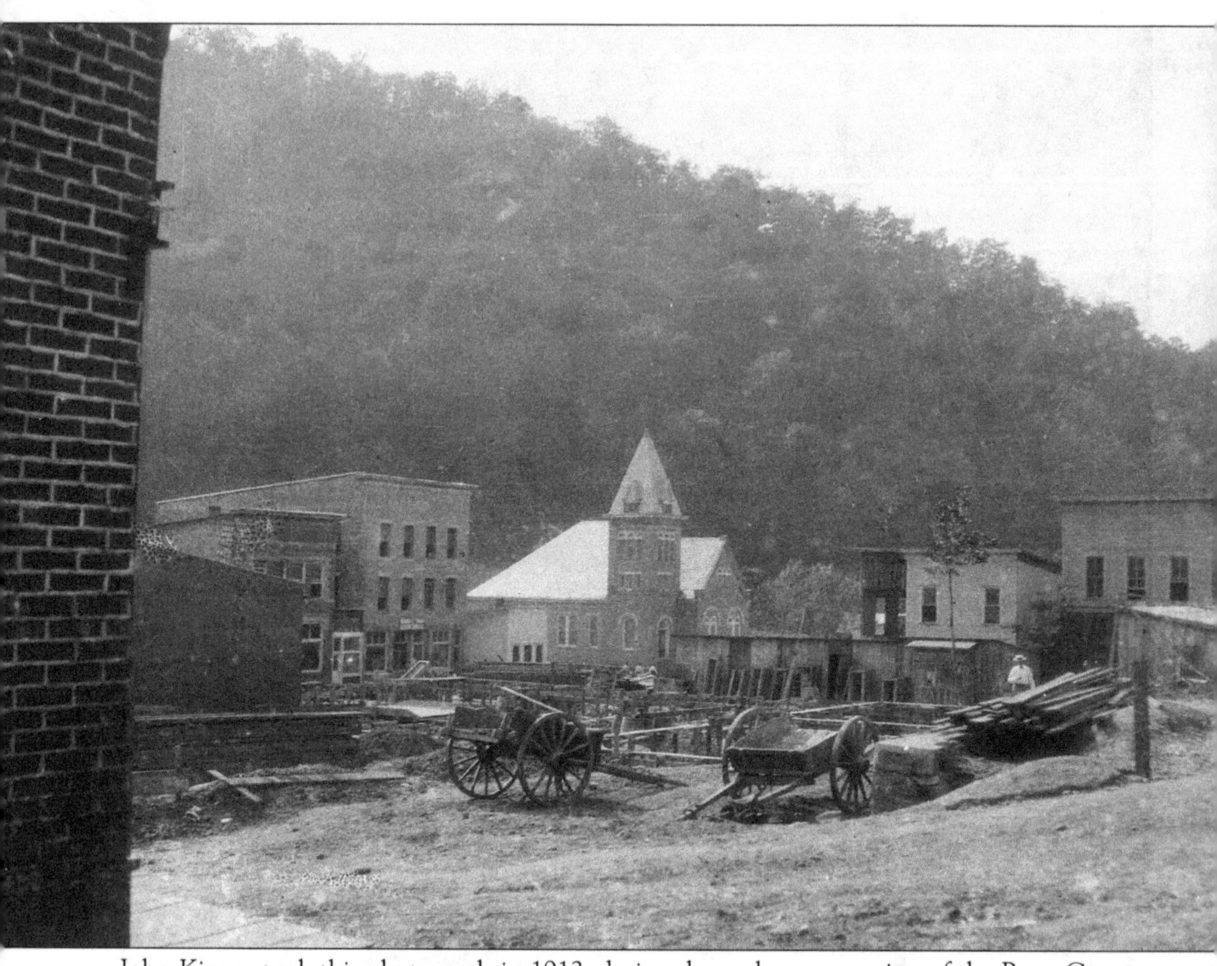

John Kinner took this photograph in 1912, during the early construction of the Perry County Court House. The structures on the right were later torn down to make way for the Austin Fields Building—the Beaumont Hotel. The First National Bank is partially obscured. The Professor S.A.D. Jones Building is located between the bank and the First Baptist Church. The Jones Building housed the fiscal court while the courthouse was being constructed.

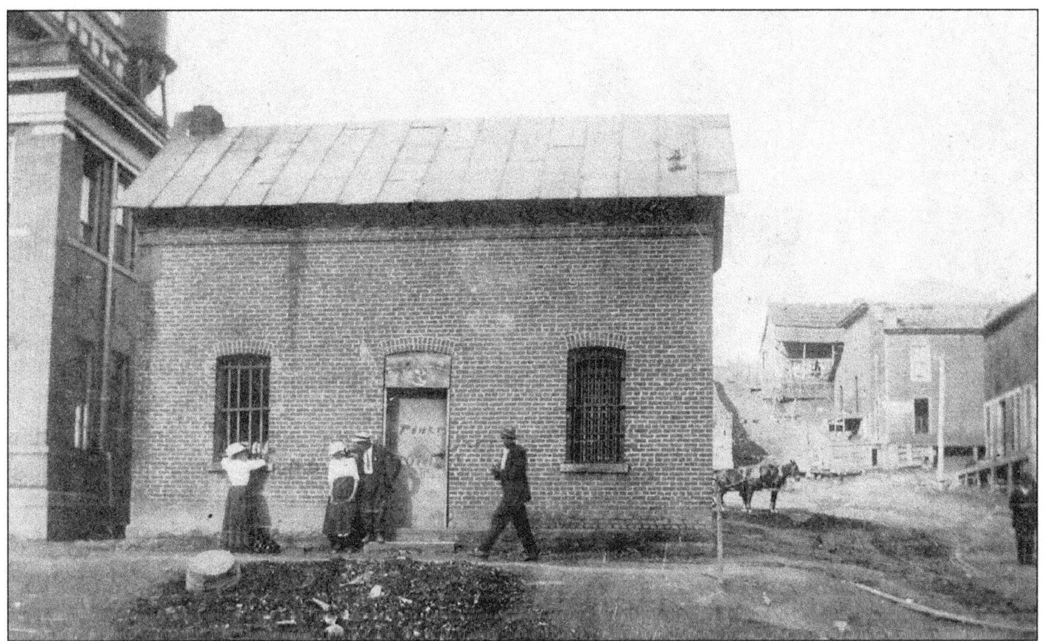

Friends and family visit inmates in the jail beside the Perry County Court House (above). This building, Hazard's first brick jail, was in use from 1899 to 1914. The view on the right is old Fleet Street. In this picture, taken about the turn of the 20th century, it appears to be a very wide street. A small corner of the jail is visible on the left (below). Broadsides and posters, nailed across the side of the D.Y. Combs Building, publicized political candidates and announced coming attractions such as the circus, performers, or shows. The town government honored E.B. Lovern in 1954 by changing the name of Fleet Street to Lovern Street. Among his many contributions, Mr. Lovern, postal inspector, with Dewey Daniel, postmaster, modernized the Hazard Post Office in 1920.

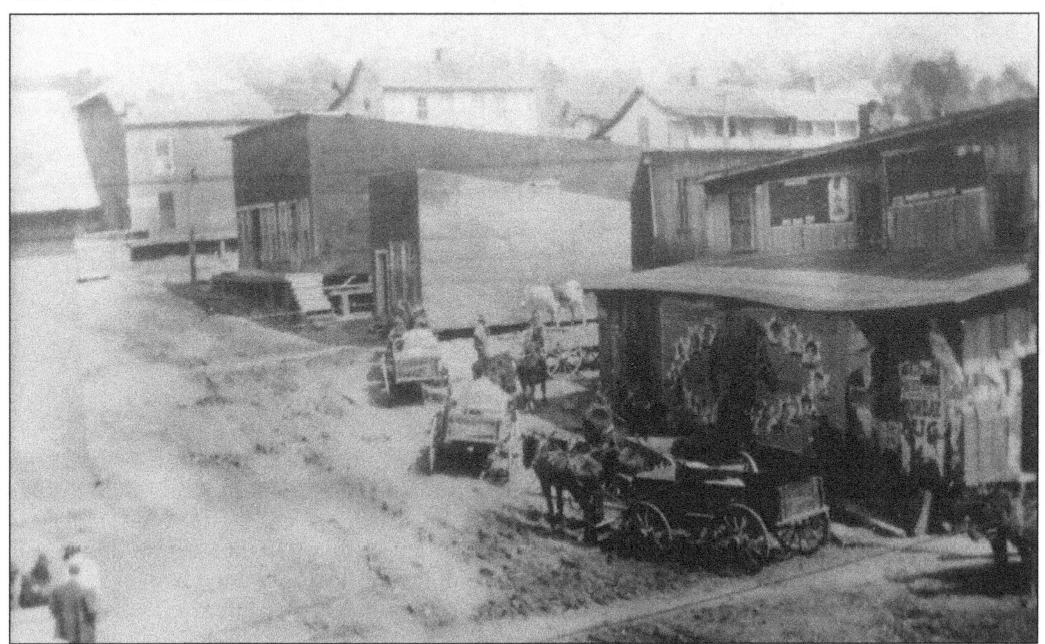

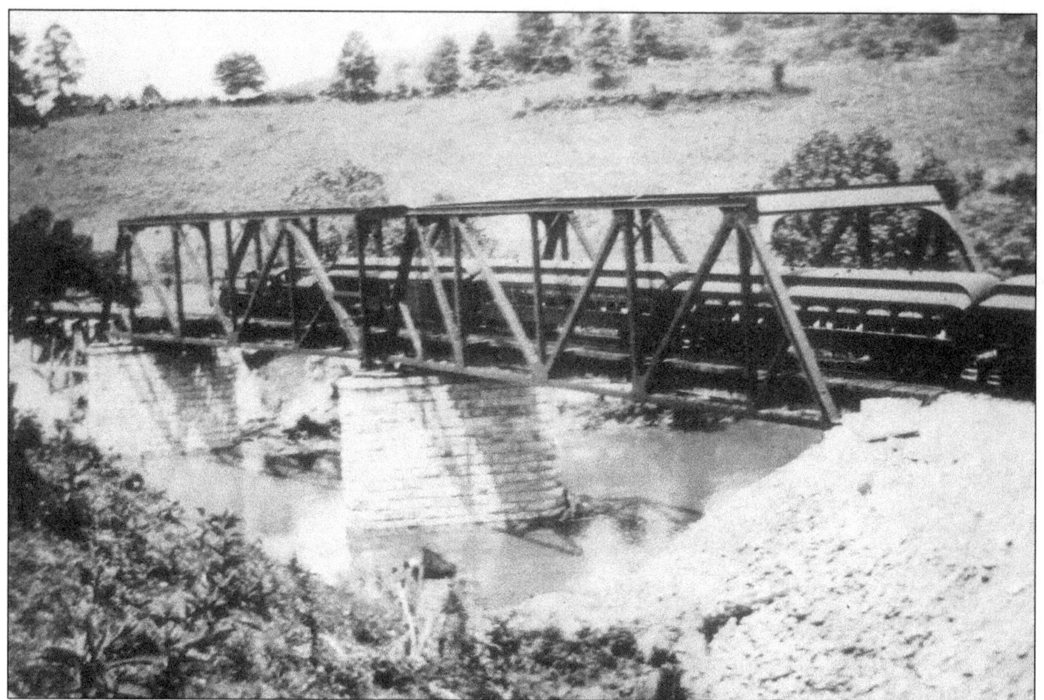

The building of L&E extension train tracks, from Jackson to McRoberts, took from 1910 to 1912. John Kinner took this photograph of the railroad bridge, seen crossing the North Fork of the Kentucky River at Combs. The European workers, who built the bridge and the tunnel that follows it, lived nearby at Camp 4. Camp 4 later became known as Lennut (for tunnel).

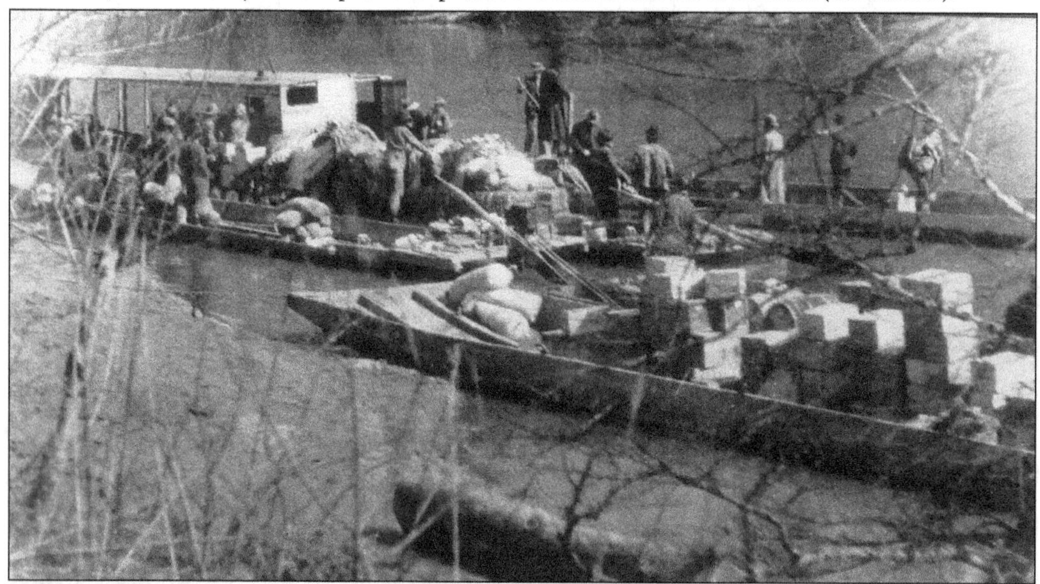

This Kinner photograph was taken at Combs, KY. Flatboats, such as the ones pictured, carried up to 30,000 pounds. The first piano in Hazard came on a flatboat. Before the arrival of the railroad, Edison record players, electric irons, dolls, musical instruments, lamps, ready-made clothing, writing paper, and all manner of household goods for Hazard merchants were laboriously pushed on flatboats loaded at Irvine or Beattyville.

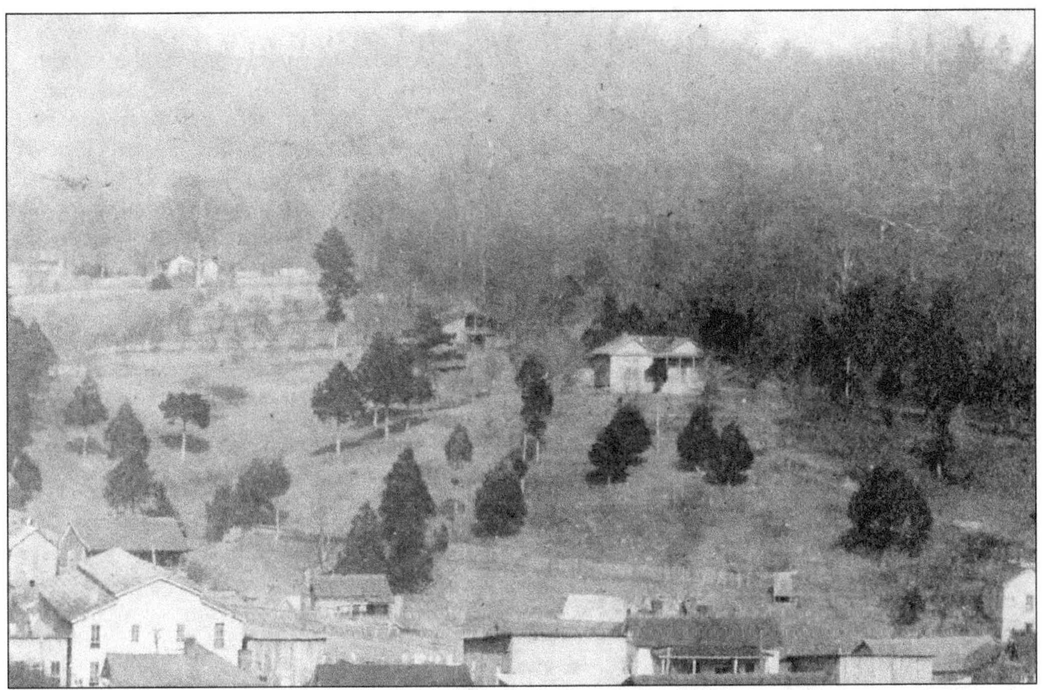

Kinner took this picture of the Isaac Baker farm, which overlooked the east end of Hazard. The Baker orchards are in the background. Now in the year 2000 descendants of the Baker family still live in the neighborhood there.

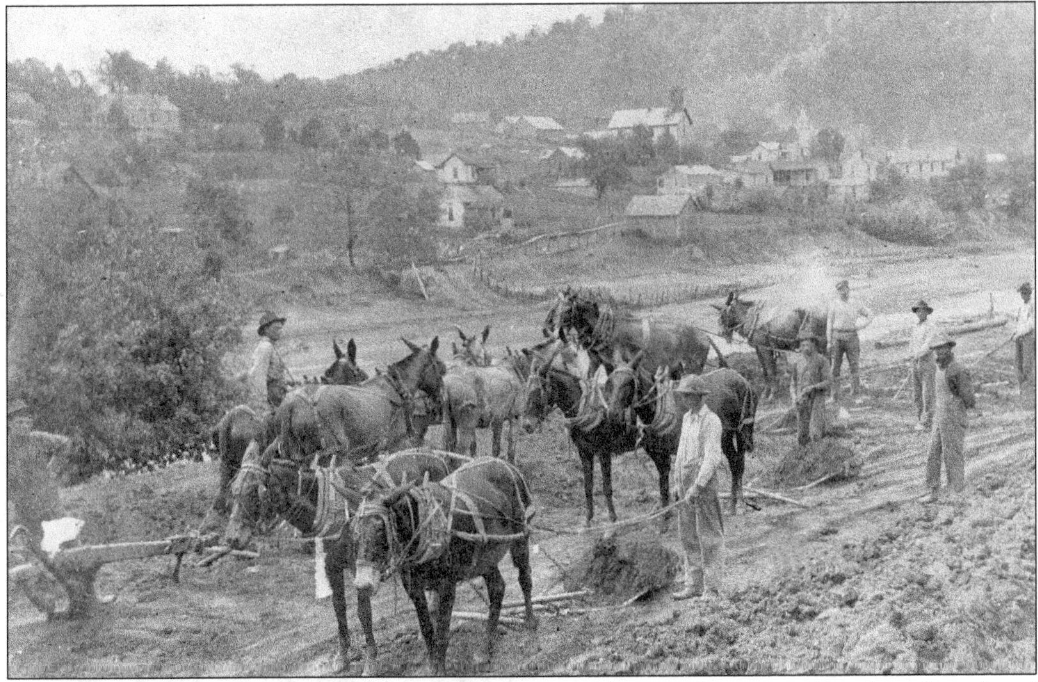

Railroad workers pause for photographer John Kinner. They are plowing and leveling the railroad grade. The north end of Hazard, on the other side of the river, appears in the background. The tallest building is the Hazard Grade School.

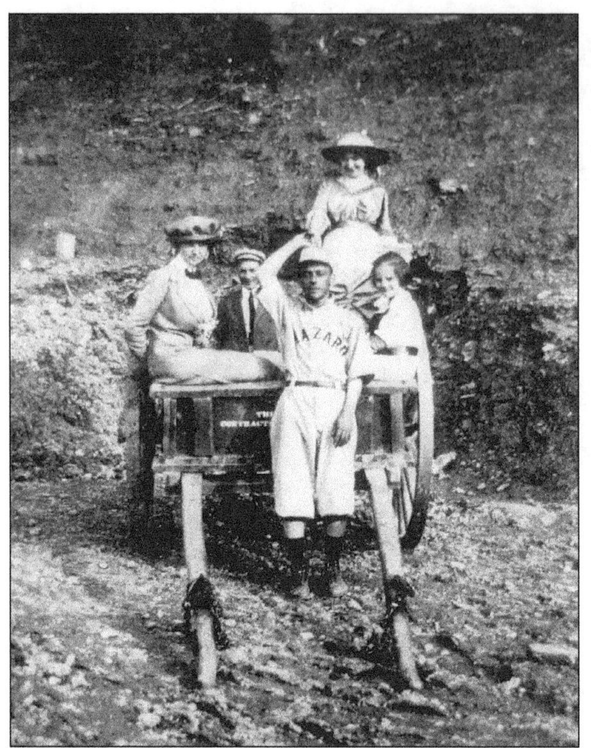

In another Kinner photograph, a member of the Hazard baseball team, with Carrie Watts (on the left) and some other unidentified young people, poses in a wagon. The Hazard team played Jackson on July 4, 1912. The new railroad had reached Hazard several days before, and the town was still making merry. The *Hazard Herald* reported: "the new terminus beat the old terminus 6 to 1."

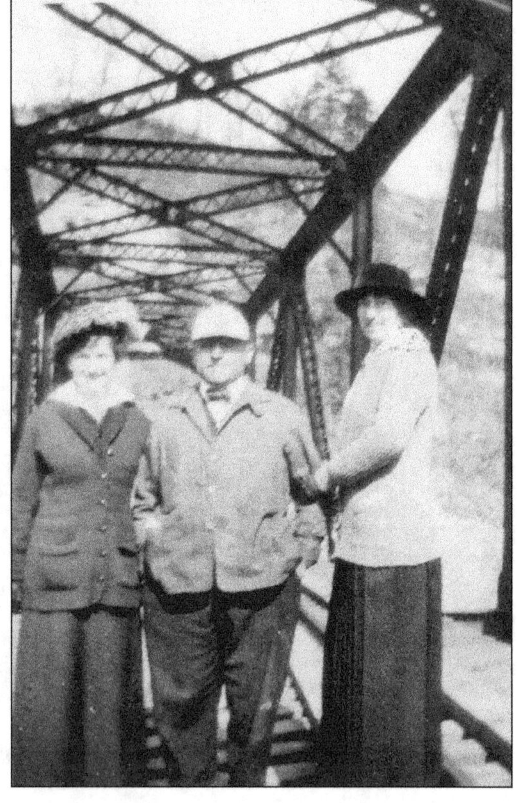

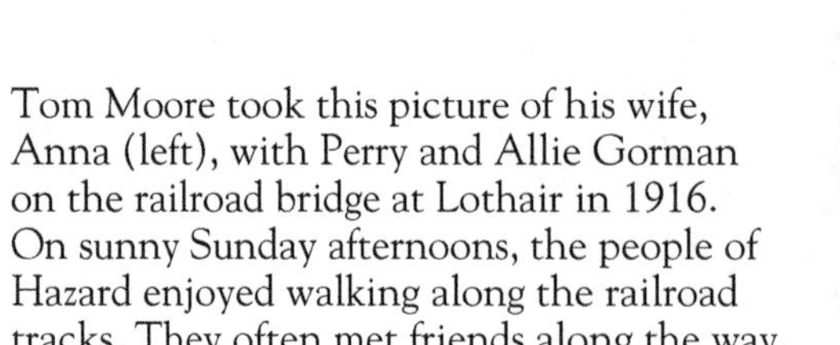

Tom Moore took this picture of his wife, Anna (left), with Perry and Allie Gorman on the railroad bridge at Lothair in 1916. On sunny Sunday afternoons, the people of Hazard enjoyed walking along the railroad tracks. They often met friends along the way.

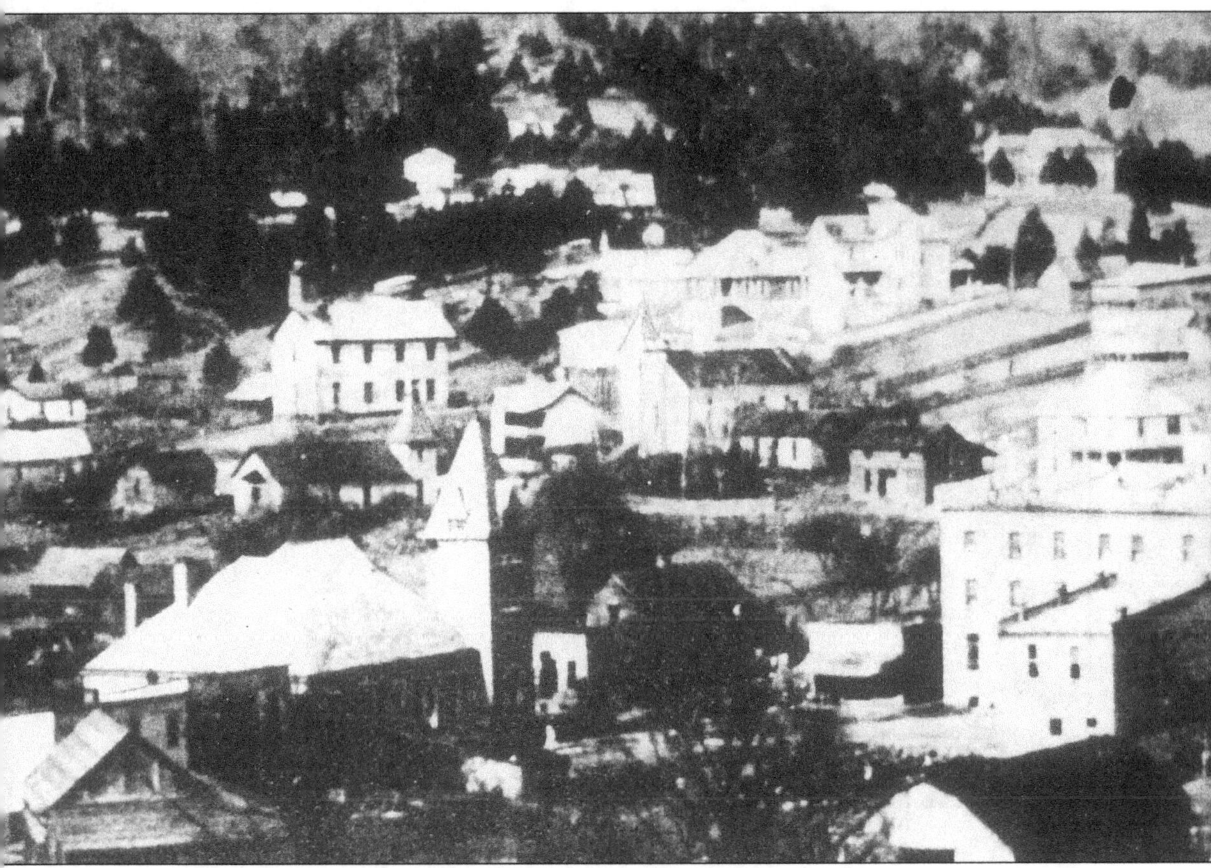

W.O. Davis started building the two-story Hazard Grade School in 1892. The first year it was one floor. Early teachers were Albert Williams and Will Ward. In 1893 G.M. Horn, a graduate of Missouri University, extended the school year in Hazard to nine months. Bailey P. Wootton joined the staff within the year. Horn was also responsible for adding the second story seen here. The town condemned the building in 1913 as unsafe. Other buildings seen here, all with steeples, are the First Baptist Church in the foreground, the Methodist church on the right, and the First Presbyterian Church in the middle.

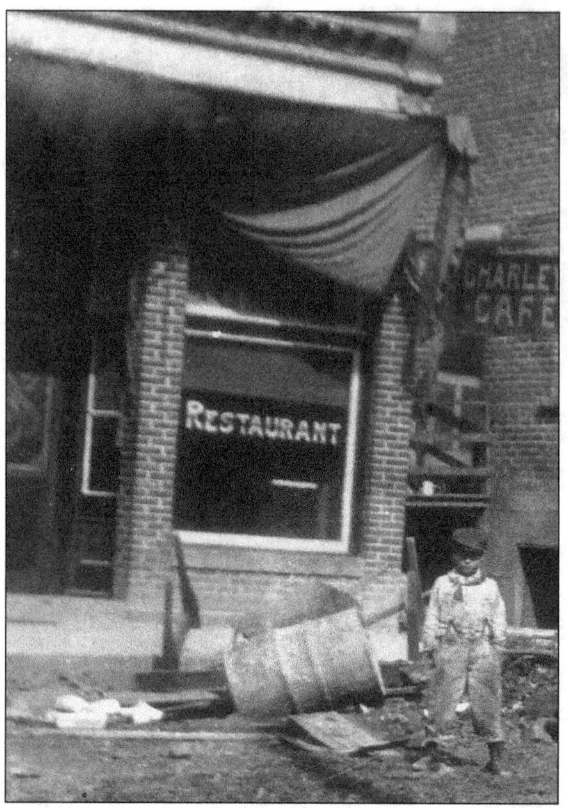

The town requested that merchants build sidewalks. In this Kinner photograph, the boy is surrounded by rubbish and mud in the street. This business, located on Main Street behind the Beaumont Hotel, started out as Charley's Cafe. In a later picture, "Vick's" was added above "Restaurant."

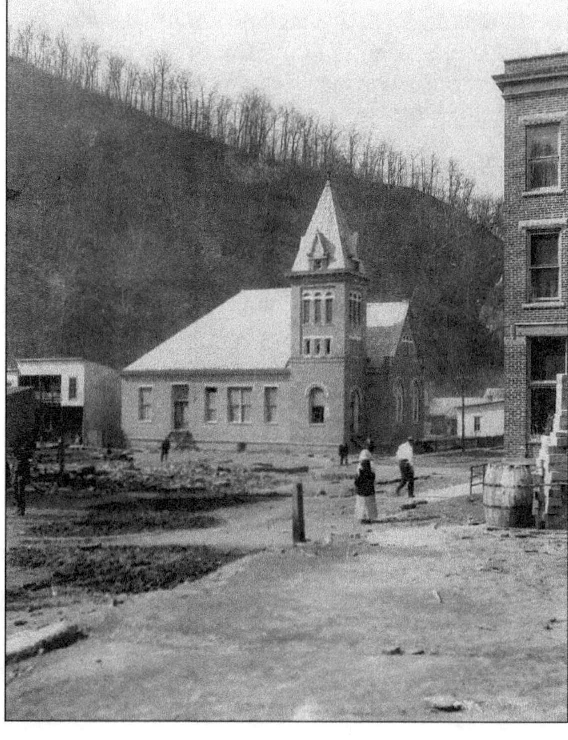

The First Baptist Church, central to this picture taken by John Kinner, was dedicated in 1912. The pews were brought in by one of the first trains to arrive in Hazard. Kinner asked Susan Combs Eversole, in the long skirt, to stand on the spot where the house of her father, Josiah H. Combs, was located in the late 1890s.

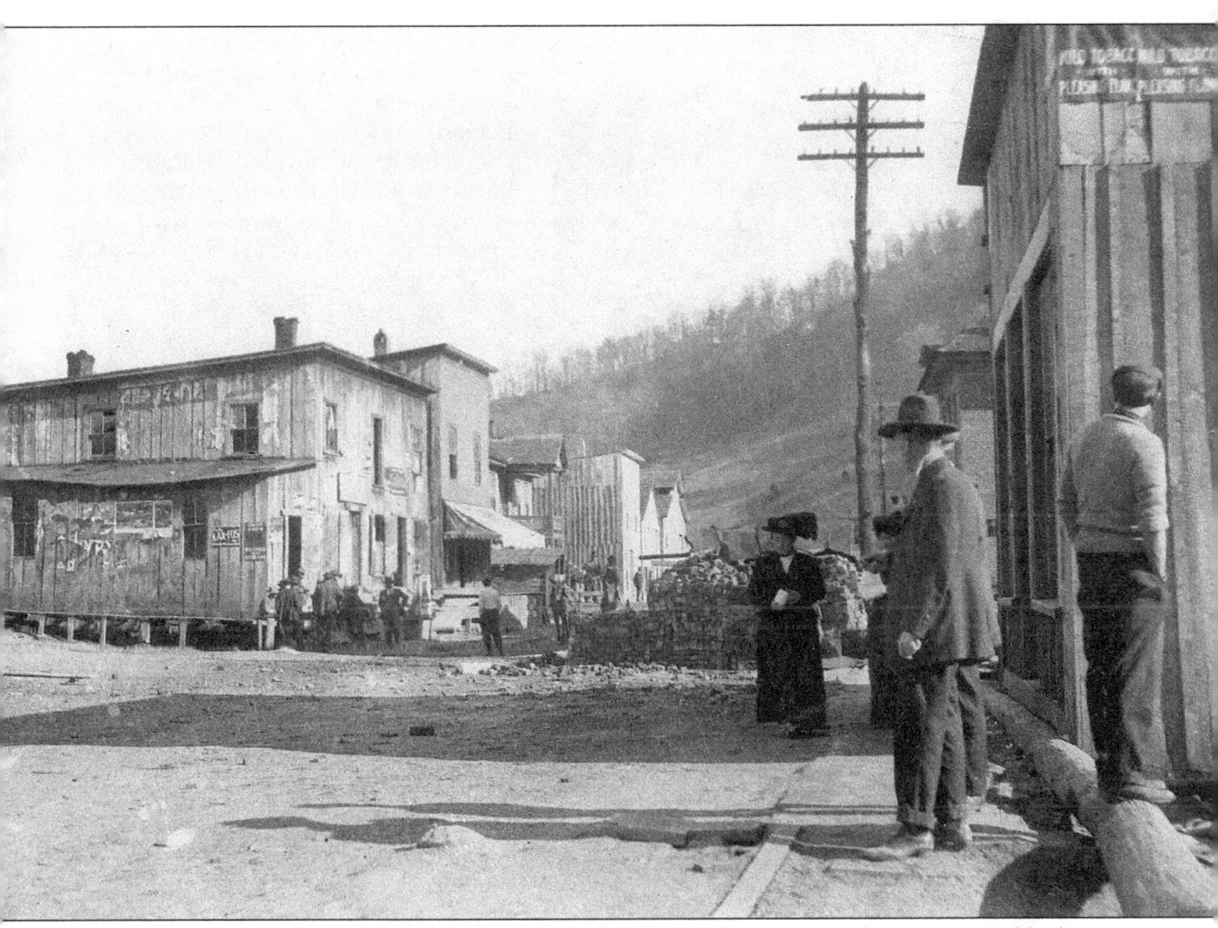

D.Y. Combs owned the buildings on the left in this 1913 photograph. The woman in black is Clara "Pet" Eversole. The man on the right, in the hat and suit, is Matt Cornett.

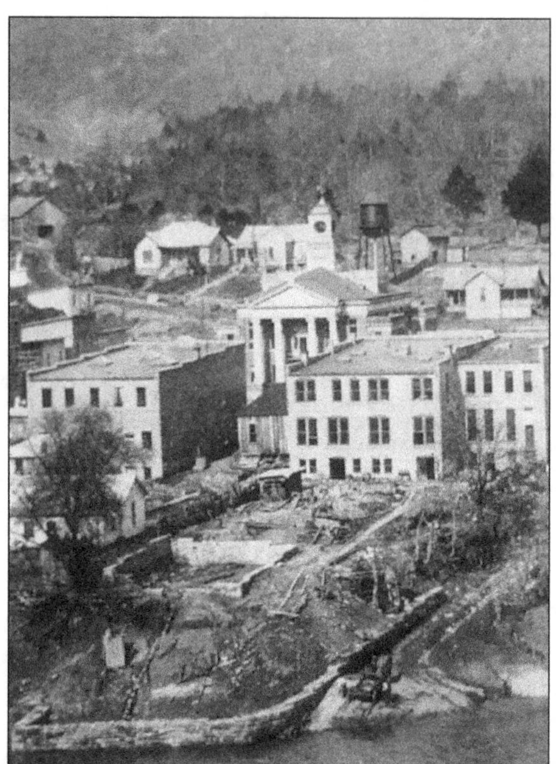

In 1913, the year following the coming of the railroad, Hazard was losing its western-frontier look, and had an increasing number of brick buildings. The water tower provided the Perry County Court House with running water. Electric lights were switched on in Hazard on May 15, 1913.

This photograph was taken around the intersection of East Main Street looking north on High Street. The large house is the Campbell Boarding House, and the building on the right is the blacksmith shop. The clock, on the left, is on top of the 1912 courthouse steeple.

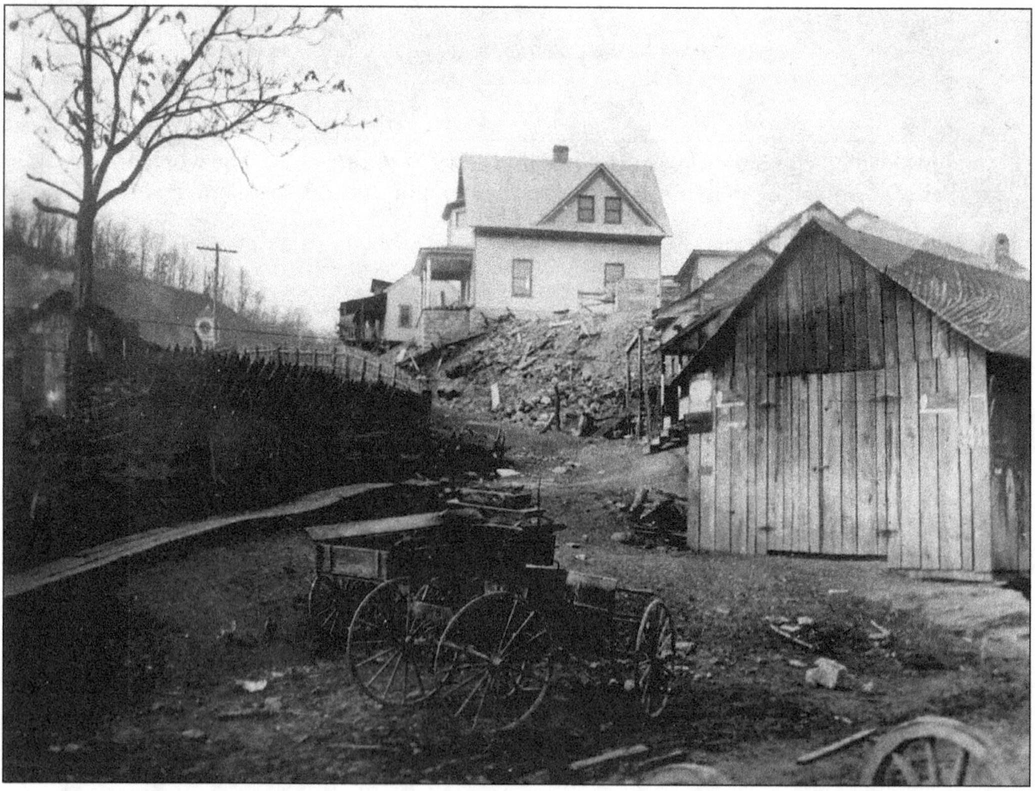

Photographer John Kinner poses with his camera on a board sidewalk on Broadway. While in Hazard, he was under contract with the L&N Railroad to document the construction of the right-of-way. Kinner also took pictures of Hazard people and places. After the railroad completed the tunnels, bridges, and railroad track near Hazard, Kinner and his family moved down the line with the rest of the workers.

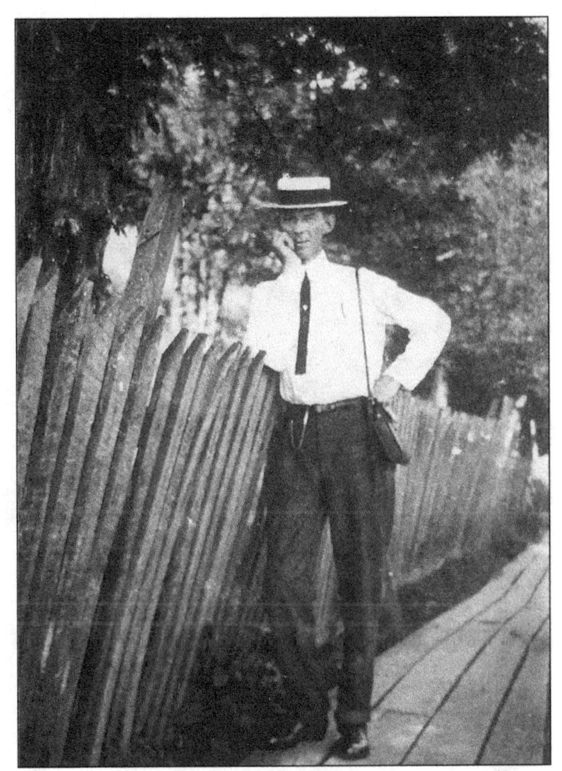

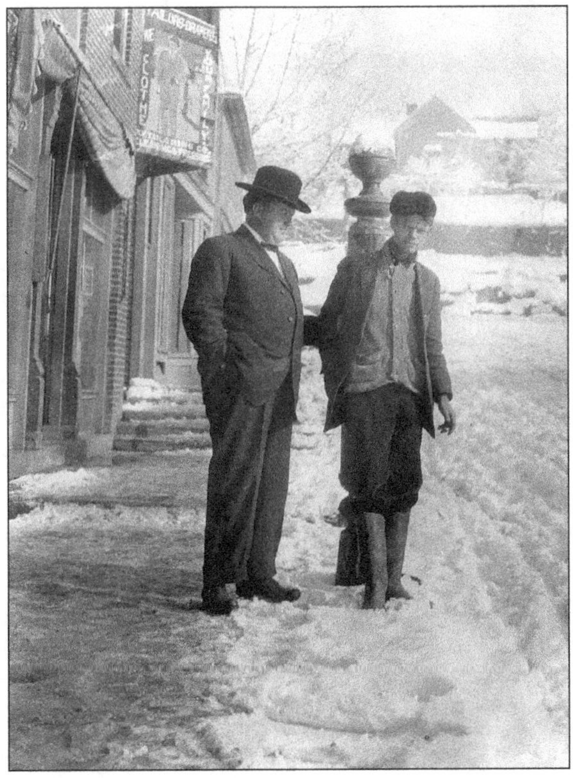

In this photo, taken on a cold winter day by John Kinner, Dr. Henry Maggard, a local dentist, meets Bob Cooksey on Court Street. Today the name of the street is Morgan Street, for Jesse Morgan, a Hazard attorney.

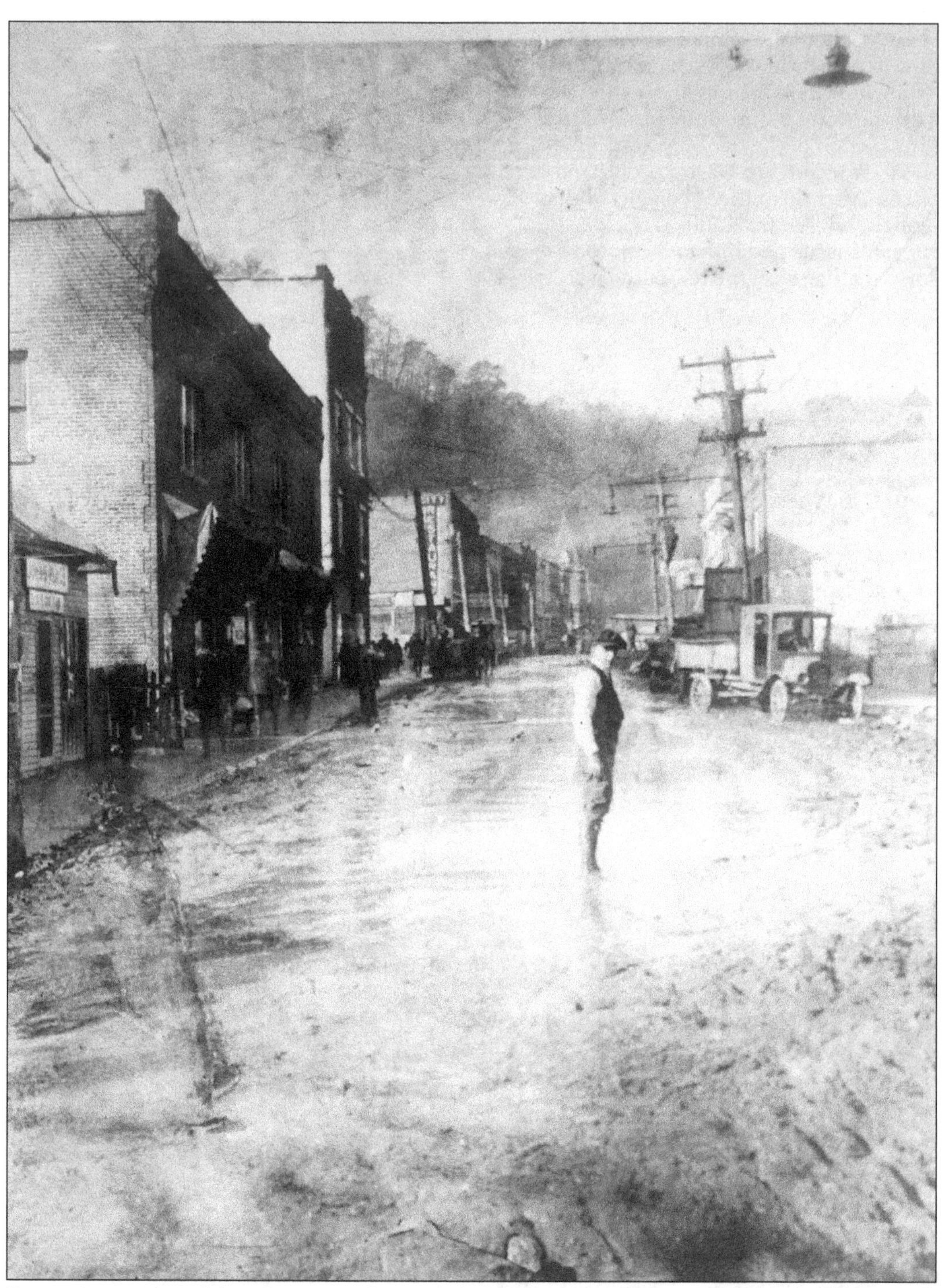

Signs of progress on Main Street are the street light, the utility poles, and the automobile. Still, the streets were deep in mud. It was the constant lament into the mid-1920s, until pavement came to Main Street. In May 1916 three automobiles, popularly known as "buzz wagons," arrived in Hazard. The trouble with having a car at the time was the lack of roads. The moving vehicles engaged in an ongoing battle with stray cows and pigs. The main figure is unknown.

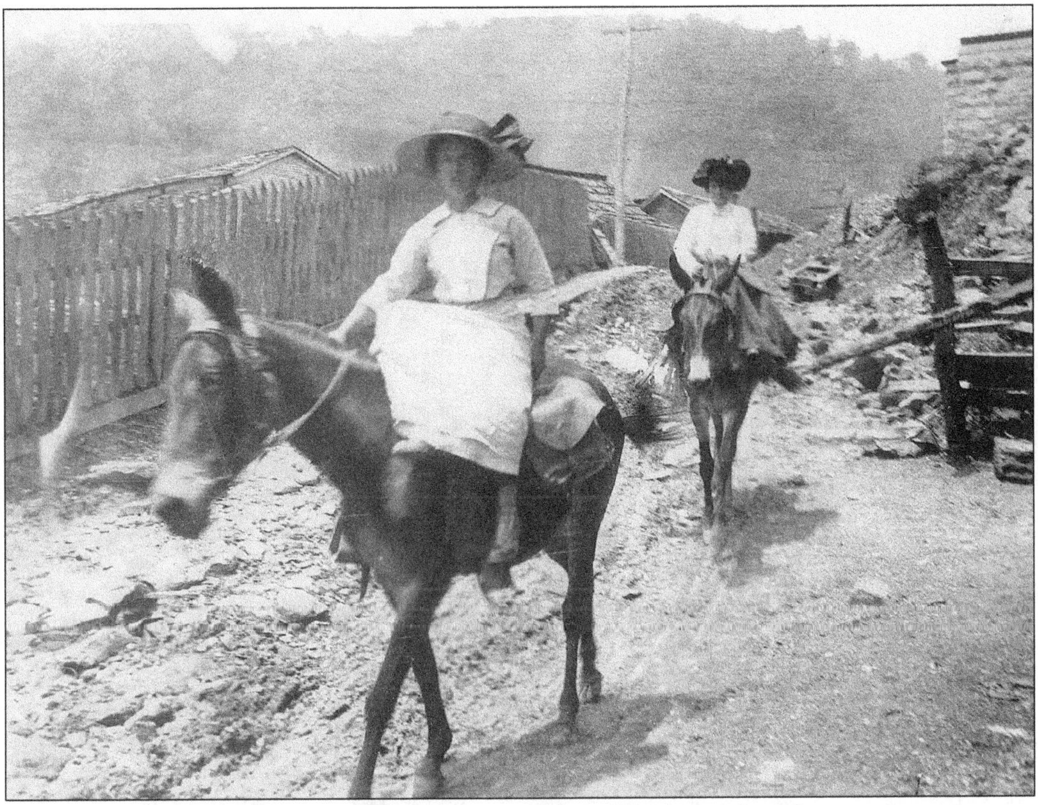

In this Kinner photo from 1911, two women on side-saddles bring their farm products to town. They are riding their mules south on High Street.

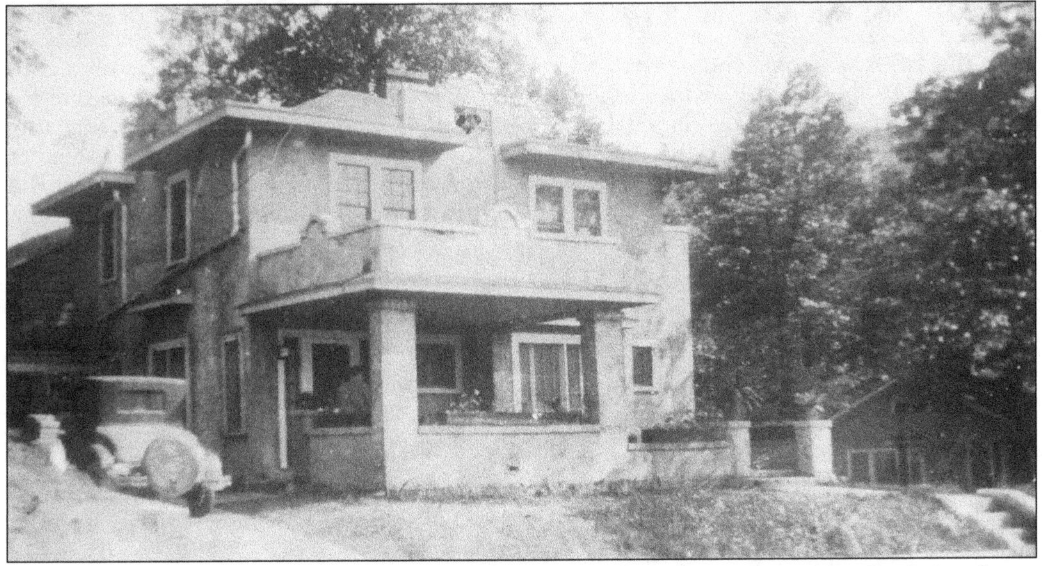

Dr. B.M. Brown, a Hazard physician, ordered this house from the Sears and Roebuck Catalogue of Houses. The model, No. P17090 A, named the Alhambra, cost $3,134 in 1926. Two other houses on Oakhurst are known to be Sears houses. So many people ordered prefabricated houses from Sears in the 1920s that stacks of crates crowded the railroad yards.

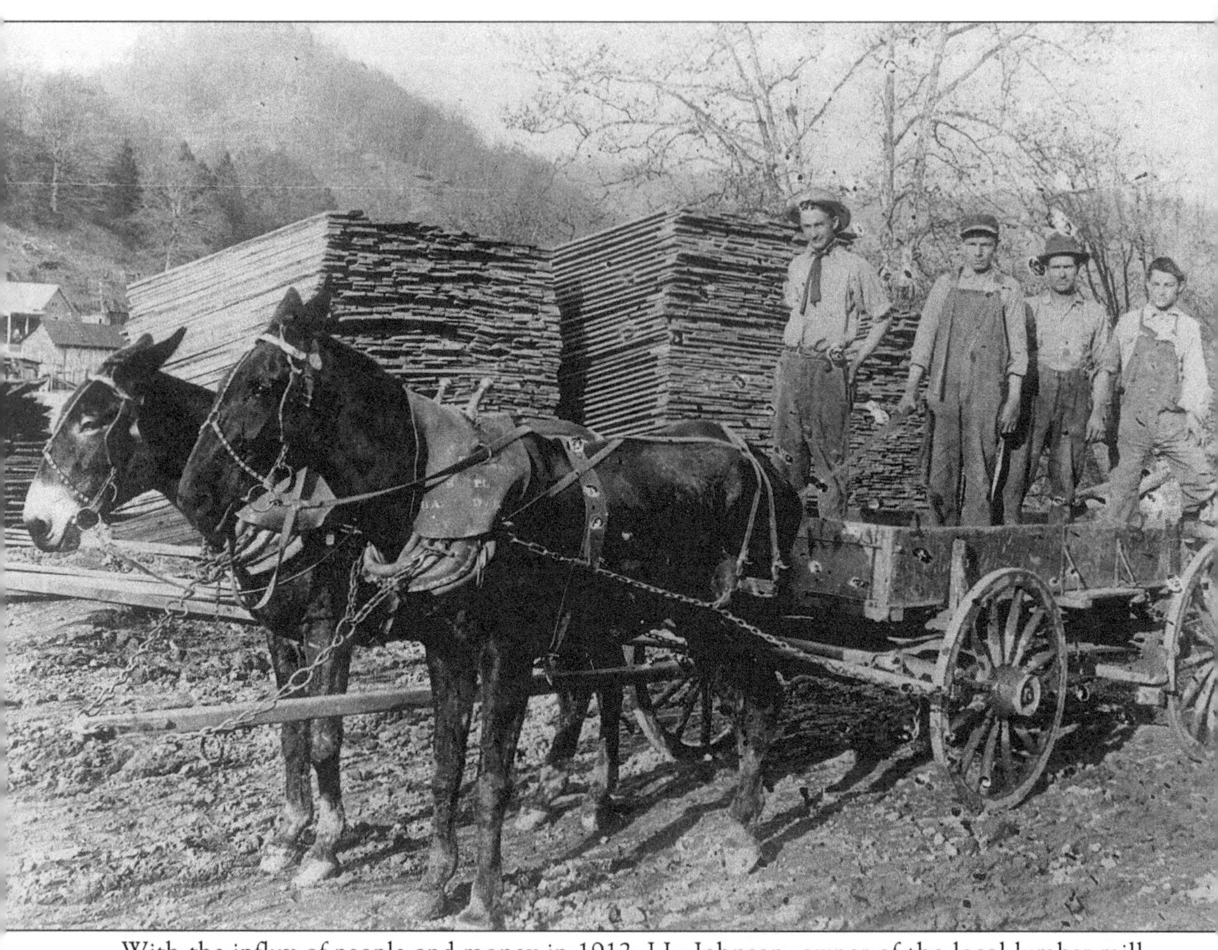

With the influx of people and money in 1912, J.L. Johnson, owner of the local lumber mill, and George Wolfe, with the Ritter Lumber Company, recognized the unlimited market for lumber. So they founded the Hazard Lumber and Supply Company in 1914. The company made deliveries on bad roads and muddy streets in wagons like the one here. The lumber stacked to dry was intended for houses in one of the many company camps throughout the region. The men here are Howard Johnson, unidentified, Bill Johnson, and Charles Johnson, sons of J.L. Johnson.

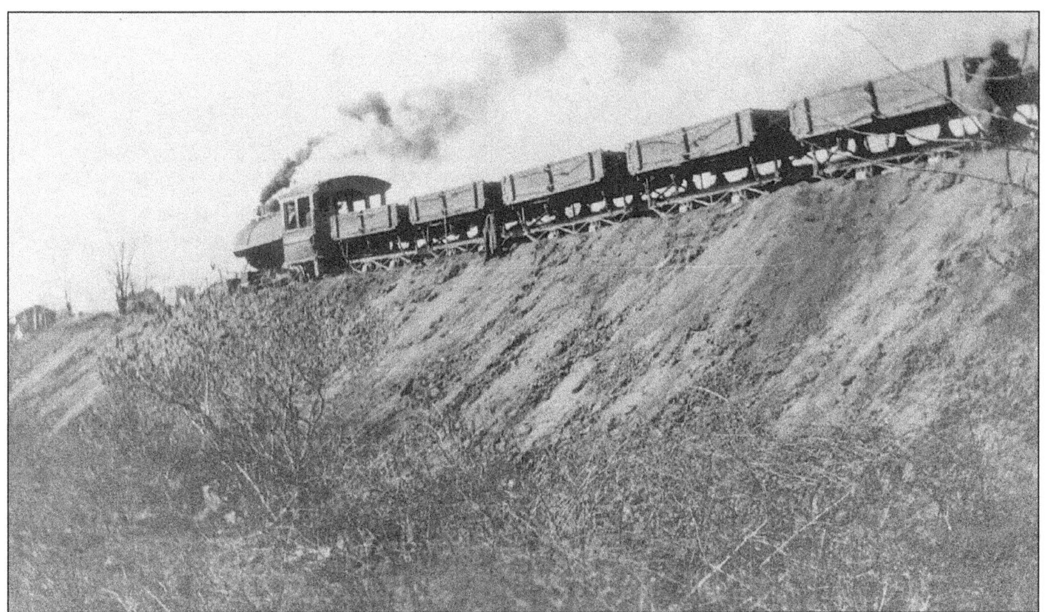

Short-run locomotives were called "dinkies." They were steam engines, with worm-gear drives, used to push and pull lumber or coal cars to the main line. They ran on narrow rails, from mines or tree-cutting sites, through hills, across streams, and over the mountains.

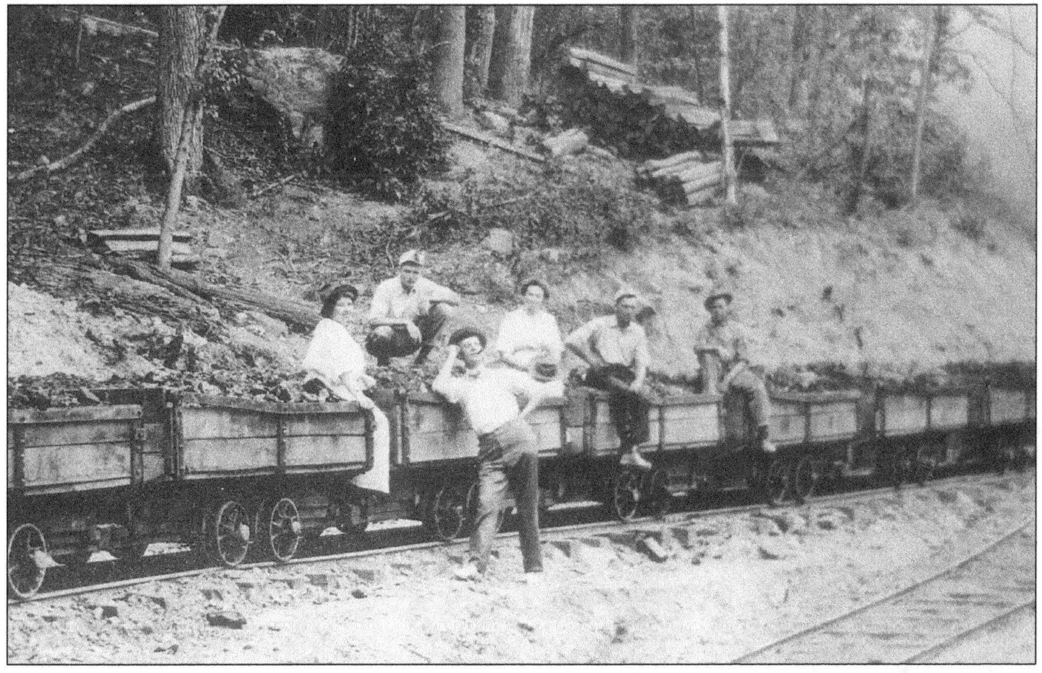

Despite the appearance of a social outing in this photograph by John Kinner, miners labored long and hard to fill the train with coal. The train is a short-run or dinky, taking coal to a tipple.

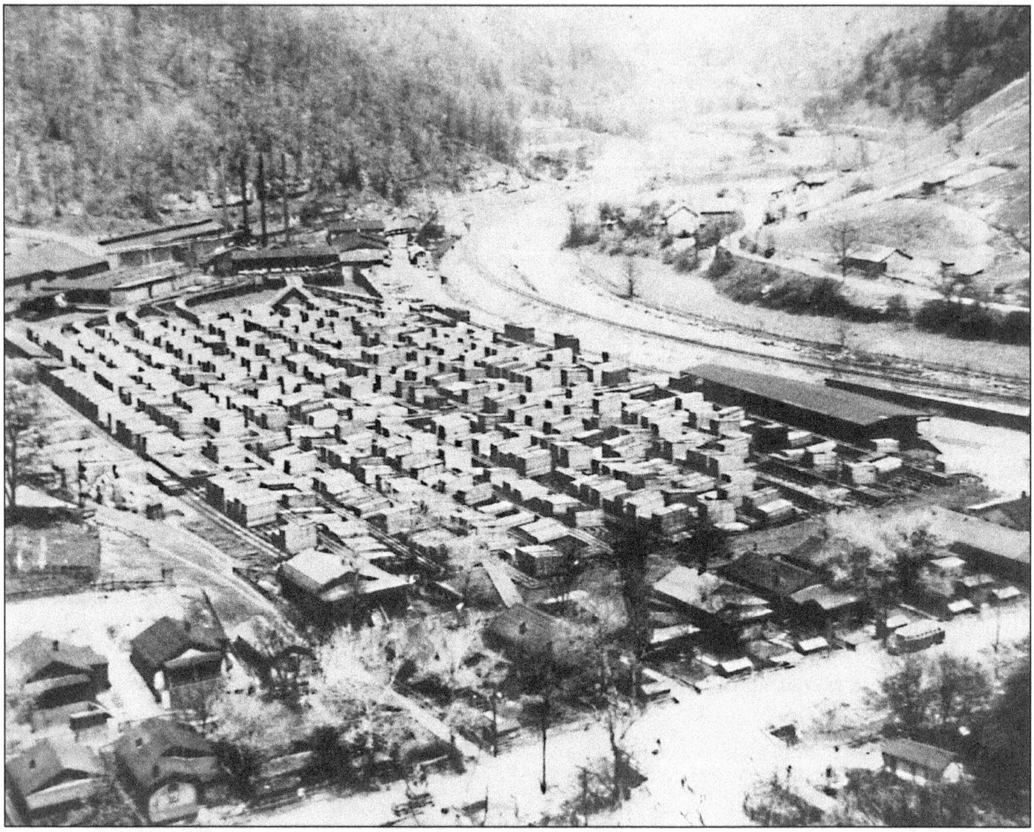

The lumber camp of the W.M. Ritter Lumber Company located in Daisy, near Leatherwood, KY, is pictured here. In 1955, fire destroyed the mill that housed all the sawing machinery. Ritter had 26 other principal sawmills in West Virginia, North Carolina, South Carolina, Tennessee, Virginia, West Virginia, and Kentucky.

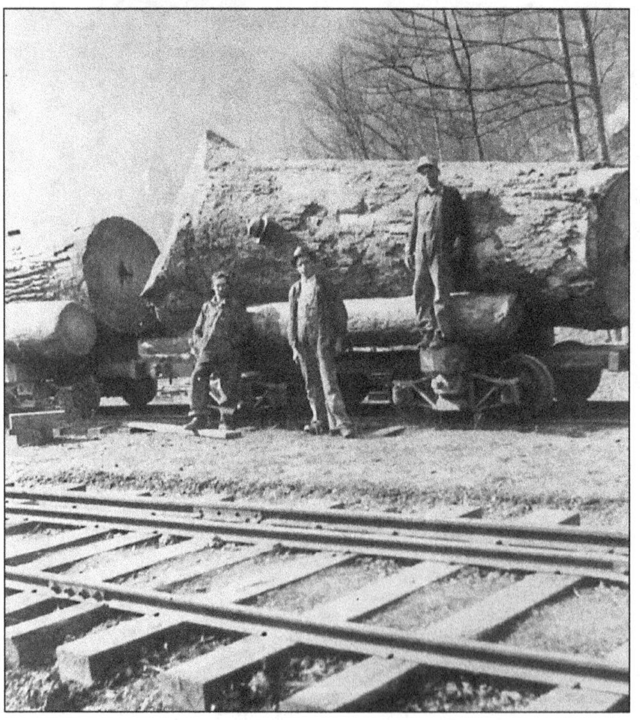

The W.M. Ritter Company cut huge stands of virgin timber. In 1937, the Kentucky Primeval Forest League attempted unsuccessfully to save a 2,000-year-old, 250-foot-high tulip poplar. At a circumference of 11 feet, people from all around knew it as "The King."

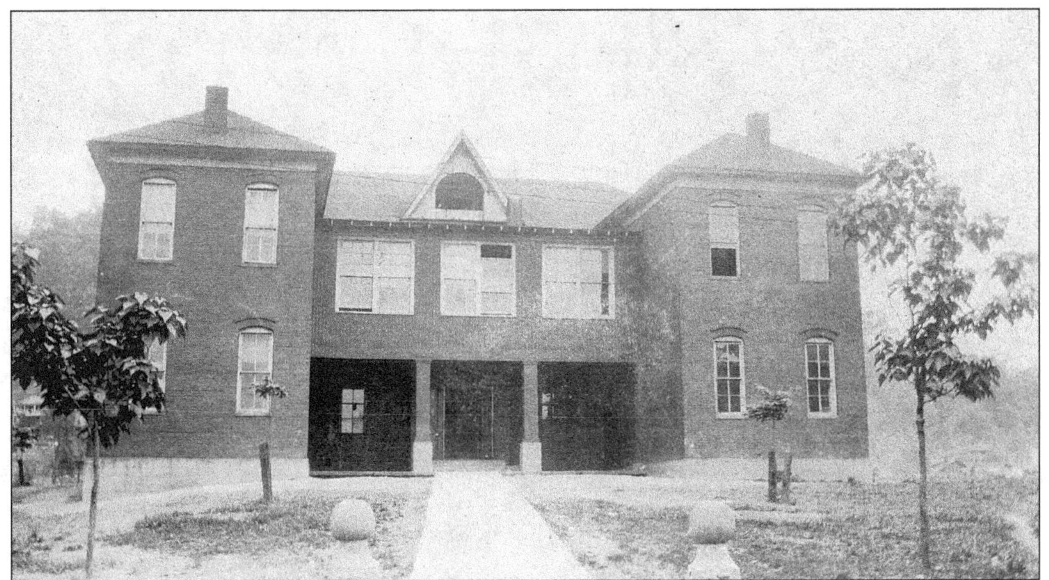

After the dedication in 1909, this HBI structure became the classroom building. Teachers and students used the other building as a dormitory. The campus became Hazard Junior College in 1934. The Hazard Independent School District purchased the college in 1941. The other buildings were cleared away for a football field.

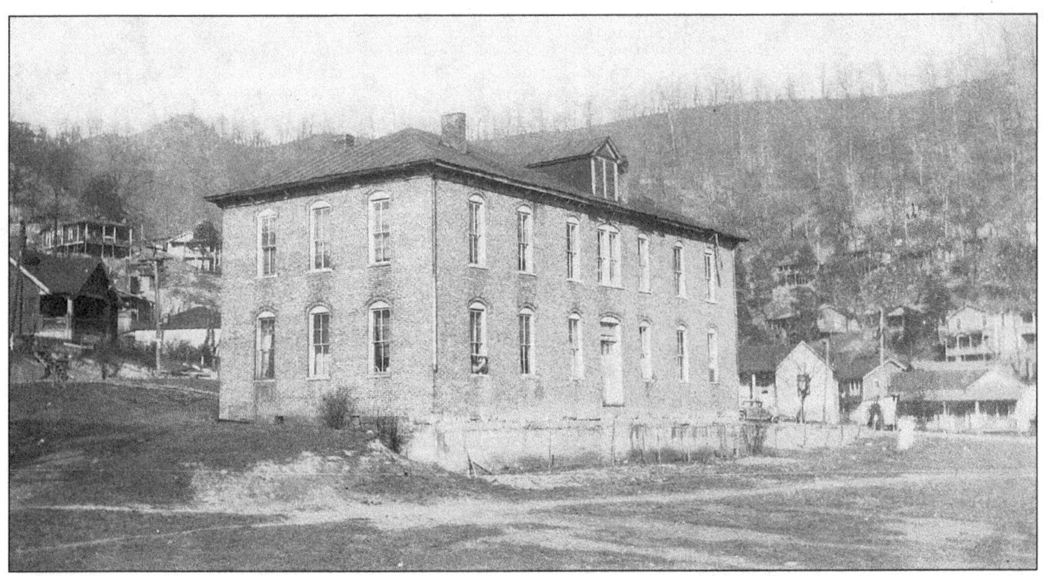

In 1903 A.S. Petrey established the Hazard Baptist Institute (HBI). This building, the original HBI classroom building, was later used as a dormitory. The brick house to the left of the HBI building belonged to Dr. Elihu Kelly. The hilltop in the background on the left is Peter's Peak. The first HBI high school graduating class, consisting of four students, received their diplomas in 1908.

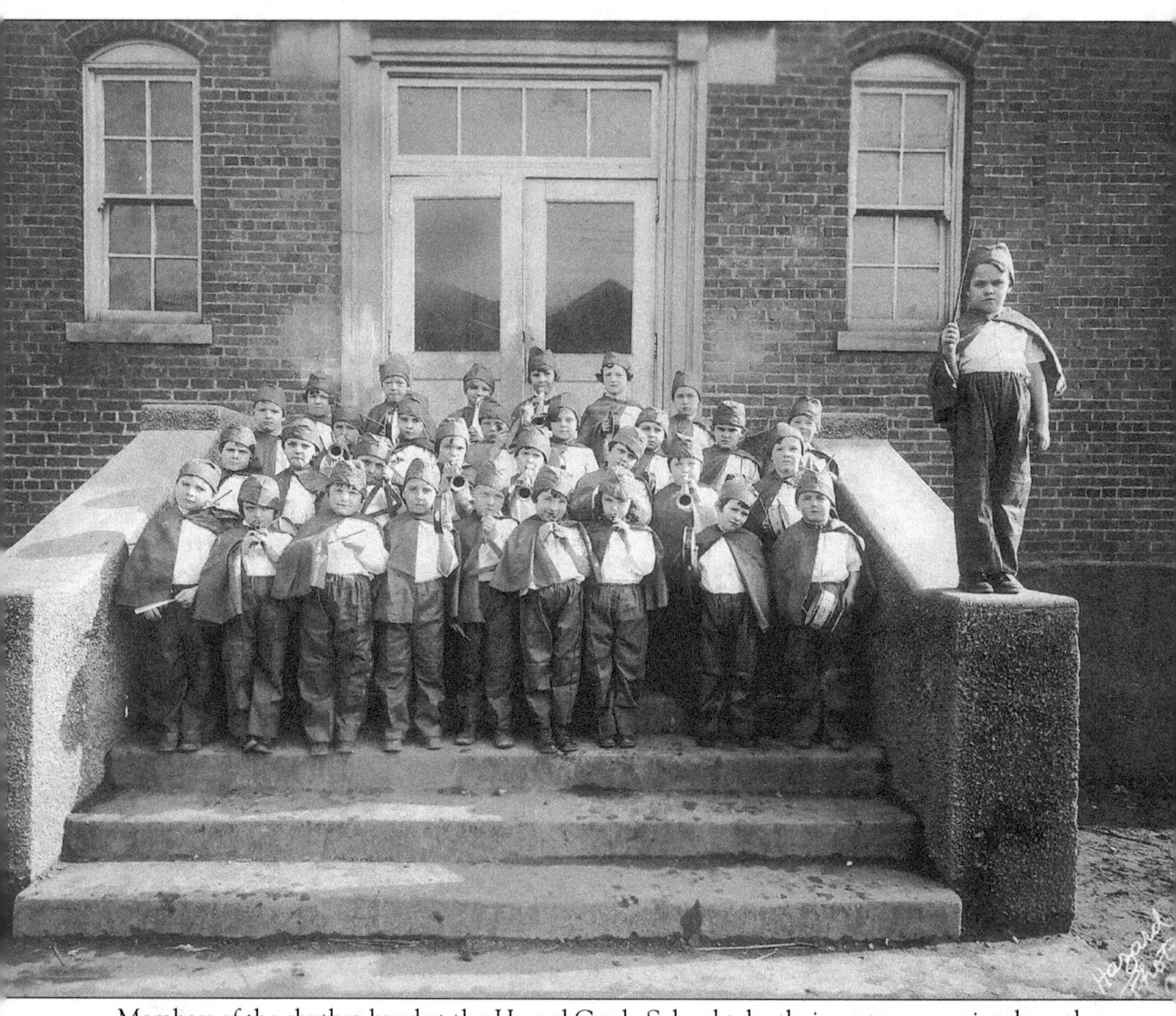

Members of the rhythm band at the Hazard Grade School take their parts very seriously as they pose in front of "Lower Broadway," built in 1914. Students moved from this building to the R.G. Eversole Elementary School (currently the R.G. Eversole Middle School) in 1962.

Two

Main Street, East End Transitions

Main Street and East Main Street meet close to the mouth of Town Branch on the North Fork of the Kentucky River. The mouth of this once-large feeder, which cut Hazard in two in the early years, is one of the first sections that floods in high water. A newspaper article in September 1919 expressed appreciation that Mr. Fulp was going to build on the low place that "had been a source of difficulty in the times of high water." The matter of high water provided an obvious reason for this corner of Hazard to receive primary attention in the later days of urban renewal.

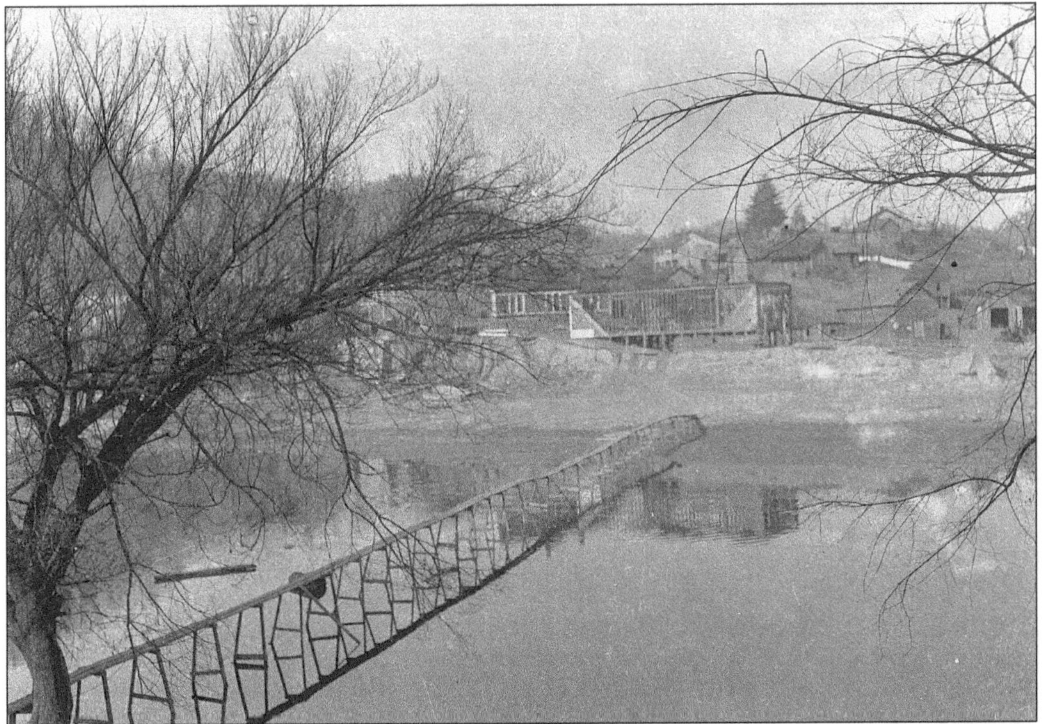

Dr. Elihu Kelly constructed this building on the east end of Main Street in 1912. He finished it by the end of the year. The walking bridge seen here was perilous in good weather and impossible in bad weather. Most people found it easier to ford the river or cross in a boat.

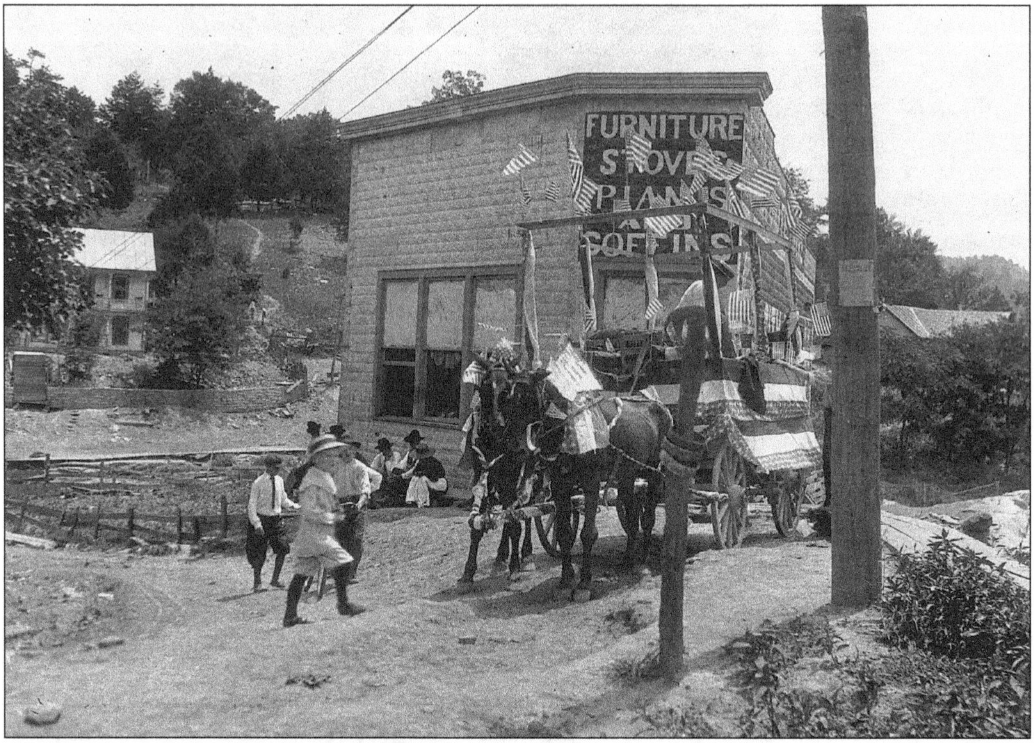

A decorated wagon in front of Dr. Kelly's building welcomed the Louisville Boosters, who arrived by train on May 22, 1913. The boosters stayed in town for an hour to make speeches, then boarded the train to go to the next stop.

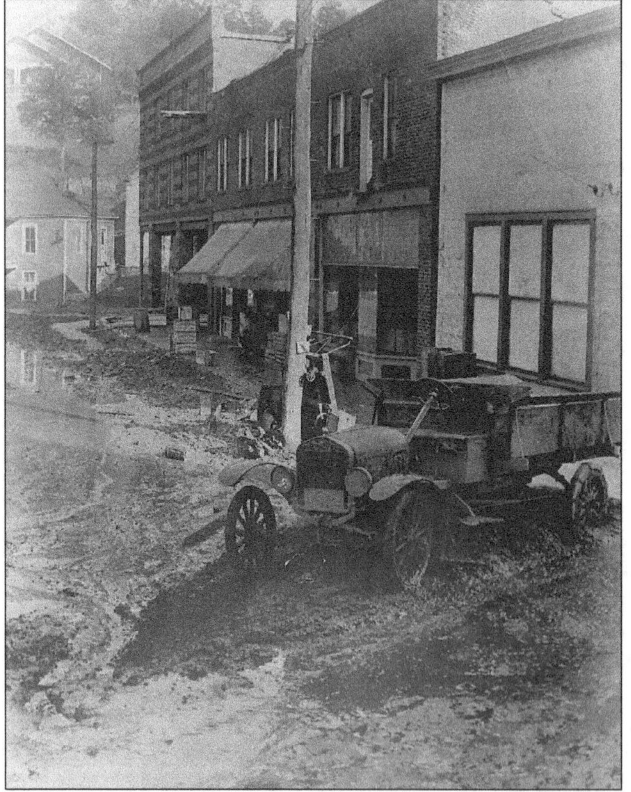

Mud, mud, mud covered the streets. According to legend, a mule drowned on Main Street. The owner of this vehicle might have to wait for a drought before driving home. The building on the right, Dr. Kelly's Building, adjoined a long block of six brick buildings built by D.W. Fulp before 1920. It appears in the following four photographs.

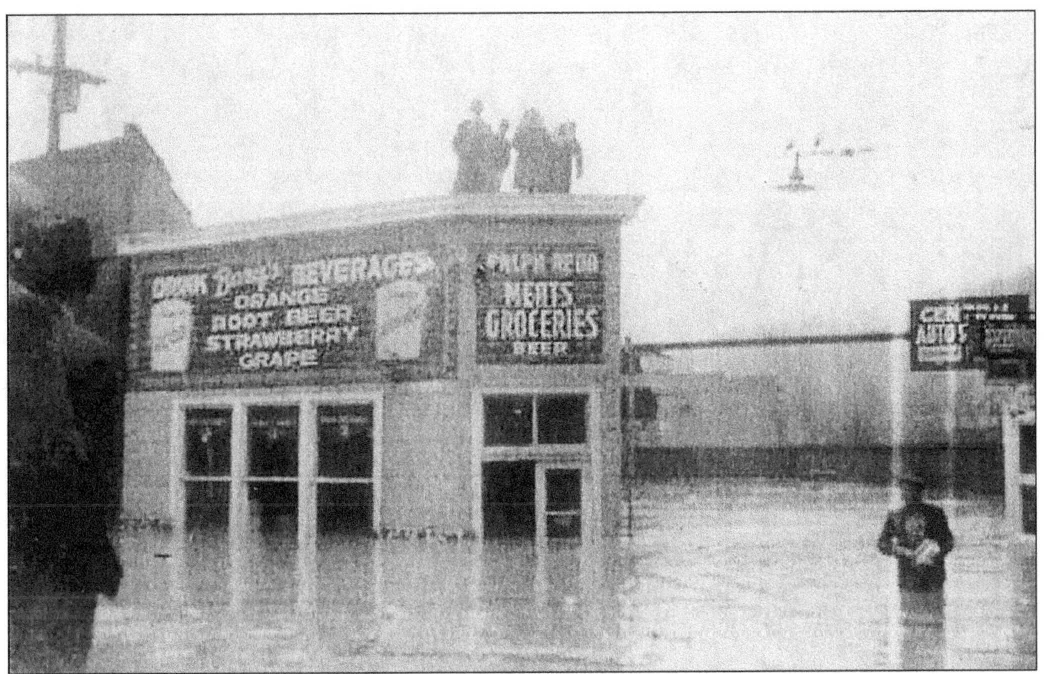

Ralph Reda operated this grocery for many years in Dr. Kelly's Building. The 1937 flood, which sent several people to the roof, was not as high as other tragic floods.

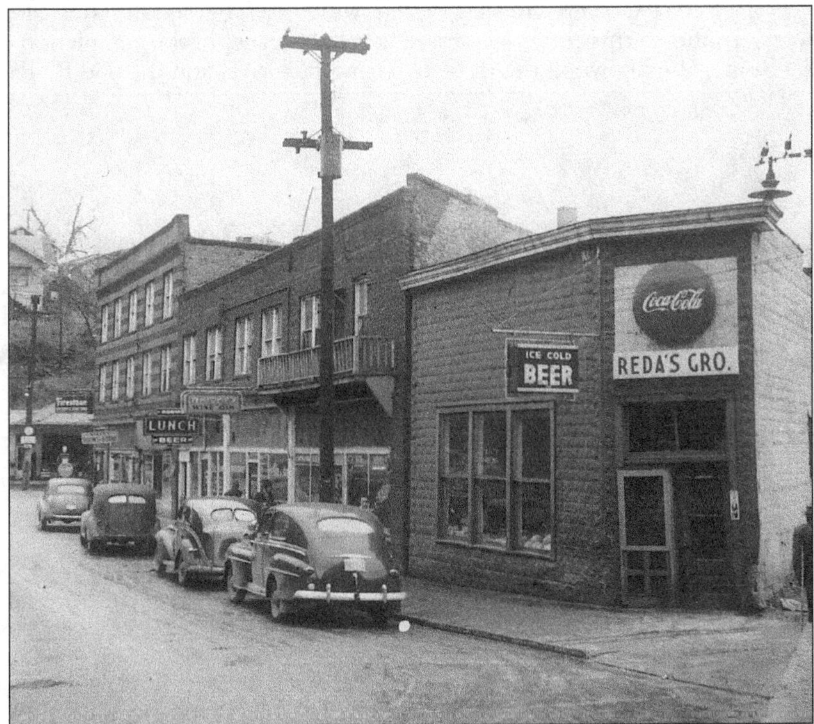

In the late 1940s, this corner was busier than ever. In 1947, there were nine bus lines using Main Street as the only way in and out of town. All the buses traveling south had to take this corner and turn right.

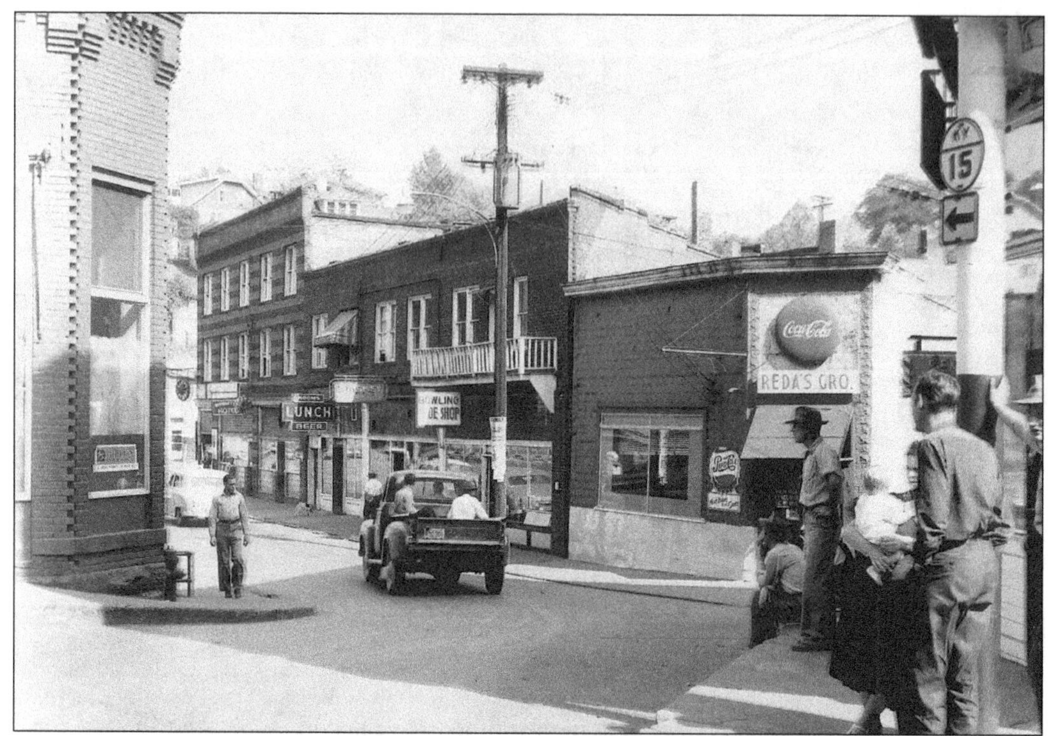

In the early 1950s Reda's Grocery got new picture windows. The building next door painted their woodwork. Traffic on this corner decreased in 1950 because of the completion of the new Hazard Relief Route, also known as the By-Pass, Memorial Drive, and the Old By-Pass.

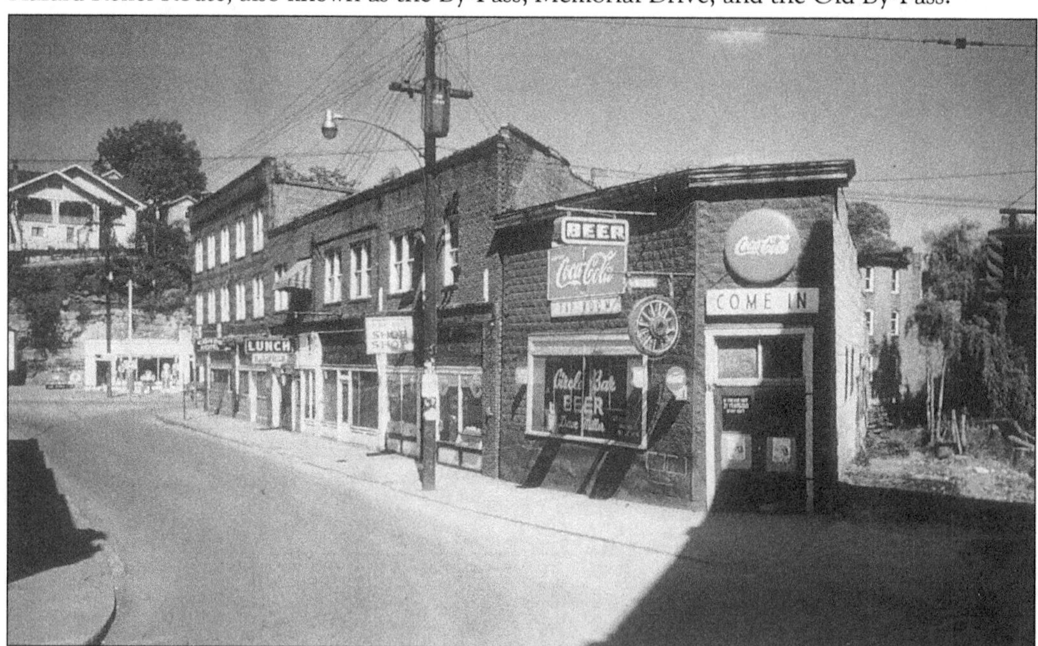

This picture shows Dave Miller's Circle Bar in place of Reda's Grocery. The Combs Hotel is on the other end of the block. The vacant lot to the right is part of the original estate of Elijah Combs and Jesse Combs.

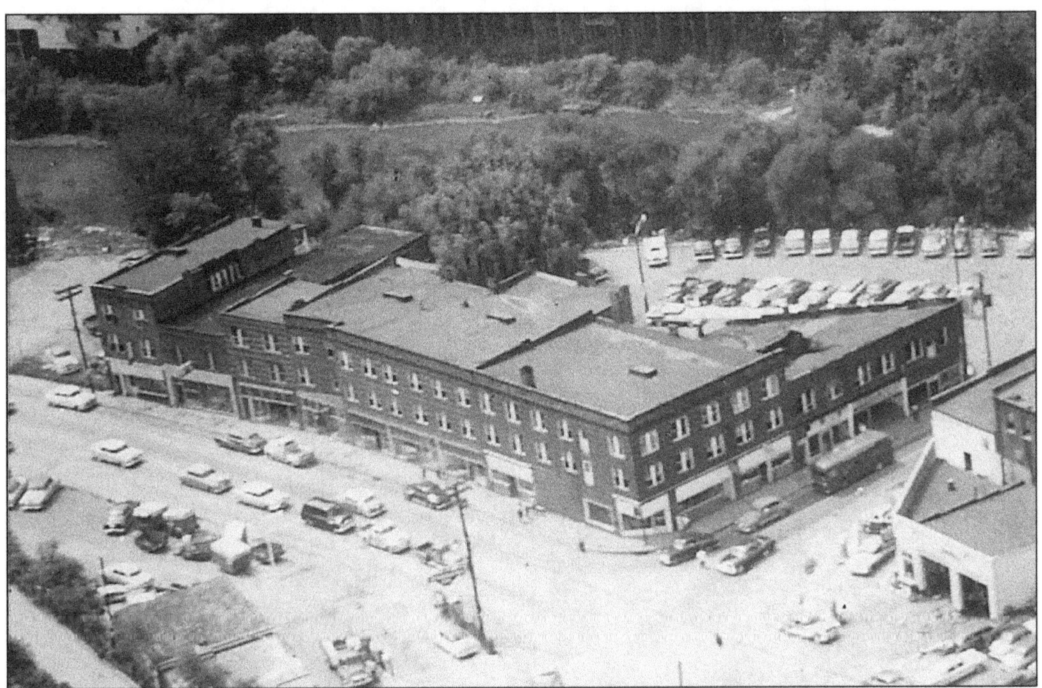

In this aerial photograph taken in 1959 Dr. Kelly's Building is gone. Plans were underway for removing Fulp's six, three-story, brick buildings, which had been occupied for about 40 years by stores, offices, and living quarters.

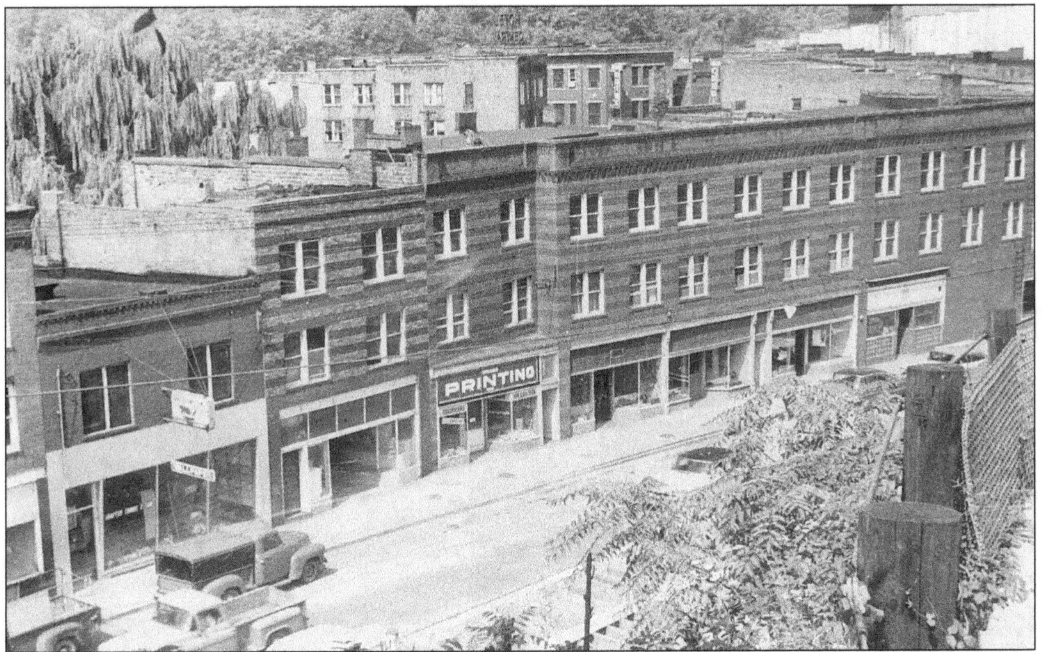

A photographer, standing on Baker Hill, captured the section of East Main Street that the city planned to tear down. A few of the businesses that had to look for a new location were Sparks Printing, Shafter Combs and Son Plumbing and Heating, and Bell's Market. (Courtesy of *The Courier Journal*.)

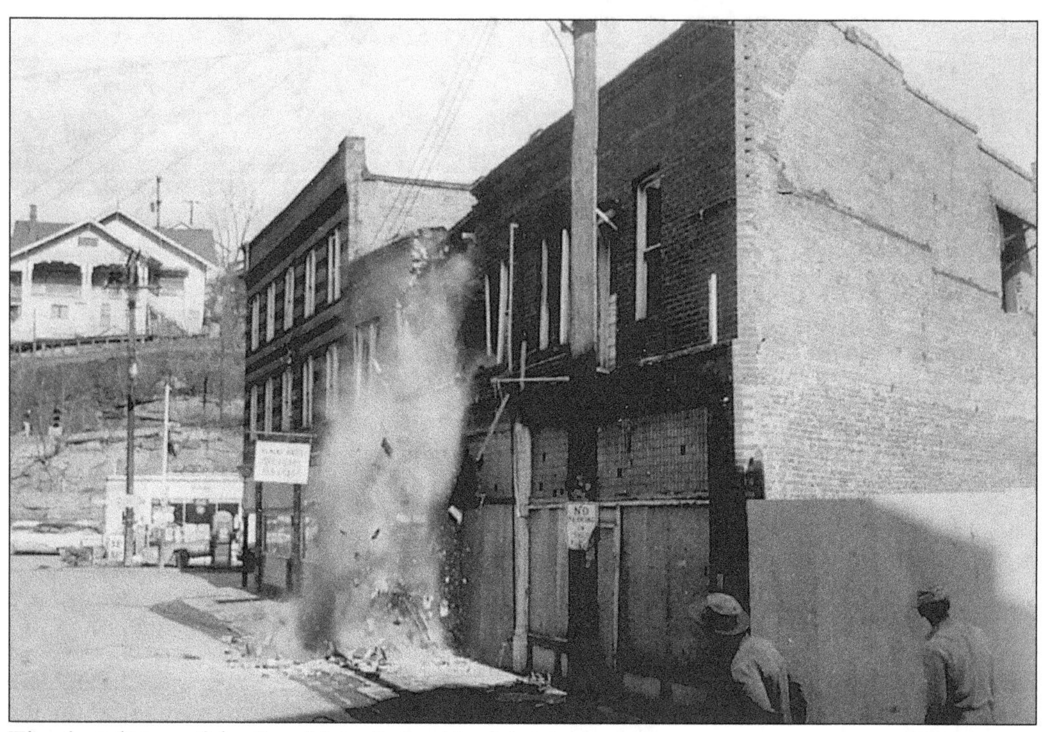

The demolition of the East Main Street block begins.

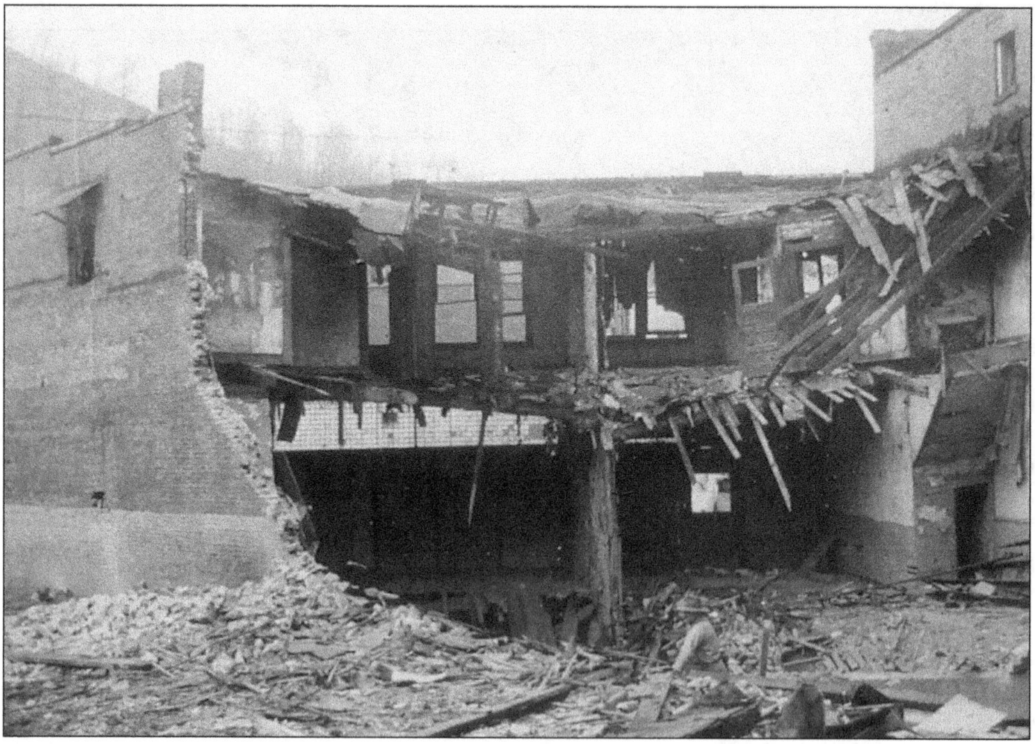

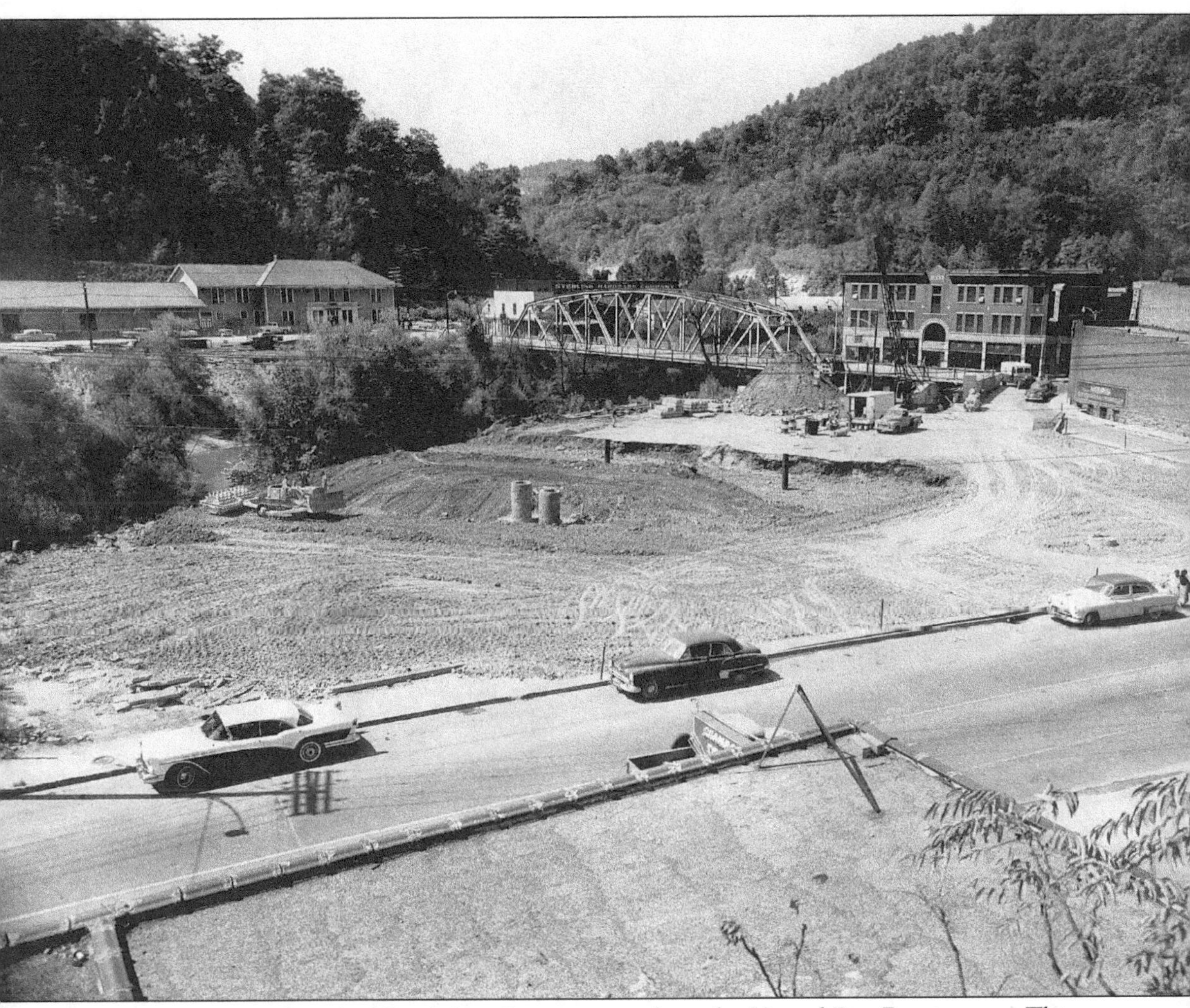

Main Street was to extend to East Main Street, across from the Hazard Fire Department. This change improved the traffic pattern and provided parking for cars belonging to people who worked and shopped on Main Street. The depot is at the end of the bridge, on the left, and the Hibler Hotel is on the right. The mouth of Town Branch is visible where culverts are standing on end.

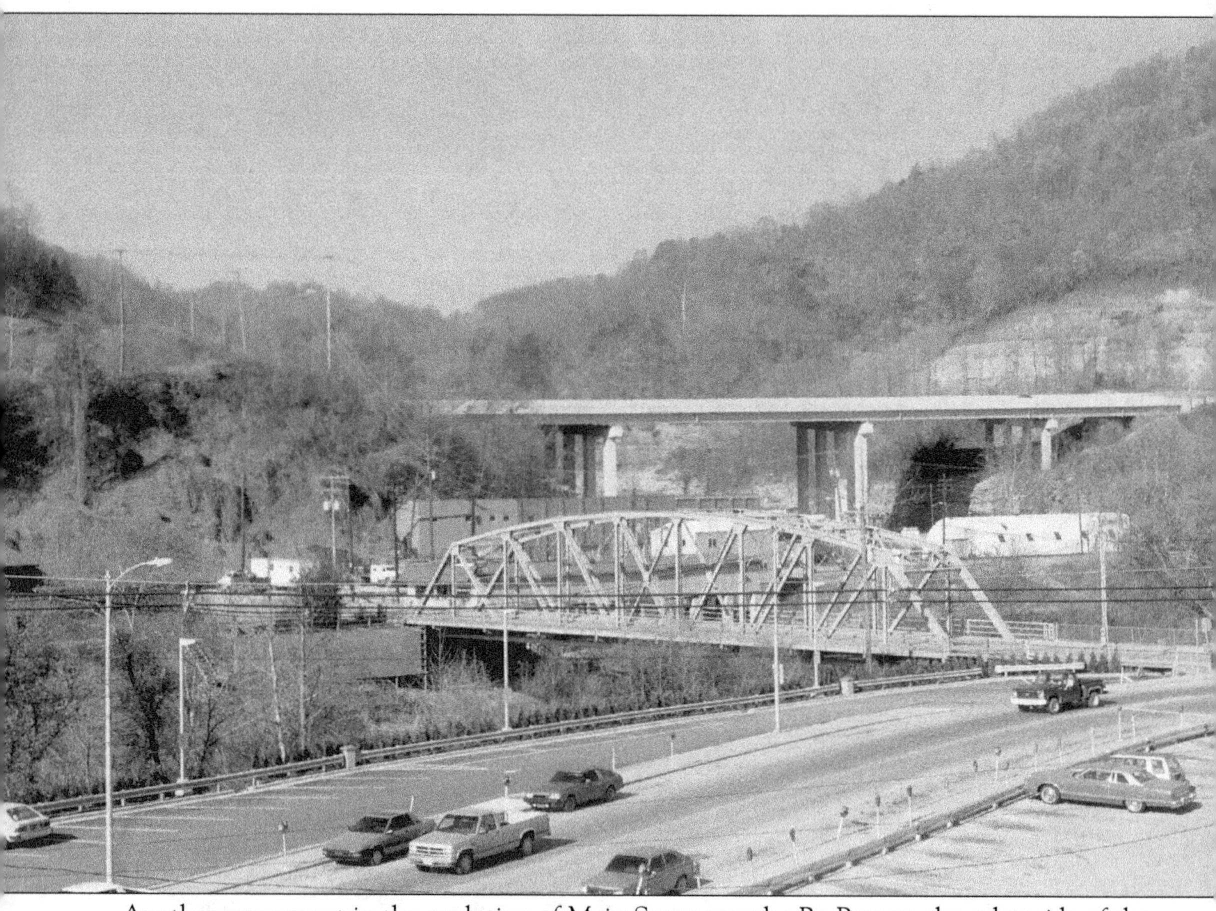

Another component in the evolution of Main Street was the By-Pass on the other side of the river. The bridge over Messer Creek is in the background. The new Hazard By-Pass, finished in 1981, connected Highway 15 on both ends of town. The route now takes traffic away from downtown to the other side of the river. The Hibler Hotel, missing in this picture, burned in 1976 (see p. 37).

Three

MEMORIES OF MAIN STREET

Main Street developed outward from founder Elijah Combs' first encampment. The street was expanding 20 years before the town or county got their name. Elijah Combs wanted the county seat to be close to the original settlement. Beginning in the late 1960s, Main Street suffered along with the rest of the country as local commerce moved to strip malls and shopping centers.

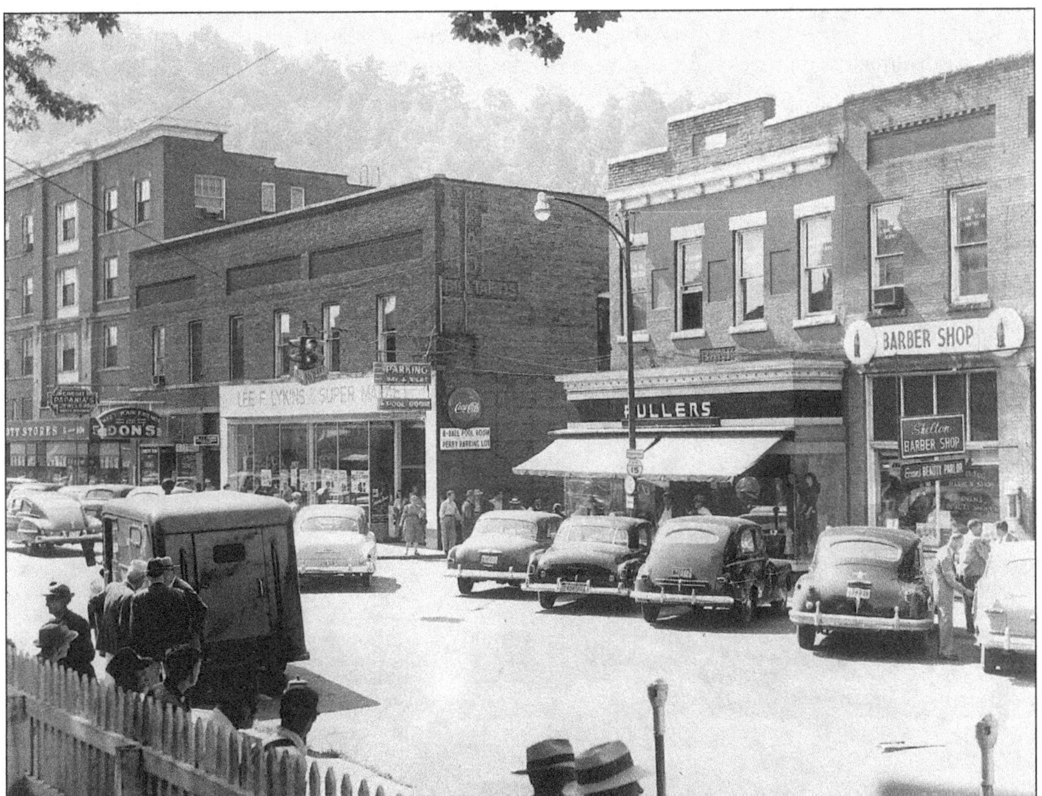

Cars and people packed Main Street almost every day in the late 1940s and early 1950s. This view is from the Perry County Court House yard. At this time, the population of Perry County was approaching 50,000 people.

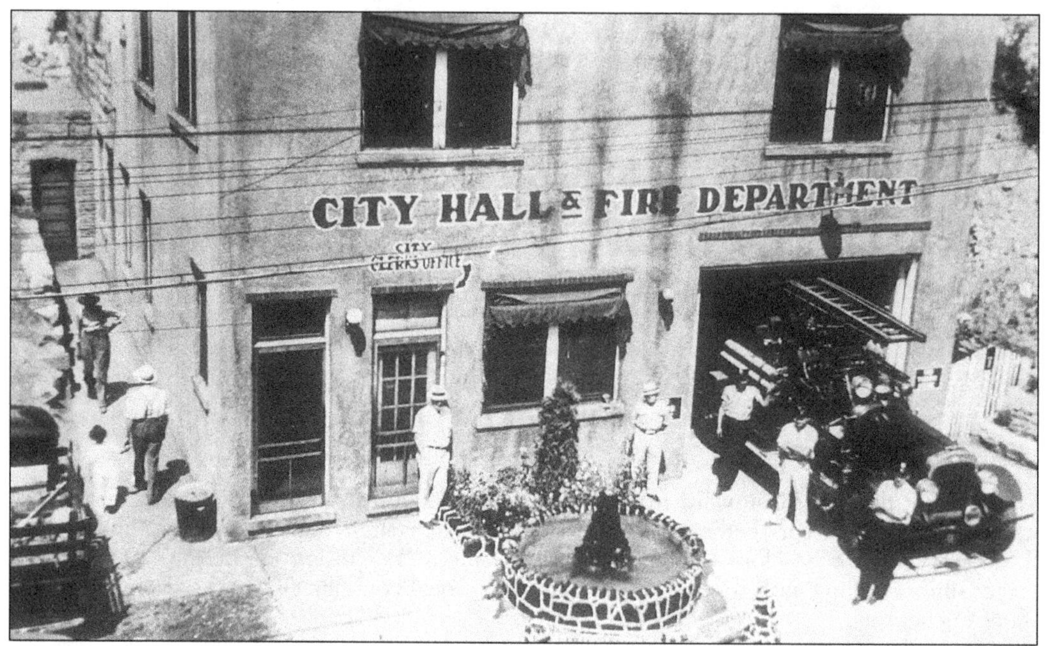

The goal of the 1937 Coal Carnival committee was to present "the greatest celebration ever in Kentucky." Pictures promoting the Labor Day event appeared on the front page of *The Knoxville-Sentinel.* Structures built of coal were displayed around town.

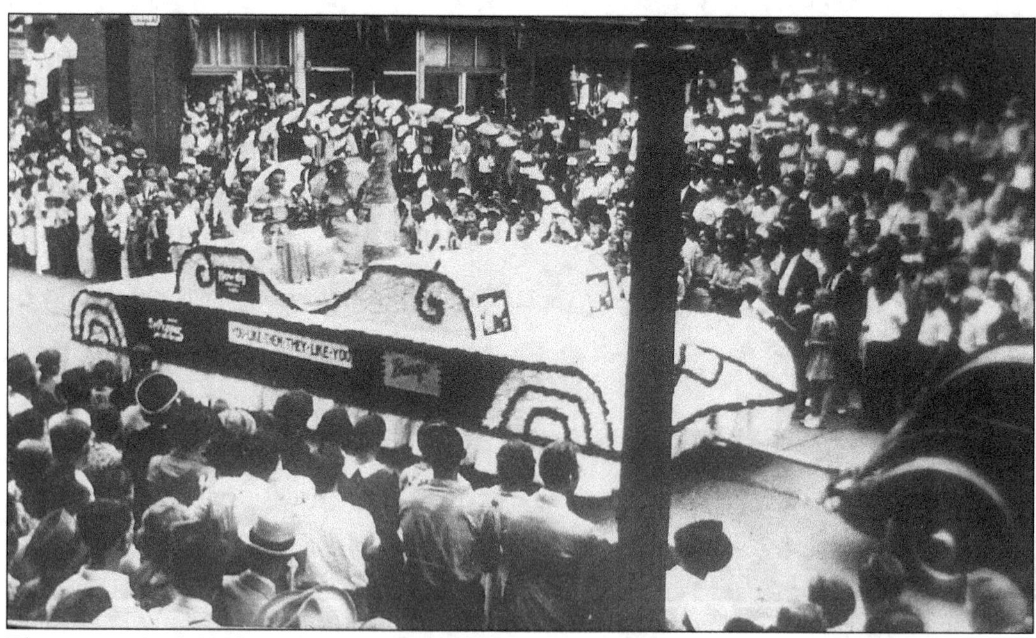

This was one of the floats in the mile-long, 1937 Coal Carnival Parade that attracted people from as far away as Virginia and Tennessee. One float designer came from Chicago.

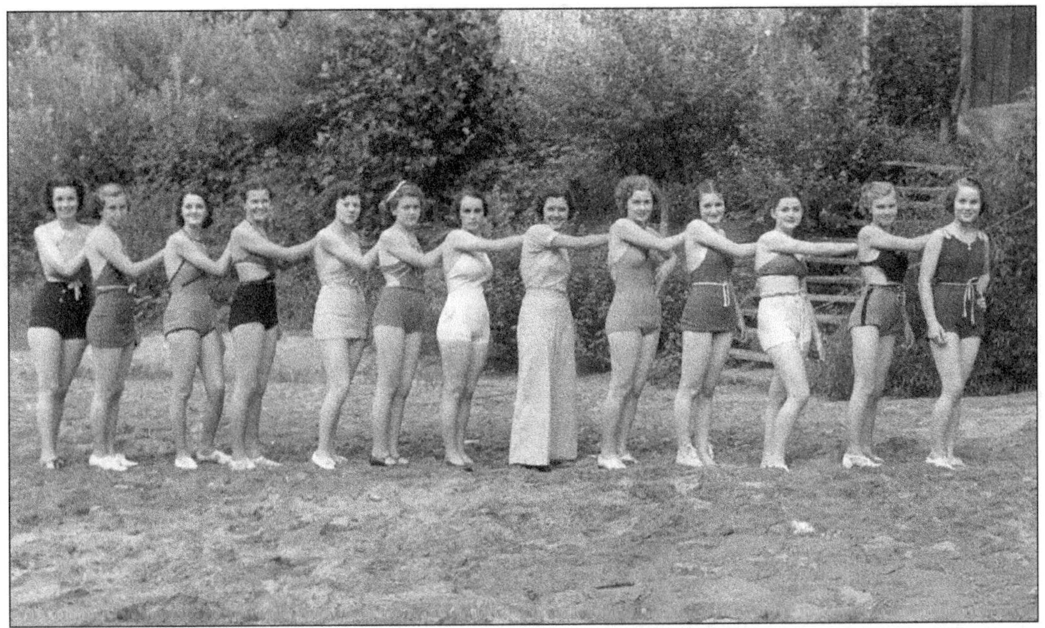

The candidates for 1937 Coal Carnival Queen pose on Sandy Beach, which is located on the North Fork of the Kentucky River near Viper. The queen, Rita Duff (ninth from left), was crowned on a stage in front of the Perry County Court House. She sat on a throne made of No. 7 coal. Miss Duff won a trip to the Cleveland Exposition, where she got to meet Johnny Weismueller, the actor who played Tarzan.

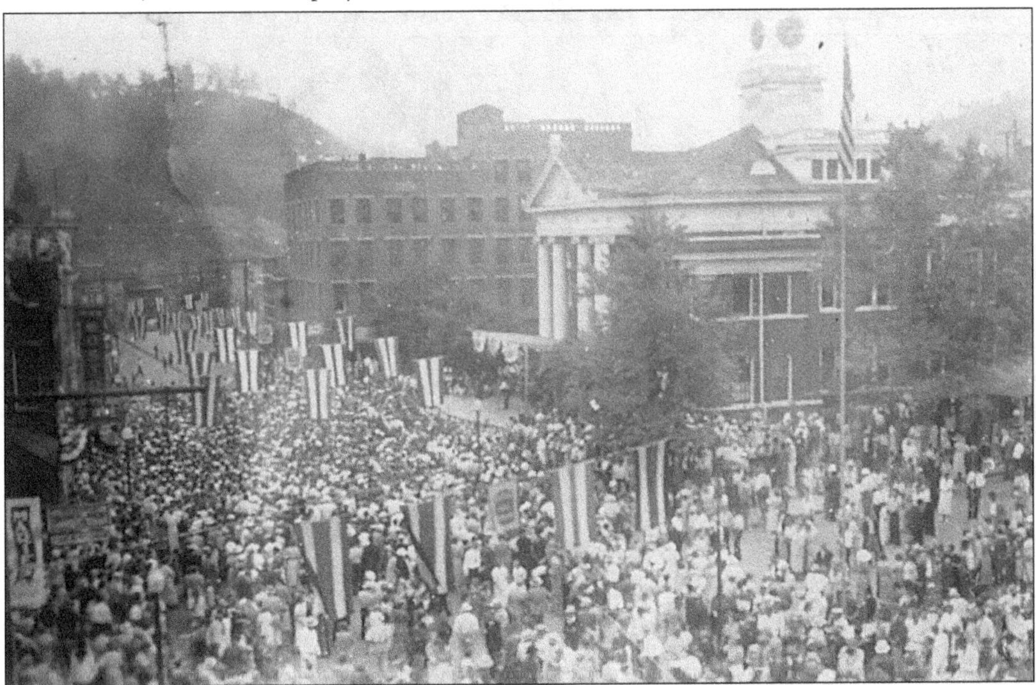

Tens of thousands of people were in town for the parade and the show. Throngs of revelers enjoyed singers from the Grand Ole Opry that performed on the stage in front of the courthouse.

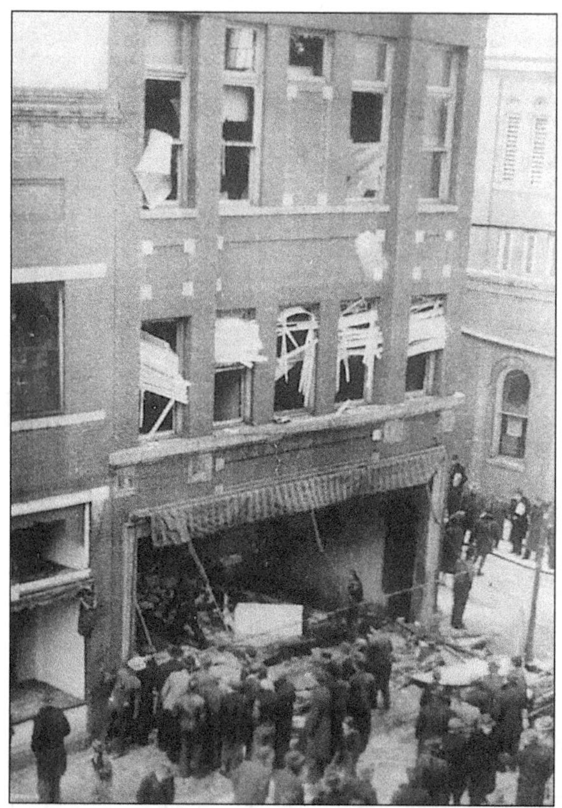

Around noon on January 25, 1940, a powerful blast ripped through the Kentucky Power Company on Main Street. A well had been sealed a few months before, in which gas had accumulated. Joe Curtis was killed. Ruth Dagley, Hope Harmon, and Jacqueline Bullard were injured. When Miss Bullard arrived at one hospital it was lunch hour, and the hospital staff was unavailable, so the injured walked across High Street to the other clinic.

Seeking shelter from light rain on Saturday morning, June 13, 1942, several people were standing under the marquee of the Family Theater. A worker overloaded the marquee, which hung by two chains, and it fell, killing Armine Sizemore, a mother of seven children. Sixteen-year-old Jesse Bowling remained in a coma for eight days as a result of his injuries. Here L.O. Davis (in front of car) views the scene of the accident. The *Hazard Plaindealer* newspaper is next to the theater.

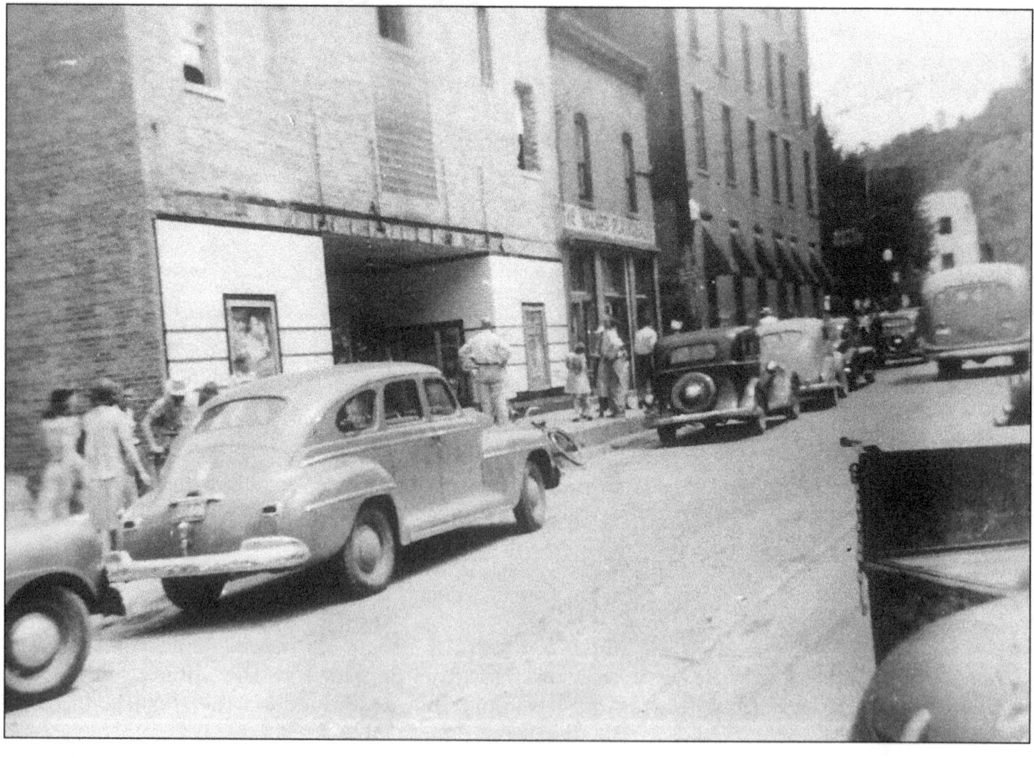

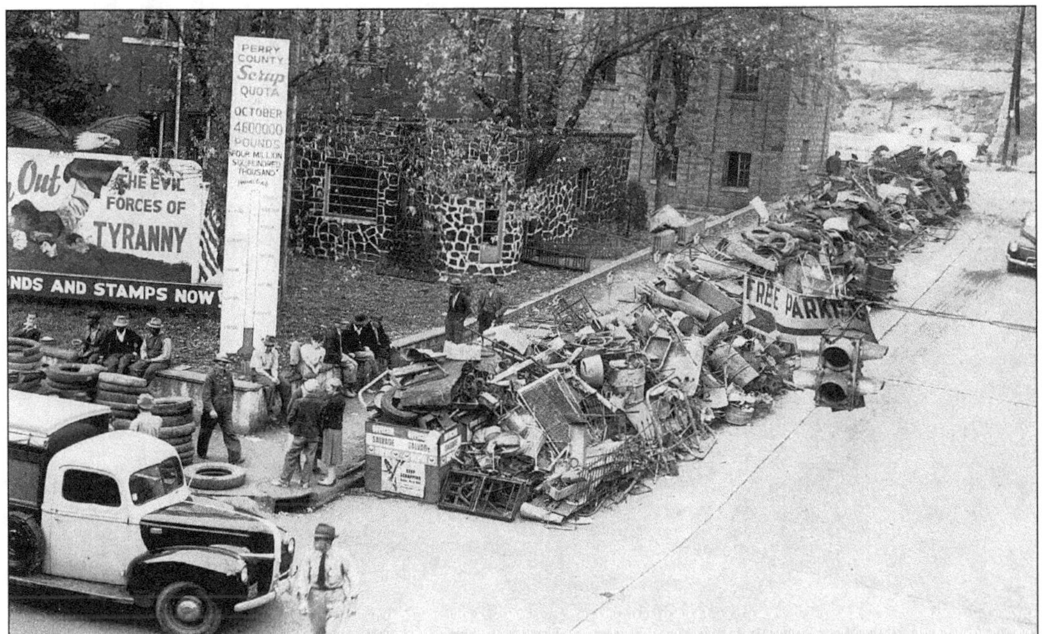

The people of Hazard and Perry County were active in the scrap drives organized by the Civilian Defense Council during World War II. Workers brought the bulk of the metal to the front and side of the Perry County Court House. The heap of metal pictured is on Fleet Street. The small building beside the courthouse was the coal house constructed of No. 7 coal during the 1937 Coal Carnival (see p. 40).

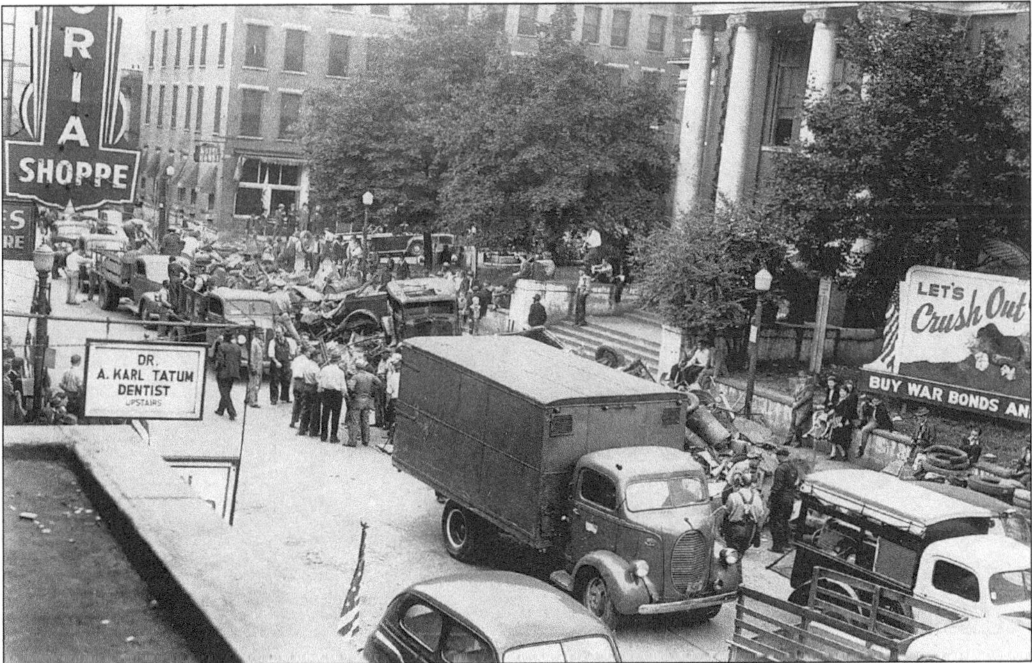

A "Junk Parade" of borrowed trucks carried the scrap metal and rubber for the World War II effort to the railroad, where it was loaded onto railroad cars and taken to foundries for processing.

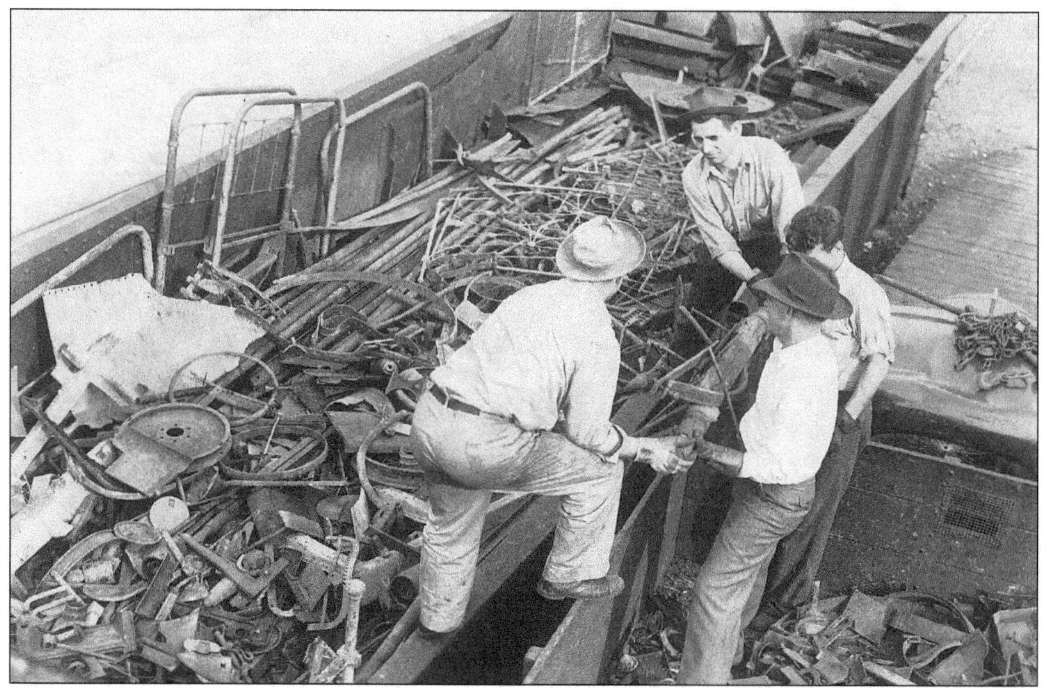

Charles Nicholson, Charles Speaks, Dan Waltman, and Roy York load scrap onto a railroad car before shipping it to a steel plant to be converted into arms for Americans during World War II. Hazard businesses closed on June 22 and 23, 1943, to allow workers to collect scrap metal. During "Scrap Days" nearly 500 tons were collected.

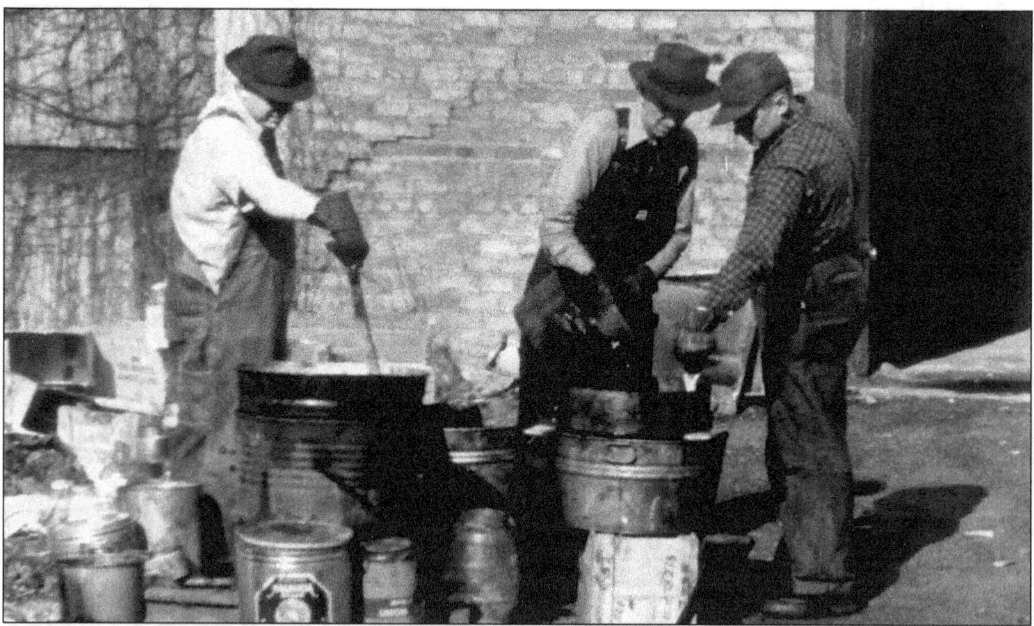

In addition to scrap iron and steel, other materials such as brass and other non-ferrous metals, rubber, rope, and fats were collected. These men supported the war effort by rendering grease and lard in large containers. Two of the three men pictured here are Bob Hall (on the left) and Charlie Howard (middle).

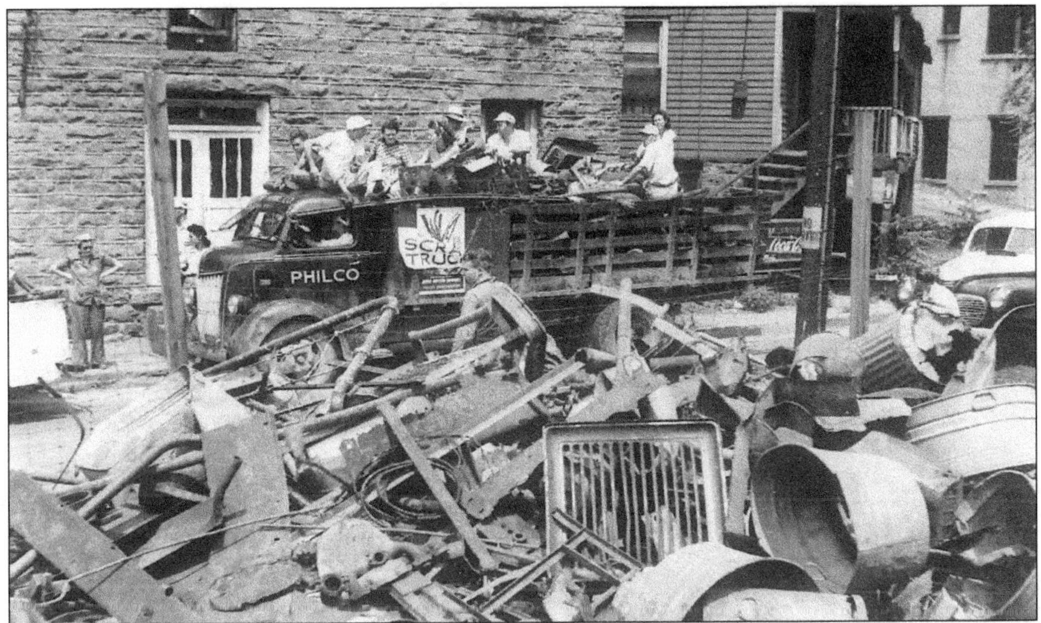

A collection point was on East Main Street across from the fire department. The spirit of patriotism was running so high some people actually sacrificed good metal objects. Workers caught up in good intentions dismantled wrought-iron fences along sidewalks and in graveyards.

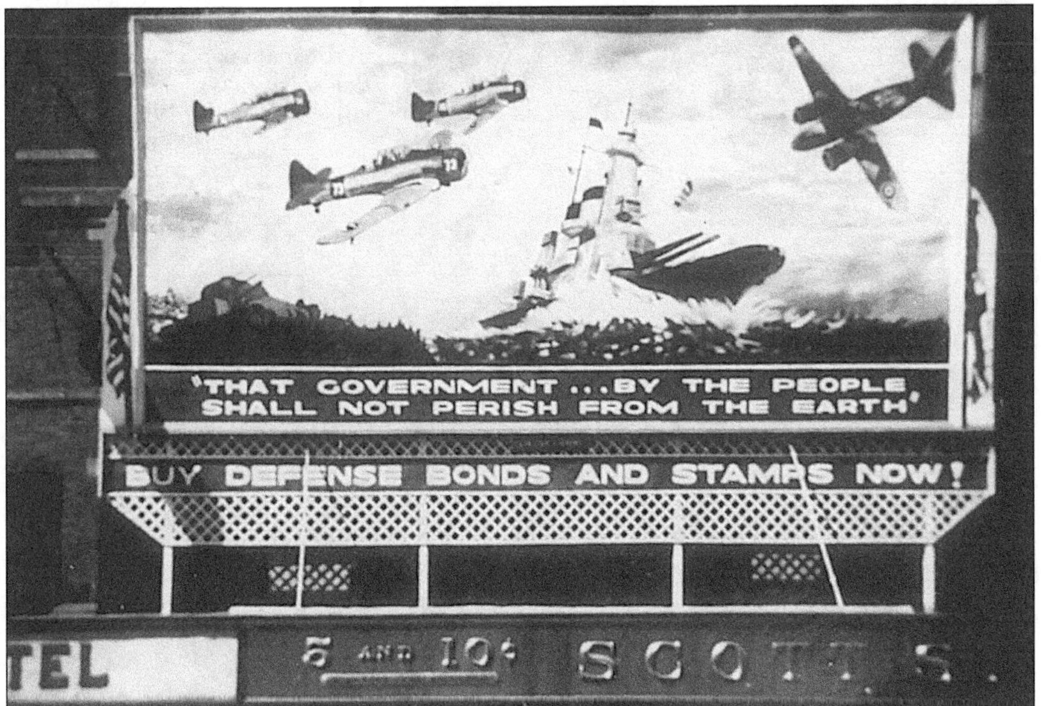

This billboard was constructed by local sign painter Chester Stevens. It inspired the townspeople, during World War II, to do what they could for the war effort. The sign was mounted on the front of the Grand Hotel.

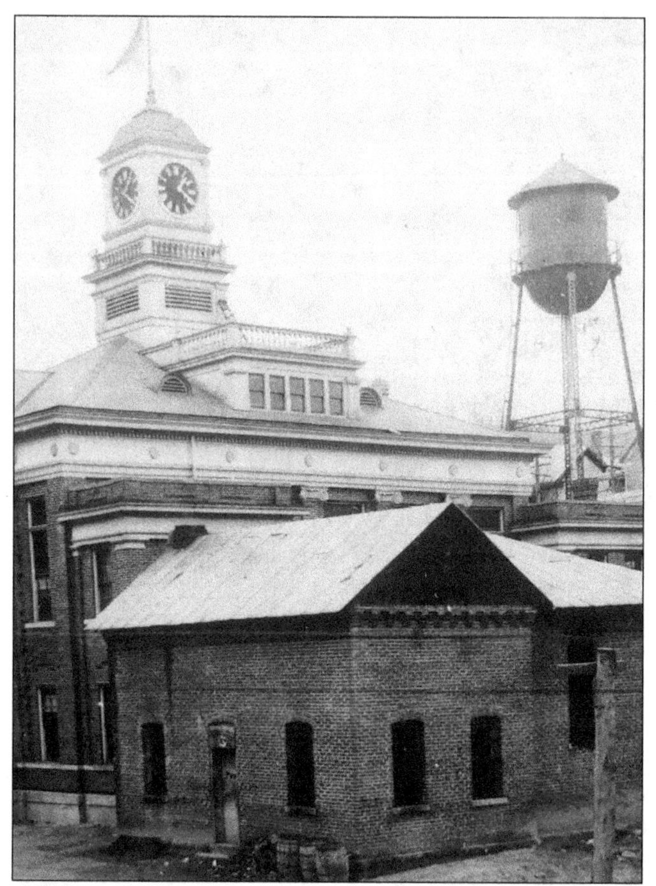

A short article in the *Hazard Herald* dated December 31, 1914, tells the Perry County jail story: "The old jail building [at left] is now an empty shell and an eyesore there beside the Court House. The county authorities will, no doubt, take steps to have it torn down. That will be as welcome as was the final removal of the old blacksmith shop from the rear of the Court House a year or two ago. Transfer to the excellent new jail building on the river front was effected the latter part of last week, under the careful management of Jailer James Holliday and his assistants. There can be no more disturbance by prisoners in the main part of town." Below is a photo of the "new jail" taken in the 1950s.

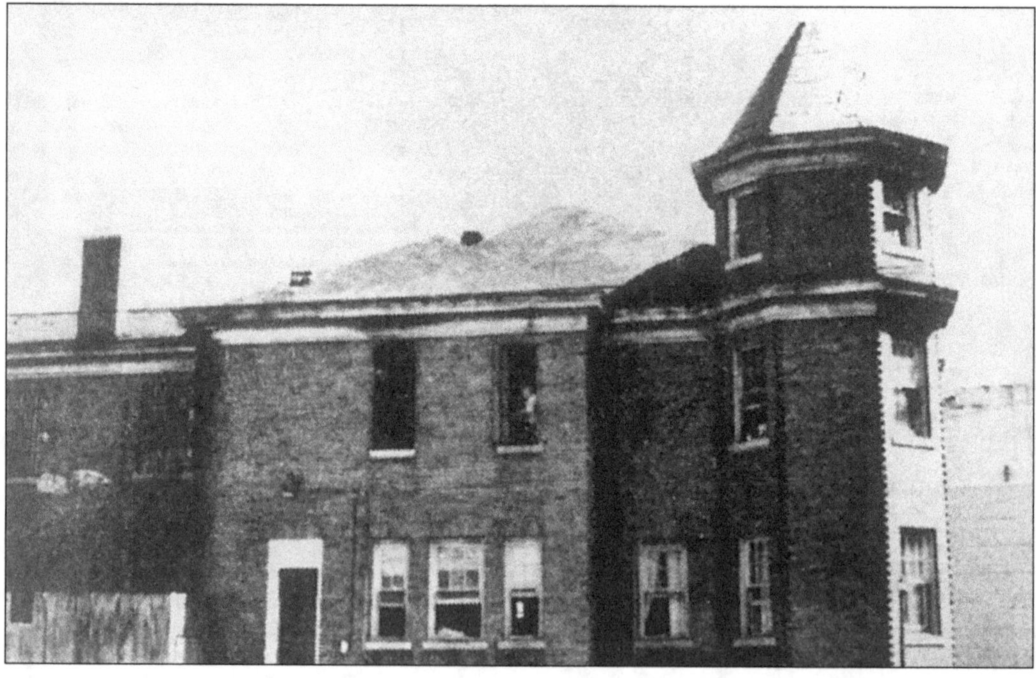

All through the 1940s traffic traveling south through Hazard could not avoid the corner of Main Street and East Main Street. Often, the downtown was so full of cars and people that it was necessary for shoppers to drive around Main Street and High Street four or five times to find a parking place.

Hazard Lunch was operated by Polly Baker Gross. Mrs. Gross served authentic country cooking such as mustard greens, soup beans, and onions, as well as chicken and dumplings. Each meal cost 75¢. She went on to open Gross' Steak House, which was simply an upscale Hazard Lunch with ice cream and sundaes. (Hal Cooner.)

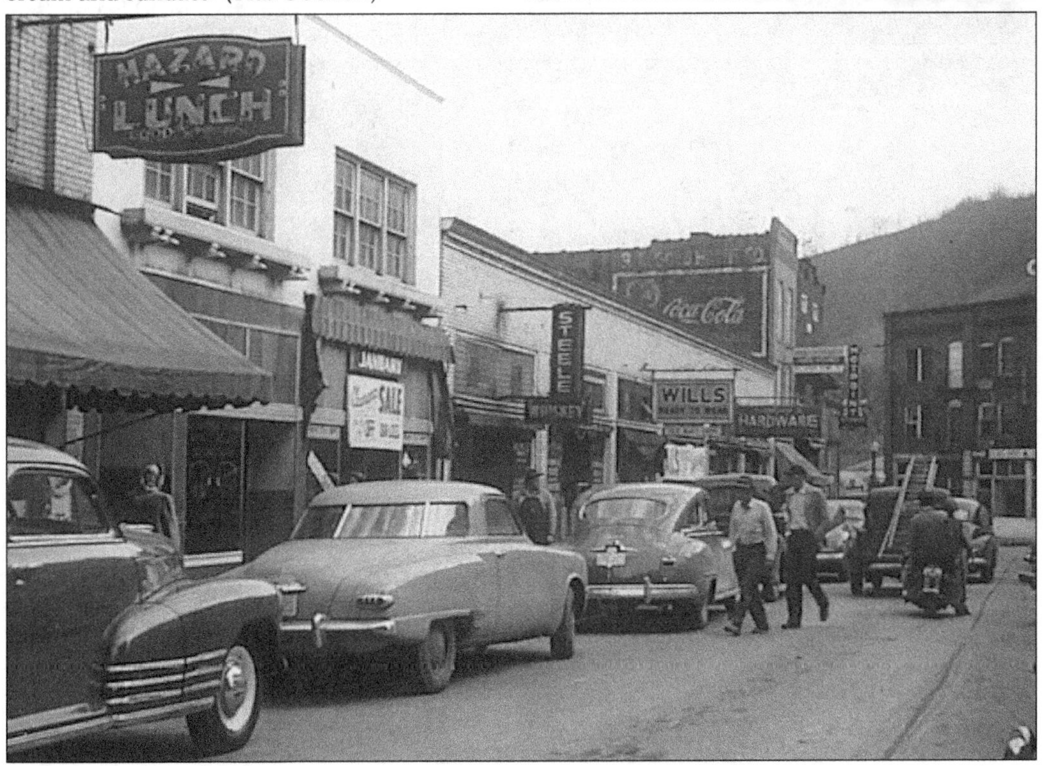

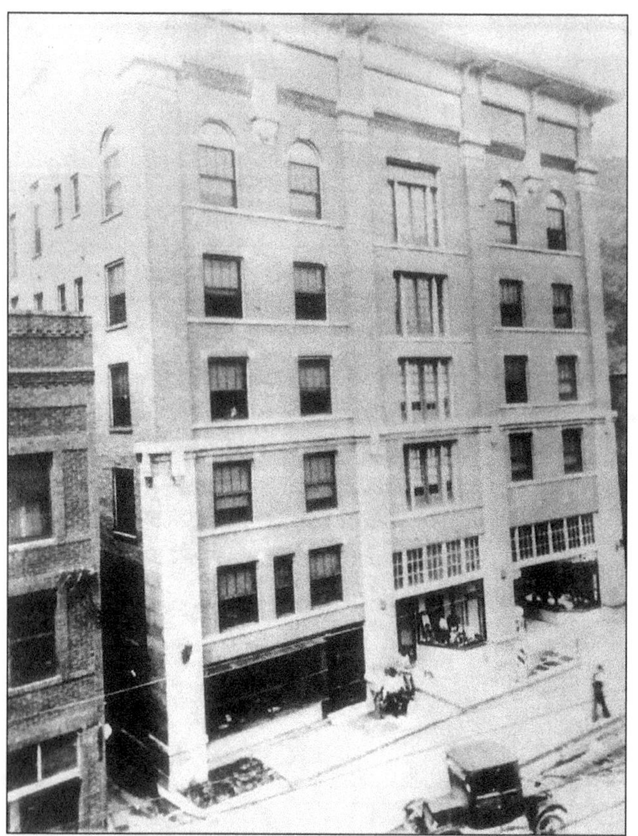

The Combs Hotel began as a six-story brick building when it was constructed in 1921. Fire consumed the tall Main Street building on December 15, 1928, killing five people. The building was in litigation and boarded up for several years. Bill Fouts bought and rebuilt the building, removing the two top floors of the original structure. He renamed it the Grand Hotel, a name borrowed from the residence rooms that were in the building next door.

This station wagon belonged to Hal Cooner. His studio and a dress shop were in the Arcade, a connecting corridor between Main Street and High Street. The Arcade could be called Hazard's first and only "indoor mall."

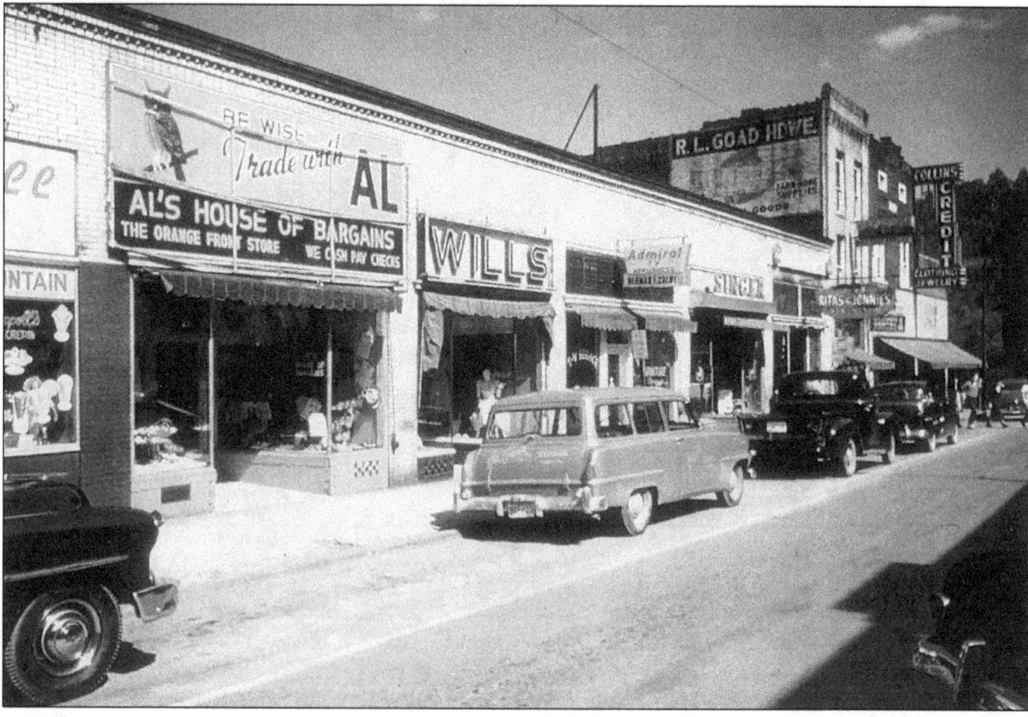

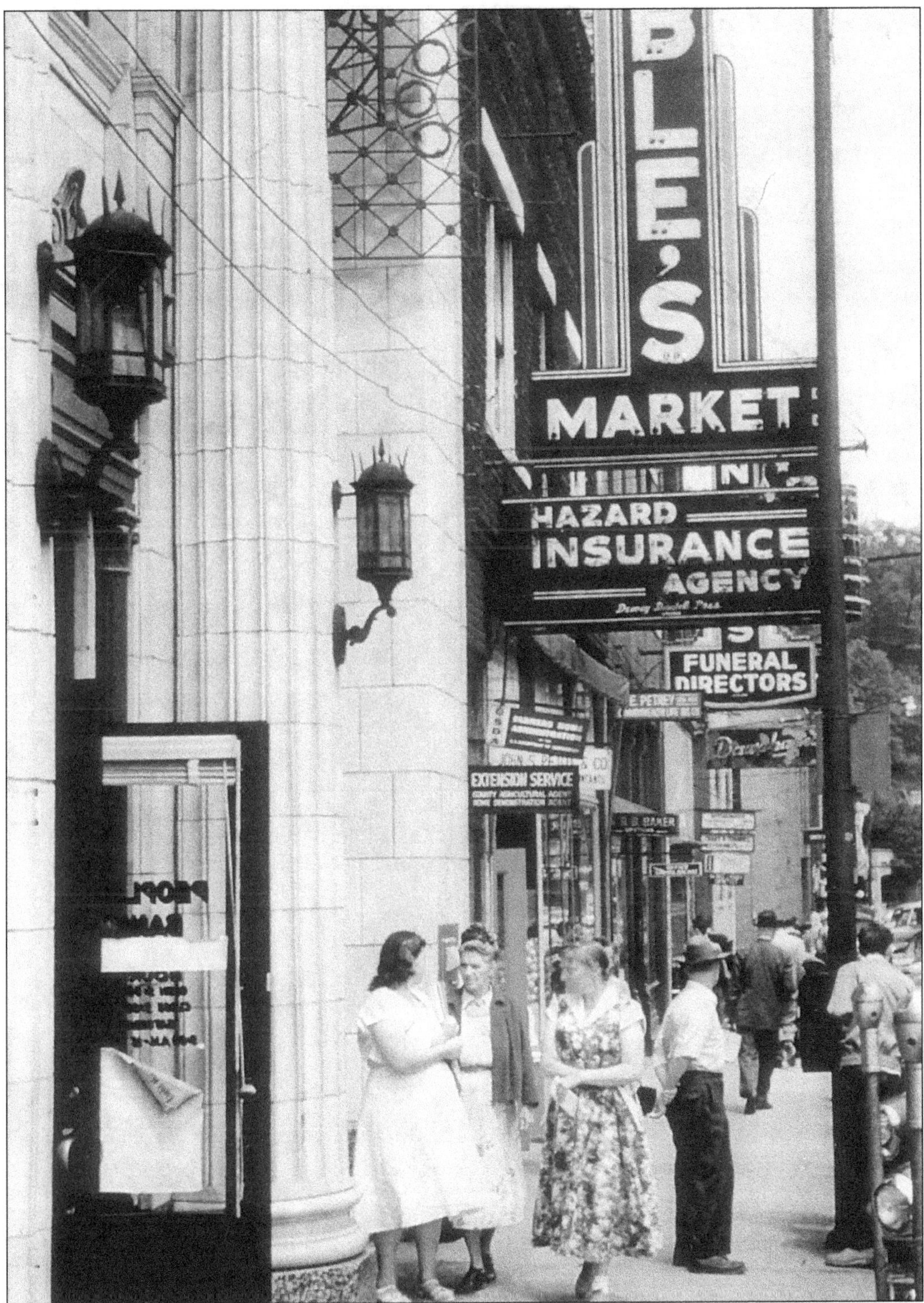

Main Street was the social center of the county. On Saturday, many people shopped on Main Street and stopped to visit with friends. The Hazard Insurance Agency and Peoples Bank are still important businesses on present-day Main Street.

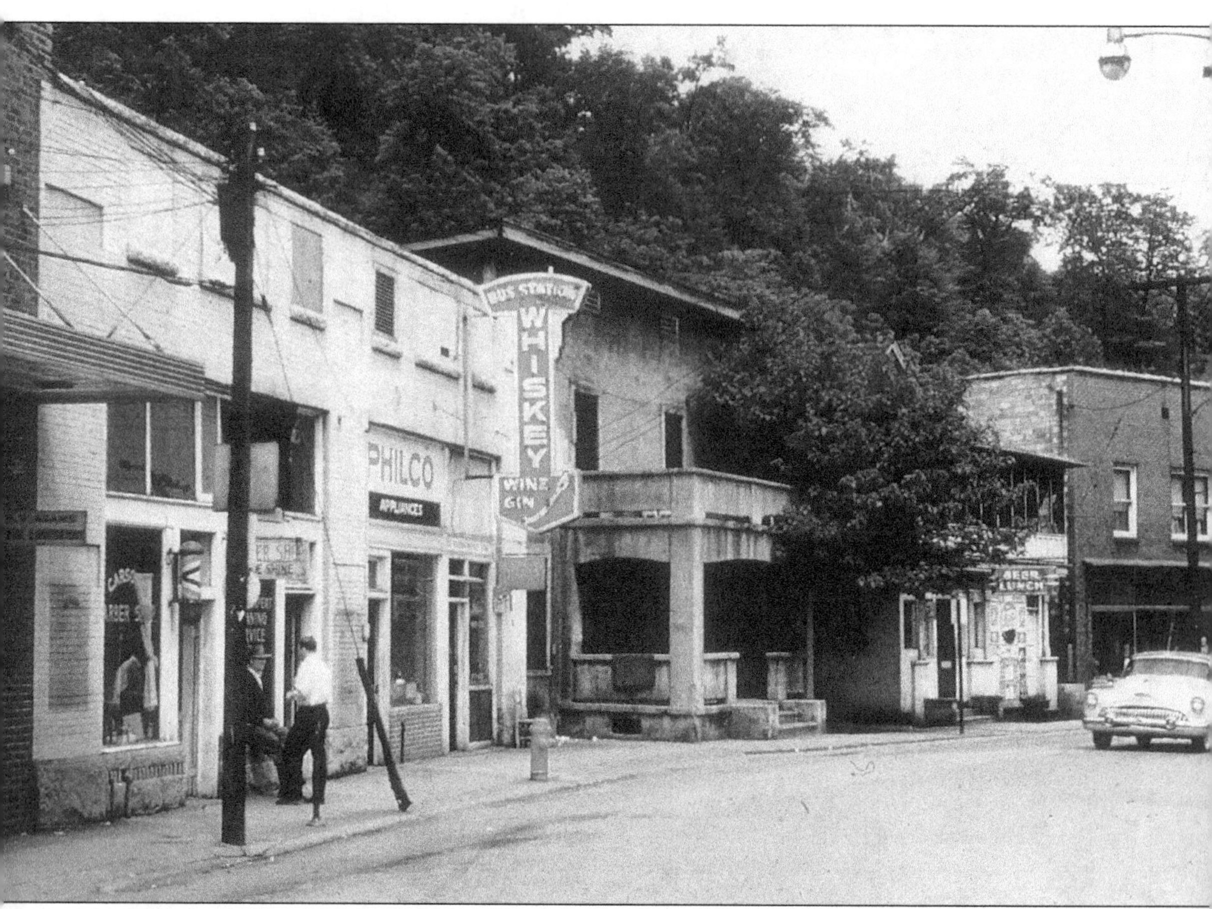

Some businesses on the north end of Main Street were Adams Dental Lab, Carson's Barber Shop (owned by Carson Cornett), Expert Cleaning Services, Philco Appliances, the Greyhound Bus Station, a liquor store, and an apartment building owned by Nell Tye Baker. (Hal Cooner.)

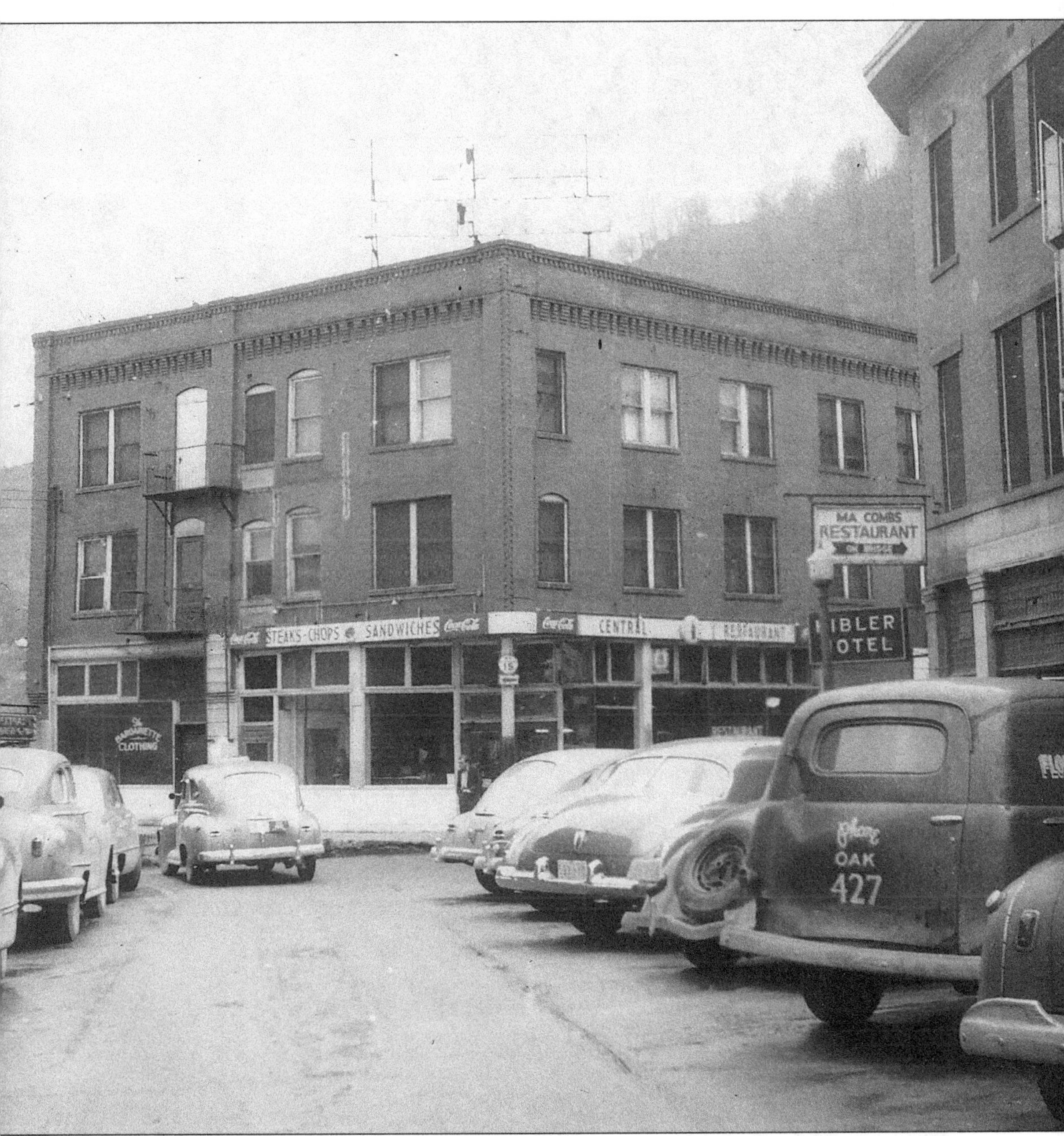

In the 1940s, a person could make a long distance telephone call on the Cumberland Telephone and Telegraph Company pay phone, located in the Central Hotel. The hotel is said to have had a theatrical air inside, complete with old-fashioned globe lights. It was also a favorite place for playing cards and placing bets on almost everything.

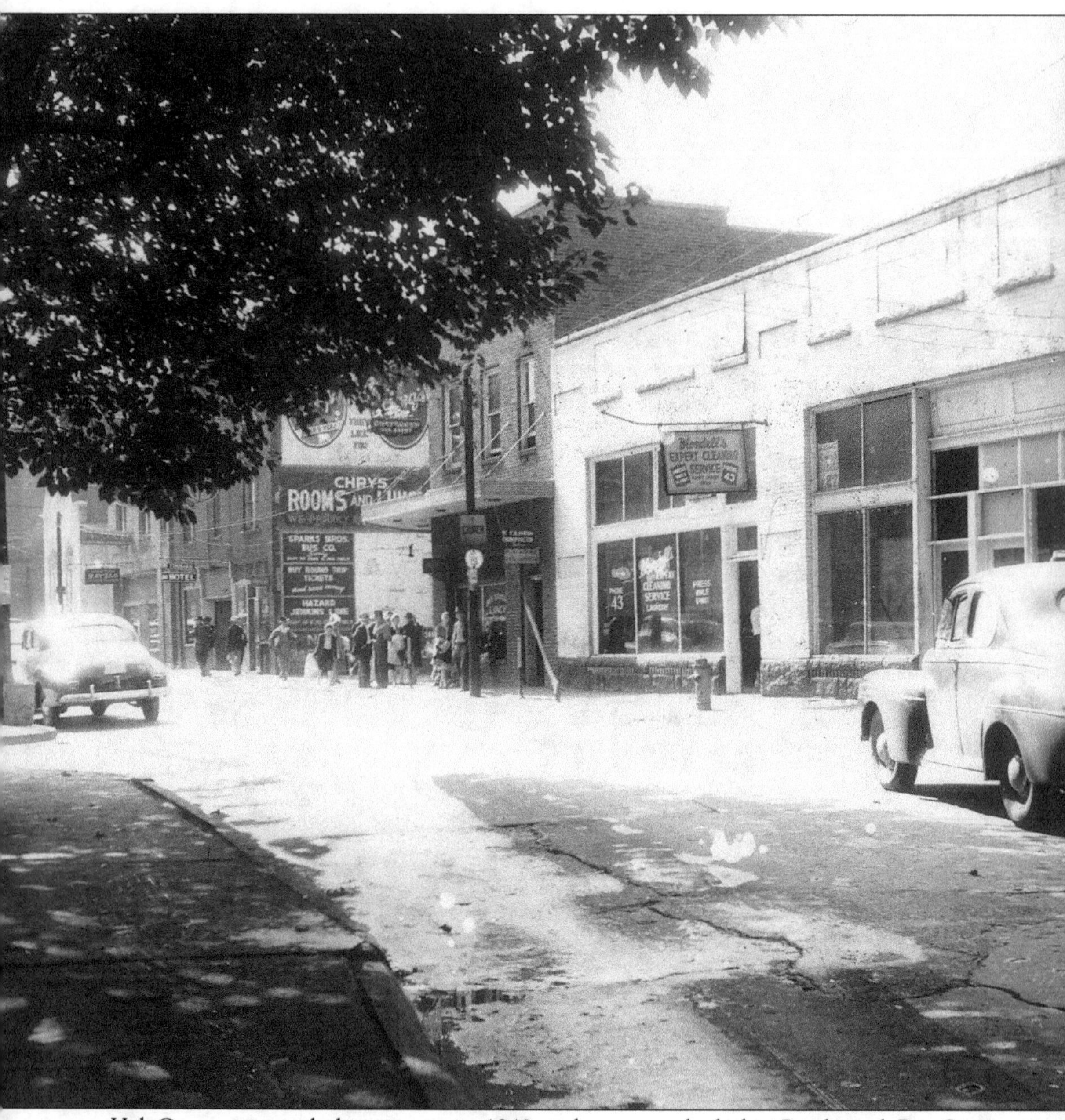

Hal Cooner snapped this picture in 1948 as he approached the Greyhound Bus Station from North Main Street. In the early days of Hazard this land belonged to Leah Feltner and others. When Main Street was joined to High Street on the north end, the business section began to grow.

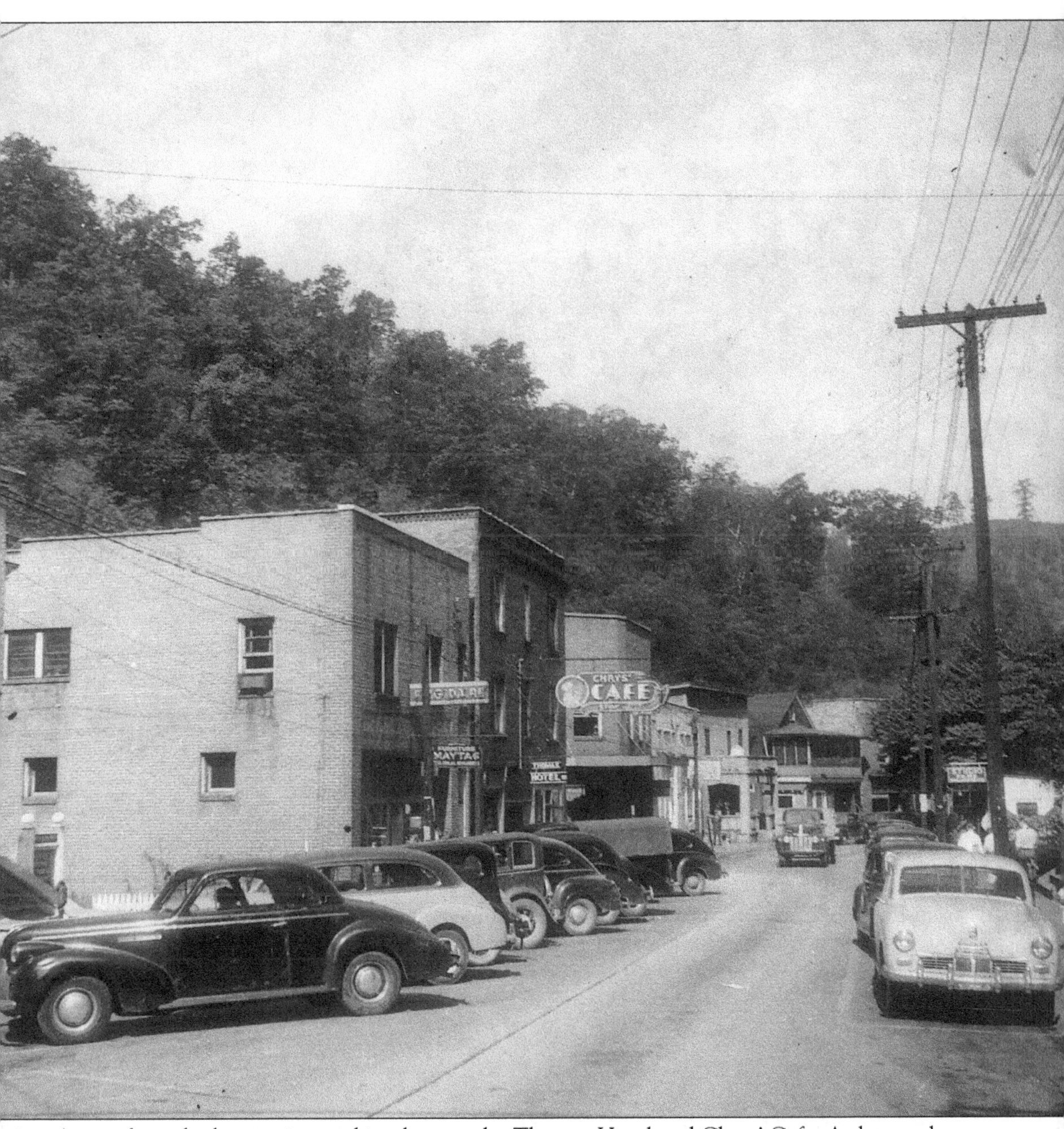

Across from the bus station parking lot was the Thomas Hotel and Chrys' Cafe. As long as bus lines ran to Hazard, this was a thriving section of Main Street. (Hal Cooner.)

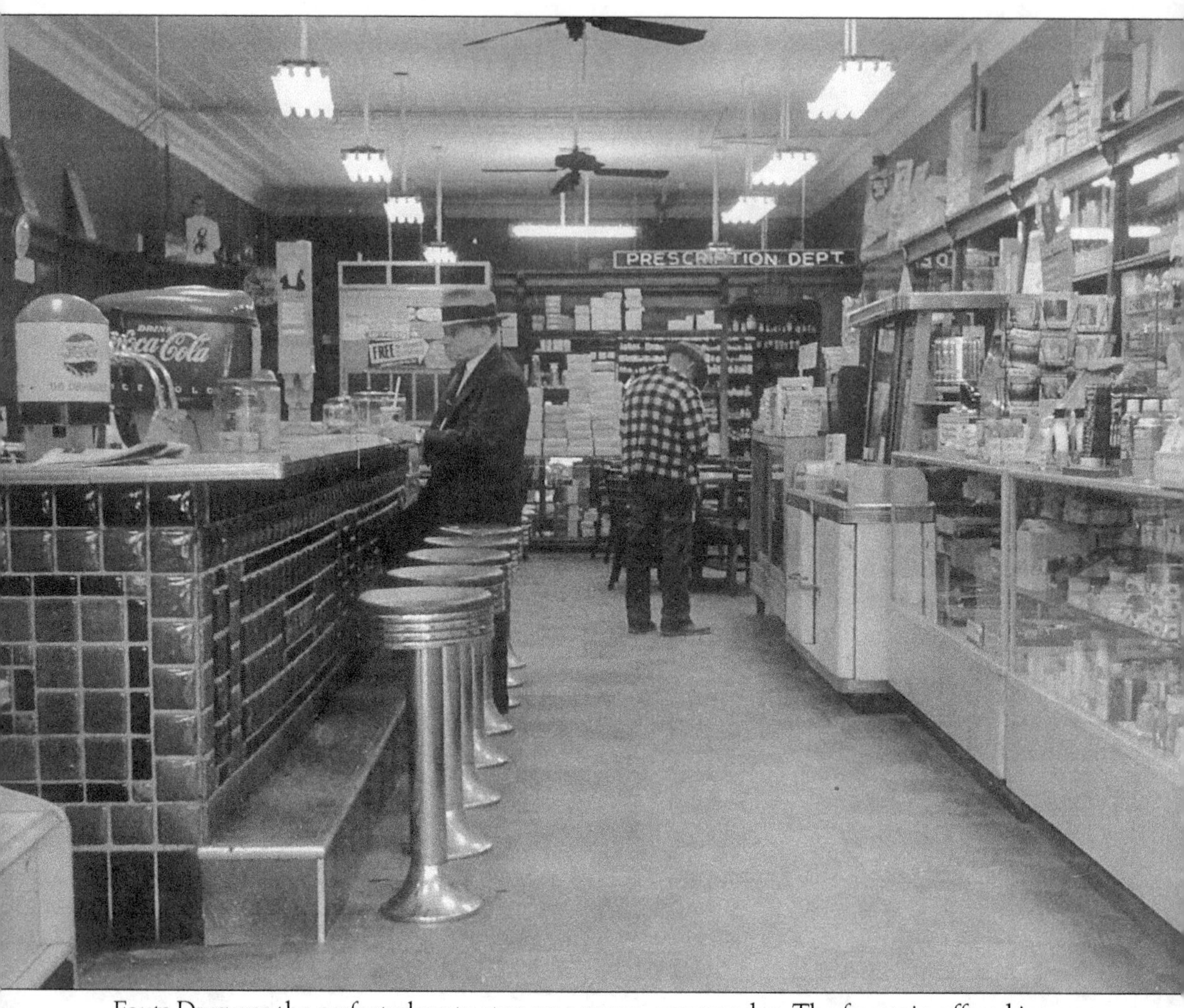

Fouts Drug was the perfect place to stop on a warm, summer day. The fountain offered ice cream cones, sundaes, and many kinds of soft drinks, including the famous "cherry Cokes." They sold cosmetics and perfumes on the other side of the store. The pharmacy was in the back. In front of the pharmacy, along with the grown-up chairs, were two sets of child-size ice cream parlor tables and chairs.

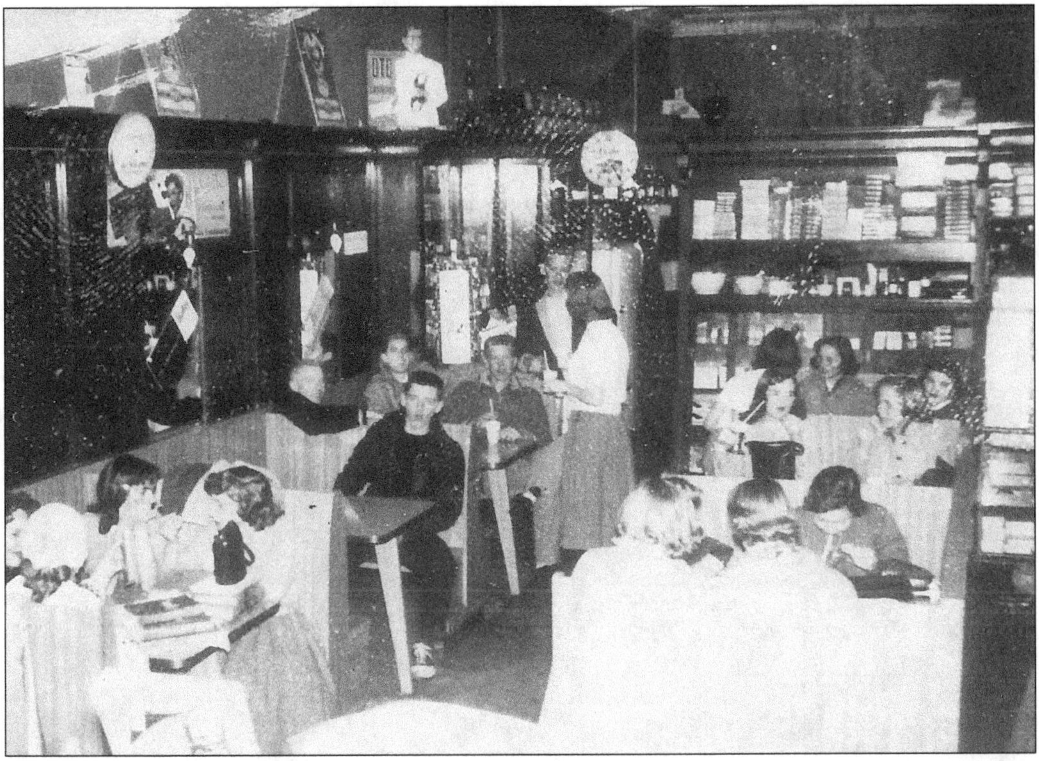

When Hazard High School was out in the afternoon, many boys and girls headed for the two drug stores on Main Street for some heavy socializing. Most of them had to be home by 4:00 p.m.

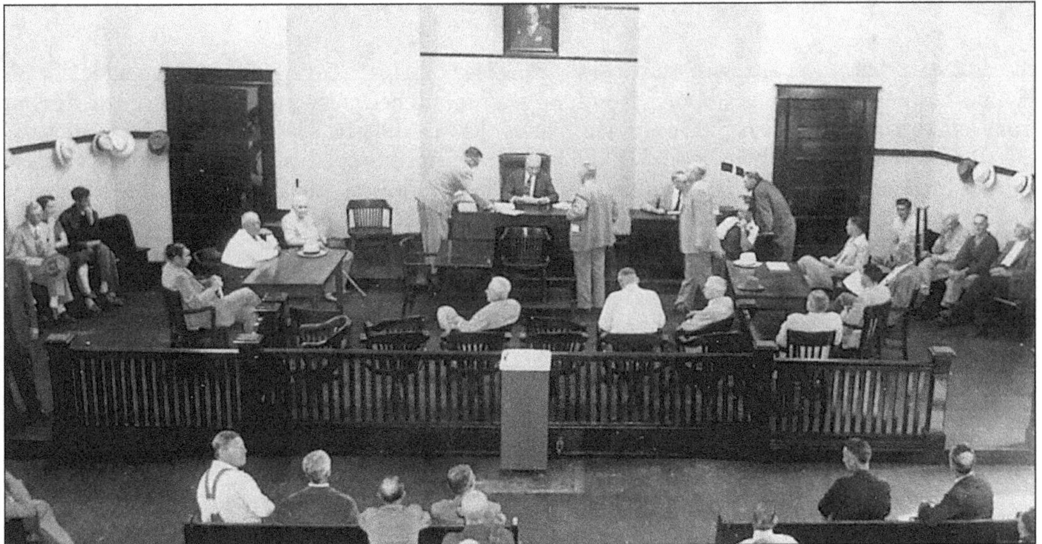

Lawyers, jurors, and others who gathered in the Perry County Circuit Court room in September 1953 were pleasantly surprised by the many improvements added since the last term of court. The rusted metal ceiling had been replaced and painted a light color. The former drab and dirty court room was the project of the fiscal court and Judge Fred Combs. The judge in the center is Courtney Wells.

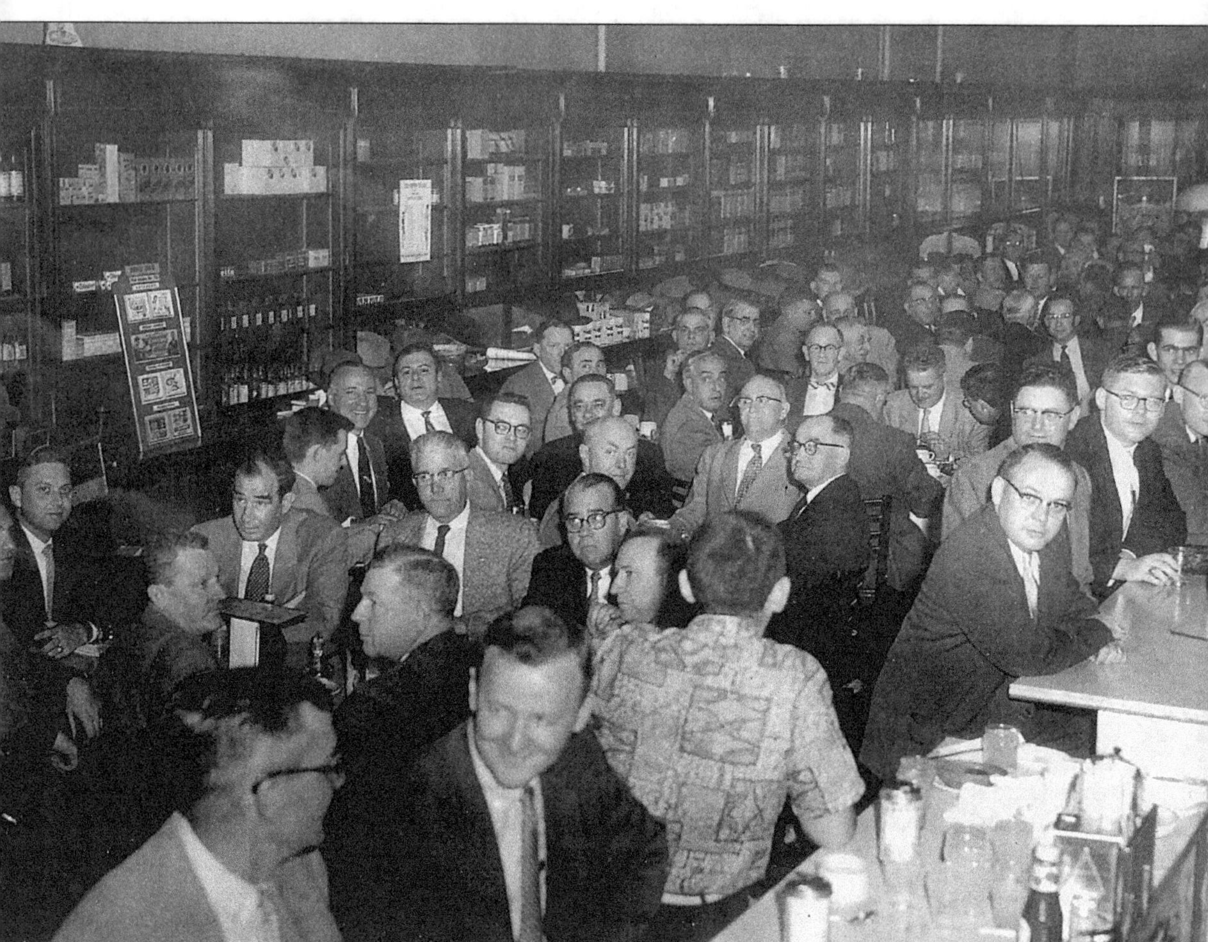

Hazard businessmen gather at Don's Restaurant for a luncheon of squirrel. Some of the diners, from left to right, are John S. Owen, Tug Fields, Joe Goodlette, Dan Mitchell, Jack Stewart, Lus Oxley, Fred Combs, Ben Rose, Willie Dawahare, Bruce Stephens, M.K. Eblen, Ern Begley, Farmer Brashear, Lewis Hopper, Paul Petrey, Charles Nicholson, Joe Eversole, Bobby Bergman, Pat Payne, Dr. Dana Snyder, Kelly Deaton, Drew Faulkner, Billy Pendleton, Roy Eversole, Bernard Faulkner, Lee Lykins, C.A. Zoellers, M.H. Alcorn, Dr. Cooley Combs, Howard Smith, Joe Duncan, Paul Tayloe, and Ben Lutes.

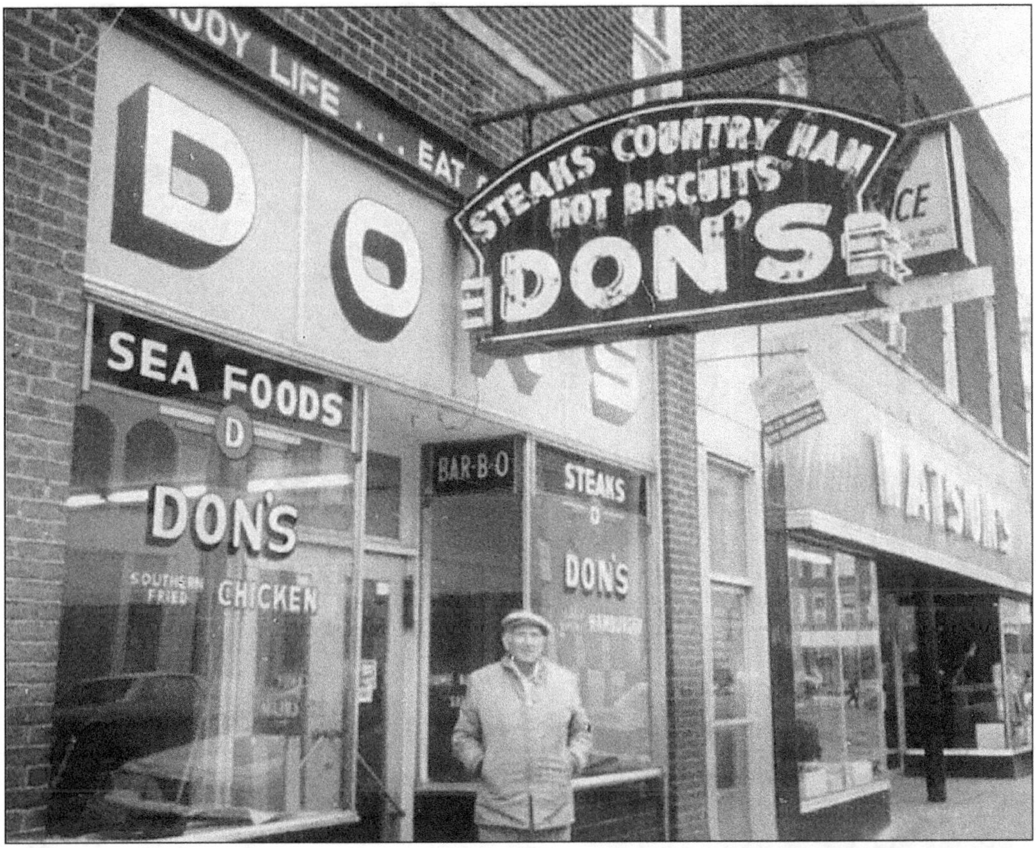

Pappy Edwards, a friend to everyone, is pictured entering one of Hazard's favorite restaurants. The restaurant opened on July 4, 1947. The picture was taken just before it closed in January 1985.

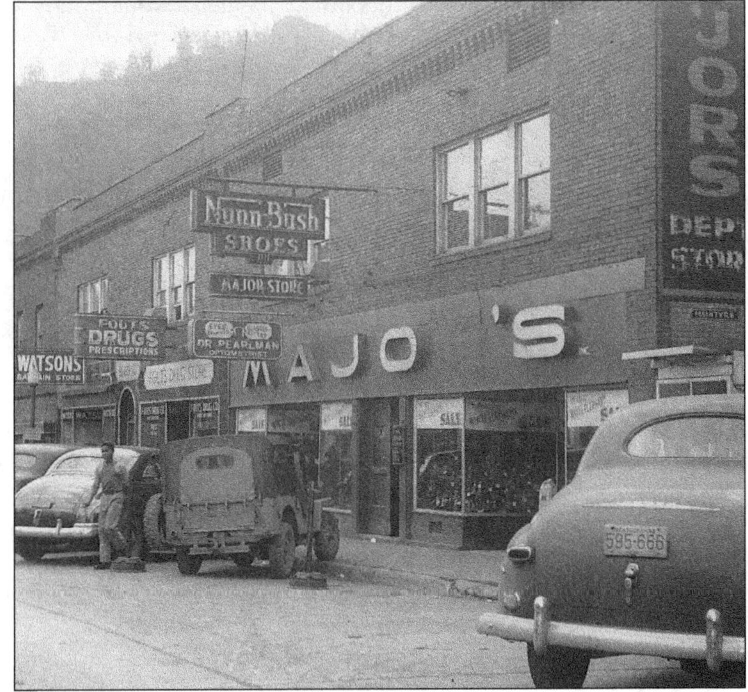

This store is Major's. Today, people still remember the x-ray machine in the shoe department. To check if shoes fit, customers would place their foot in the opening of the machine and a green screen would show the bones of the foot and the outline of the shoe. (Hal Cooner.)

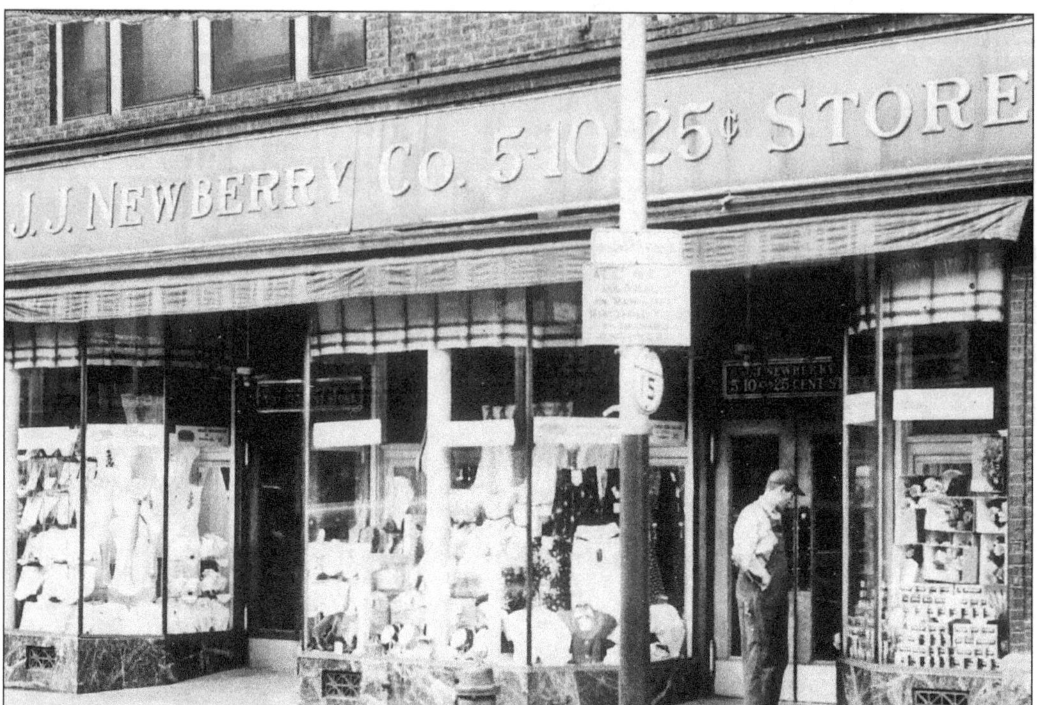

In 1955, J.J. Newberry's store underwent a major renovation. Plate-glass windows were installed so that the inside of the store could be viewed from the street. This store introduced self-service shopping. Additional aisles were installed. Air-conditioning provided pleasant shopping in the summer. Before self-service shopping, salesclerks would follow customers around the store. Self-service was a new idea that made many shoppers feel they were not getting good service.

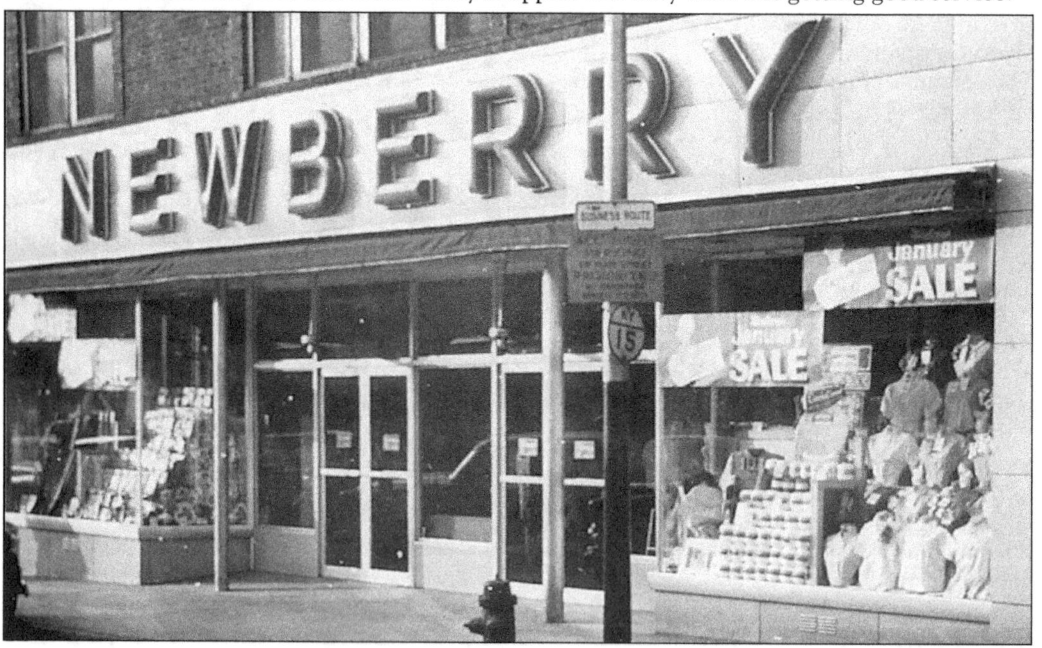

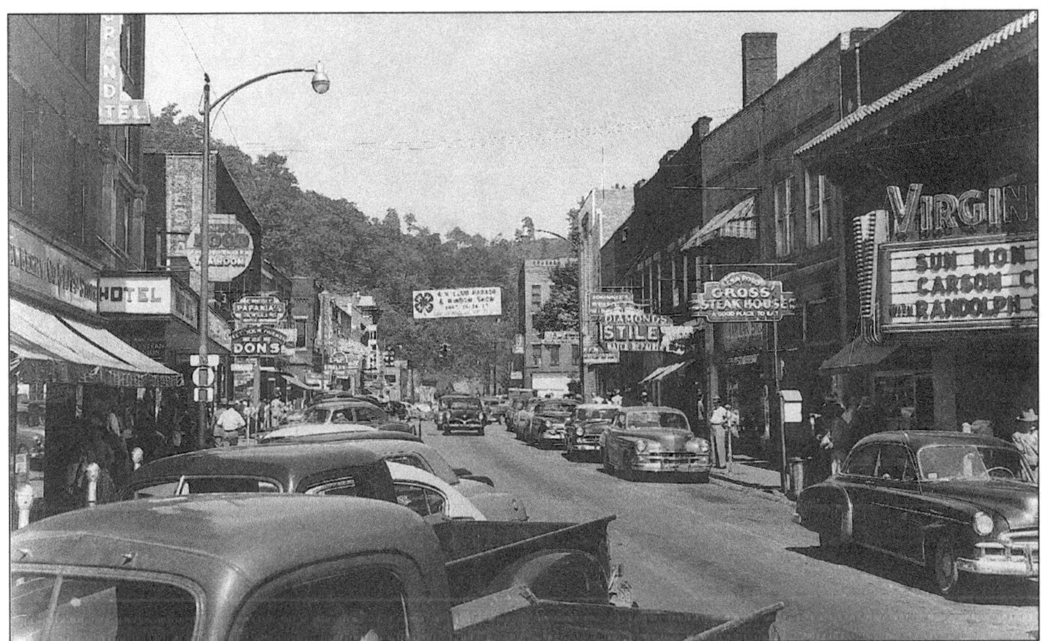

In this September 1952 photograph, the town was preparing for the annual 4-H celebration. Each store window had an exhibit prepared by 4-H clubs from county schools. The windows were judged and winners were presented with ribbons and trophies. On Saturday the 4-H clubs, including approximately 600 young people, presented a parade led by local bands, including the Hazard High School Band (shown below).

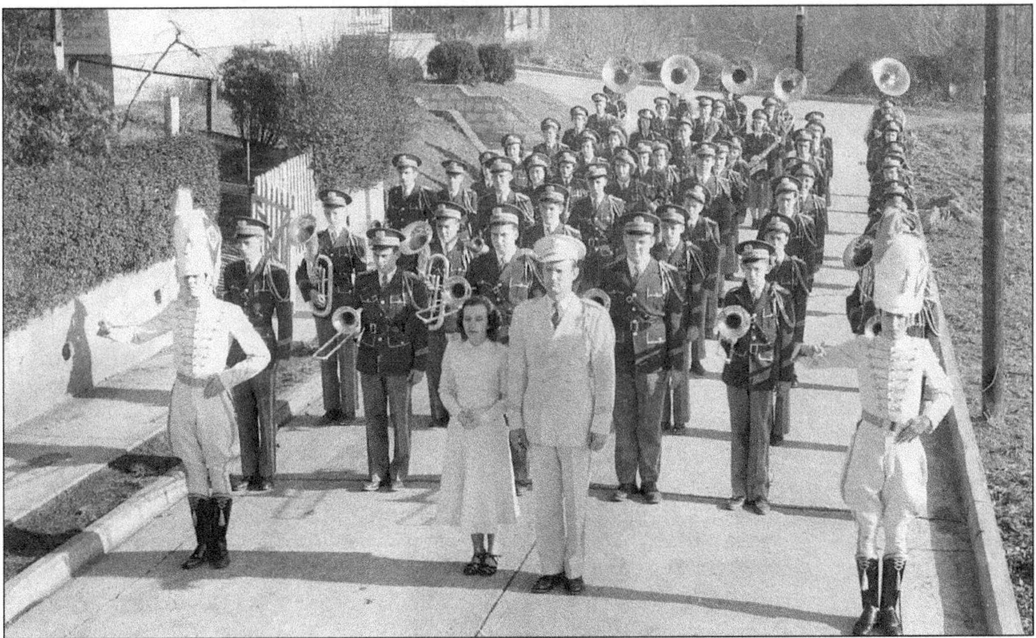

The leader of the Hazard High School Band was Walter Hall (in white suit). The band formed on Ward Street and met the parade in front of the Hazard High School. The parade marched down Baker Hill, up High Street, turned left on Campbell Street, and continued down Main Street. The band stopped at the courthouse to serenade the onlookers for the rest of the parade.

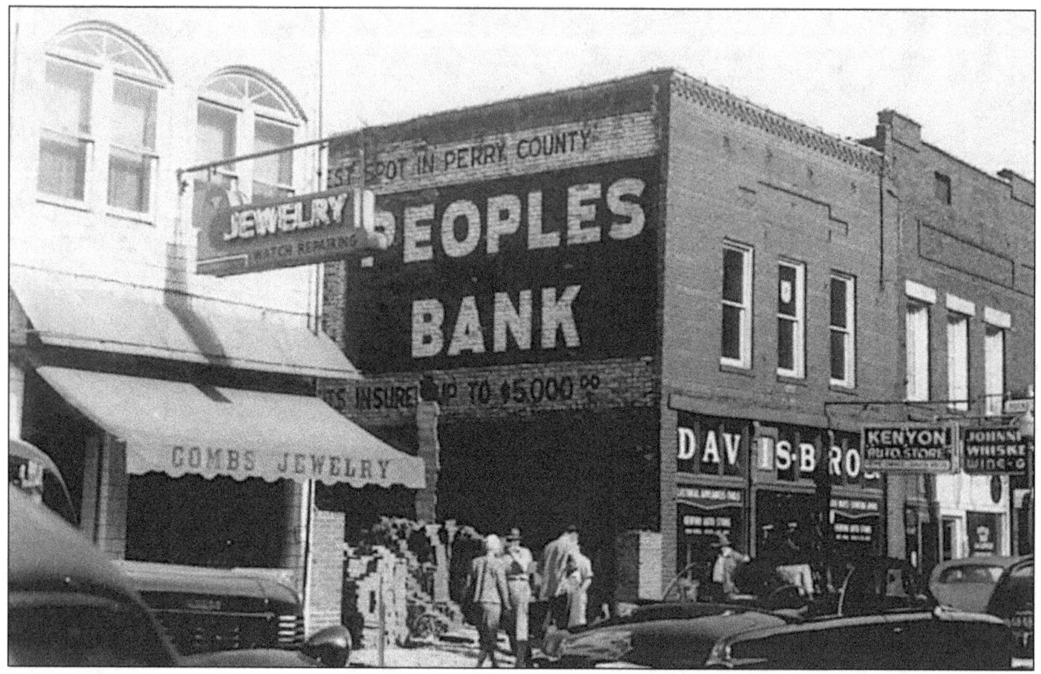

Davis Bros. Store sold a large variety of items, such as hardware, fishing tackle, fishing licenses, and sometimes aspirin. Those who grew up in Hazard were familiar with Davis Bros. because they went to the store with their fathers. The Davis Bros. Kenyon Auto Store opened in 1945. (Hal Cooner.)

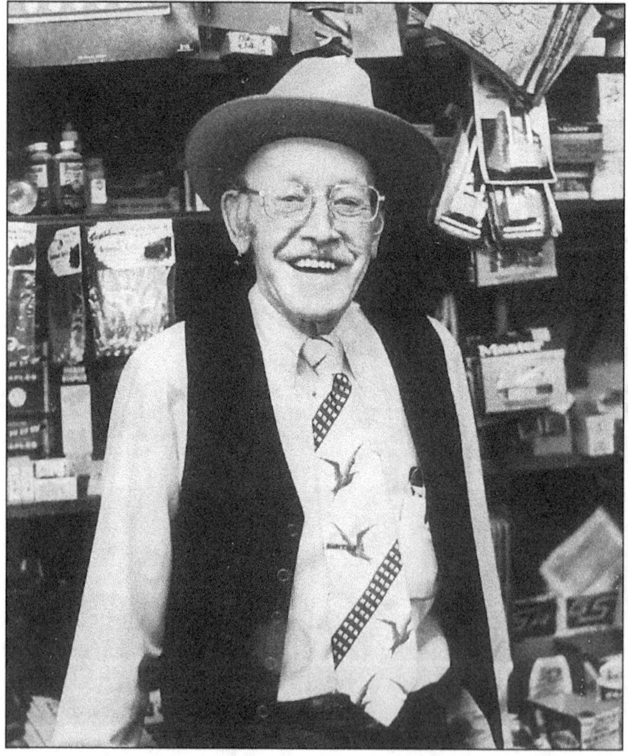

Roscoe Davis stands behind the counter just as he is remembered by hundreds. Roscoe and Bill owned and operated Davis Bros. for over 30 years.

Four

HAZARD FROM THE AIR

The following aerial photographs come from the collection of Lawrence O. Davis. He built the Bobby Davis Library and Park in memory of his son. Davis developed the neighborhoods around the park, building houses and walls. He was the president of the Civil Defense Council in Hazard during World War II, and was instrumental in coordinating the project of building the Memorial Gymnasium. His involvement with the Perry County Development Association advanced the urban renewal that took place in the 1950s.

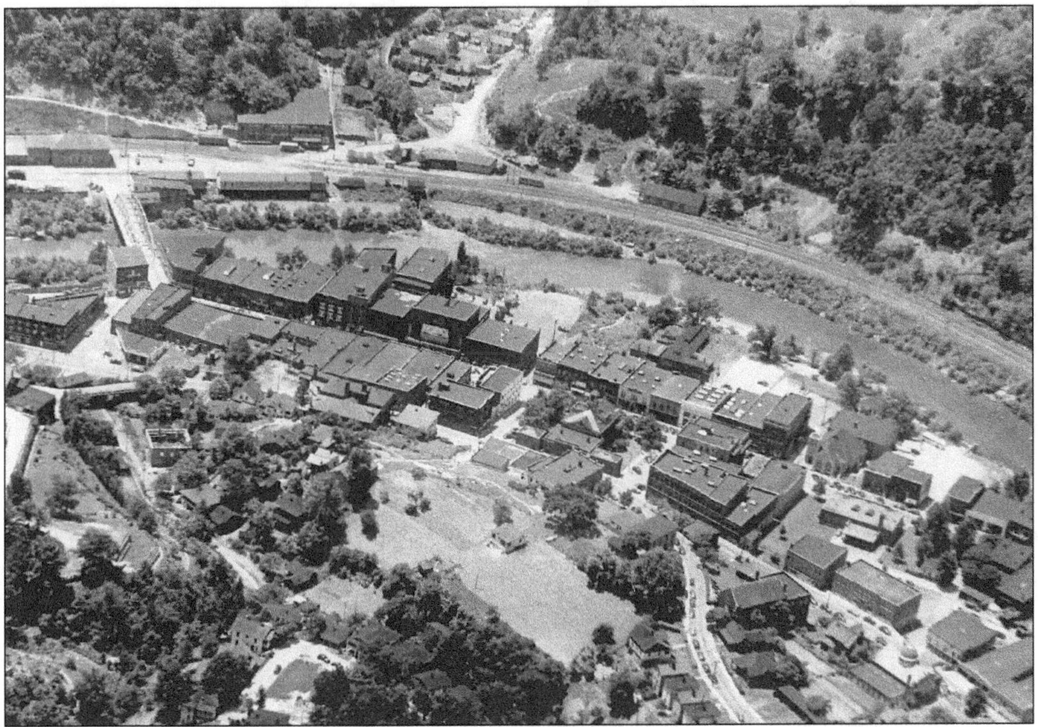

The Civilian Defense Council erected the large billboard on the front of the Grand Hotel during World War II. The large propaganda poster is visible in the middle of the photograph, dating this picture back to 1943 (see p. 45). Both sides of the track are pictured here. Town Mountain Road is visible in the upper center and to its left is Bluegrass Hollow and Messer Branch. The triangular building at the left of Town Mountain Road is the Powell Hackney Warehouse.

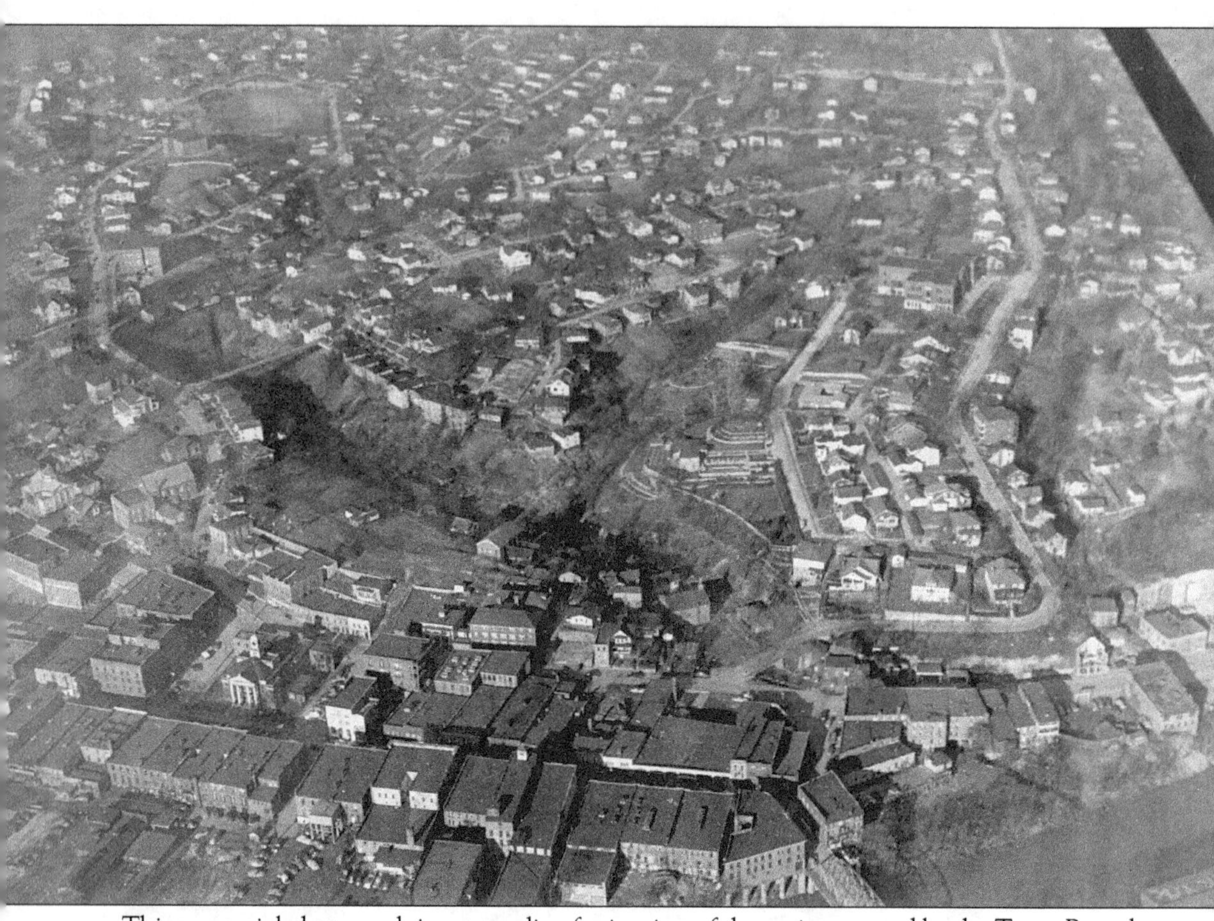

This rare aerial photograph is outstanding for its view of the ravine created by the Town Branch. Two bridges span the divide, one at Baker Hill, seen in the lower right quadrant of the picture, and the other stretching from Broadway to Lyttle Boulevard, on the left. Bobby Davis Park was completed at this time, but the construction of the Memorial Drive and Lovern Street was still in the future.

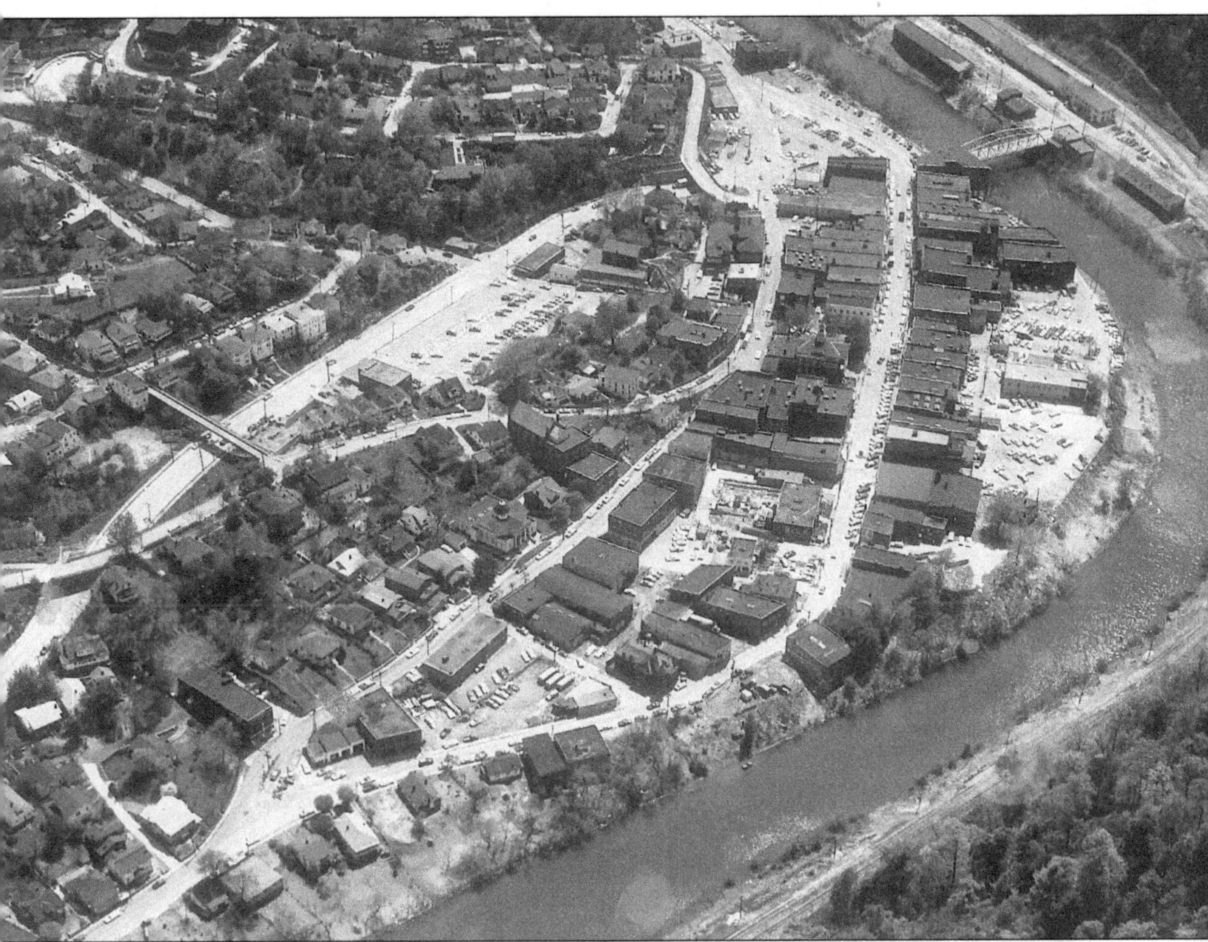

This remarkable photograph shows the completed Hazard Relief Route and the parking lot. Three overpasses carry residential traffic. The tree-covered Bobby Davis Park is in the upper left. At this stage the East Main Street buildings had been razed so Main Street could extend to East Main Street.

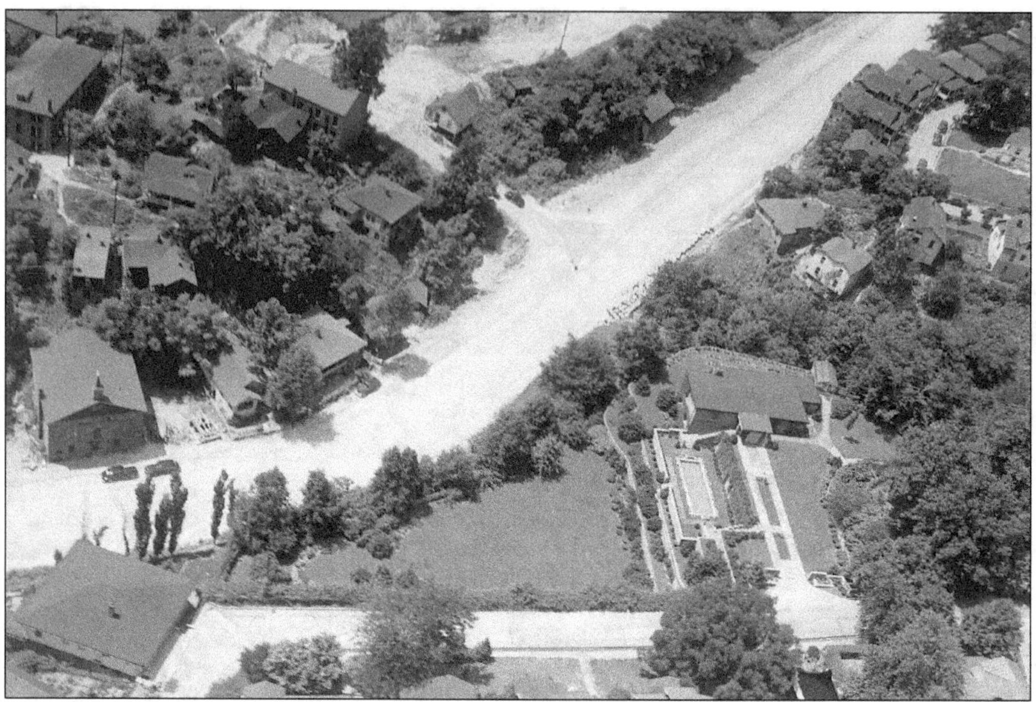

Among the many shots of Hazard from the air, this one shows the newly constructed Bobby Davis Park, overlooking the Hazard By-Pass. In this shot, excavation had barely begun for the Hazard Parking Lot, pictured at the top of the photo.

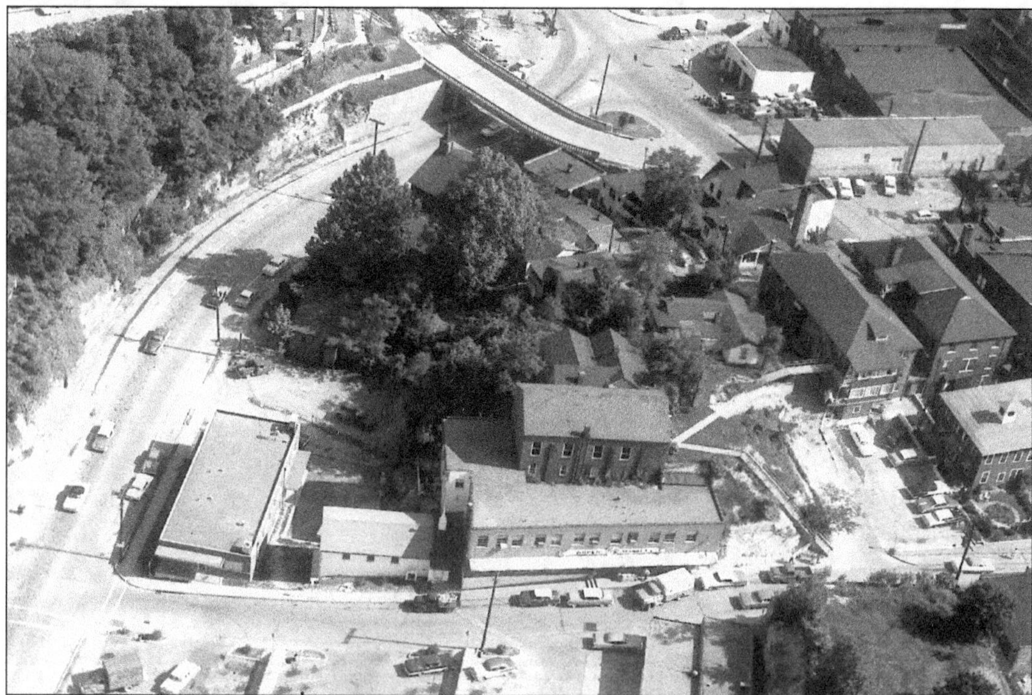

The Hazard By-Pass, Baker Hill overpass, and Lovern Street suggest the structural growth needed to accommodate the additional traffic brought by increased business.

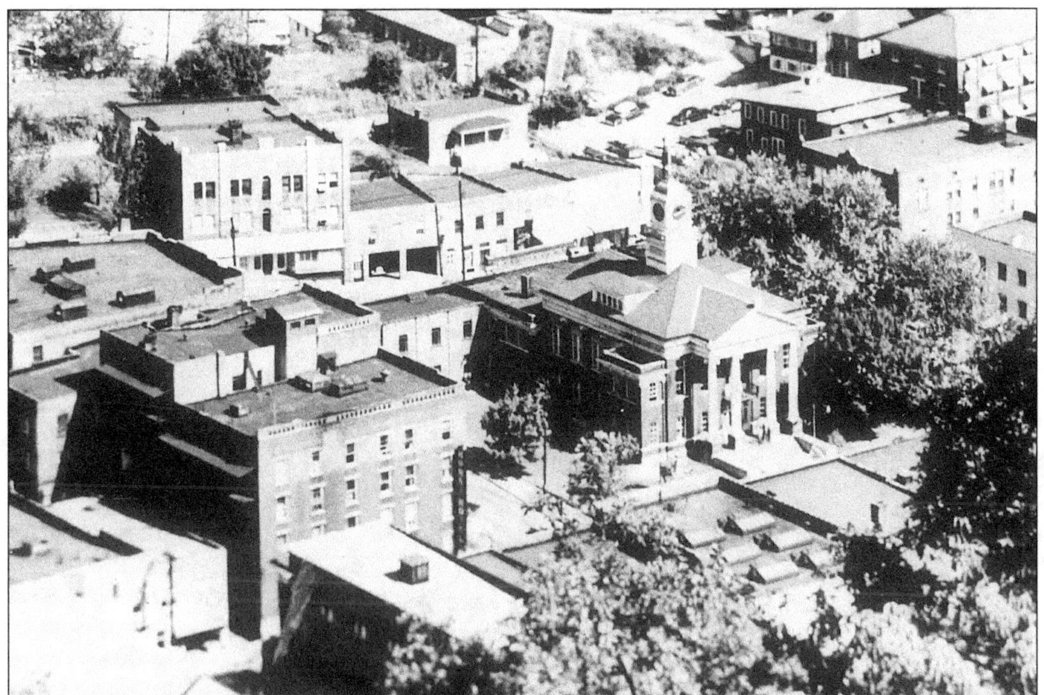

The 1911 courthouse, in the center of this picture, stood until 1964. A building twice the size of the courthouse was planned to take its place.

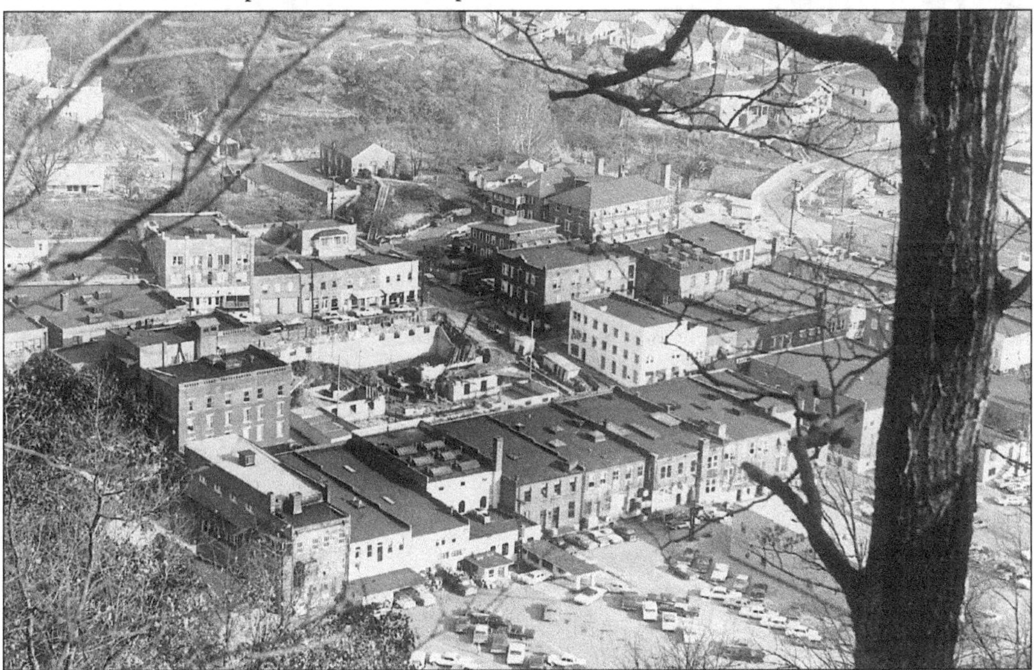

This photo around Main Street, c. 1965, shows the foundation of the Perry County Court House that was dedicated on September 17, 1966. Peoples Bank had the first drive-through window in Hazard. The drive-through, visible in the foreground of this picture, was located in the back of the bank. The large building with awnings is the Mount Mary Hospital.

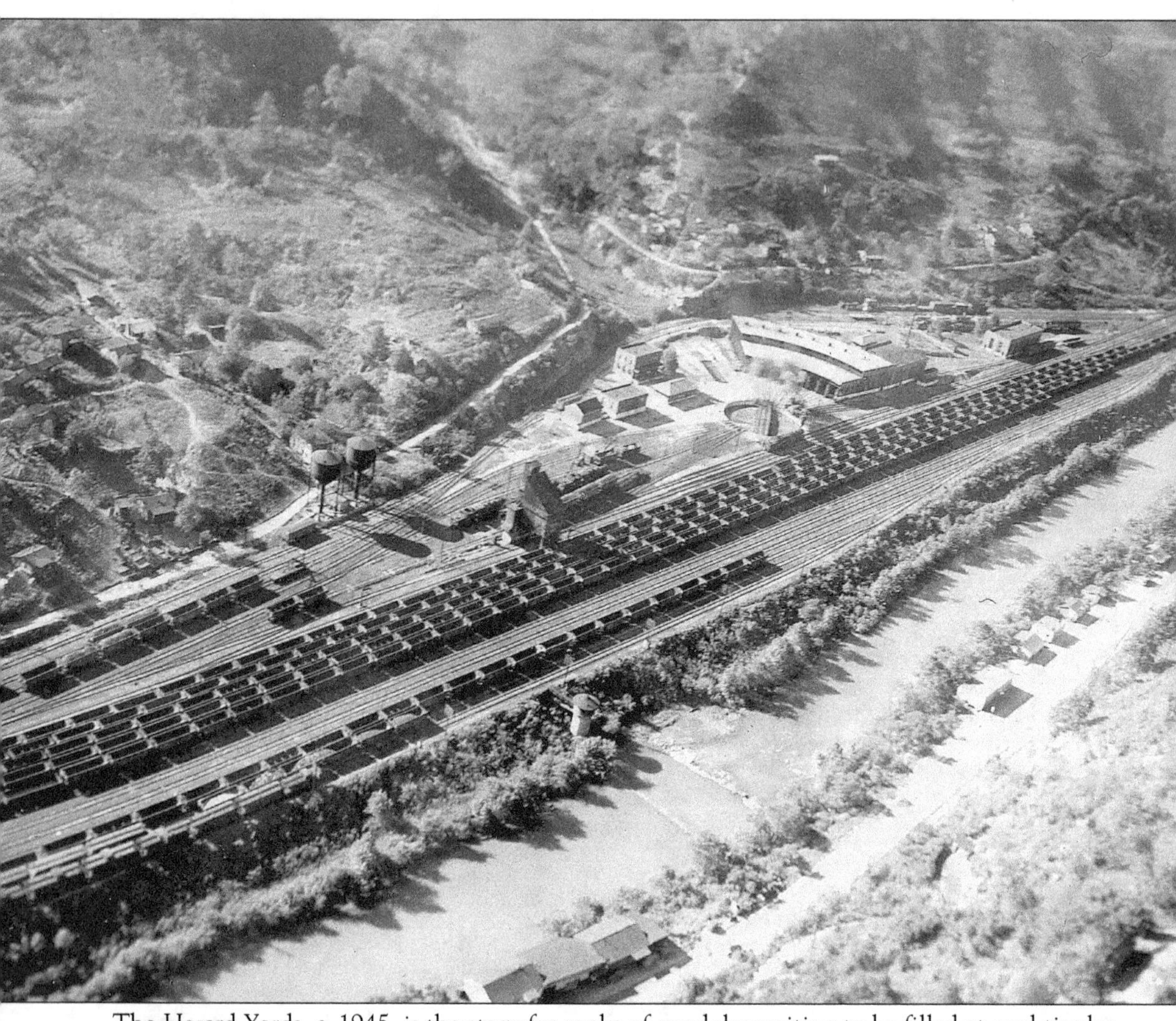

The Hazard Yards, *c.* 1945, is the stage for ranks of gondolas waiting to be filled at coal tipples throughout the area. Coal by the hundreds of thousands of tons went out each week, bound for electric power plants.

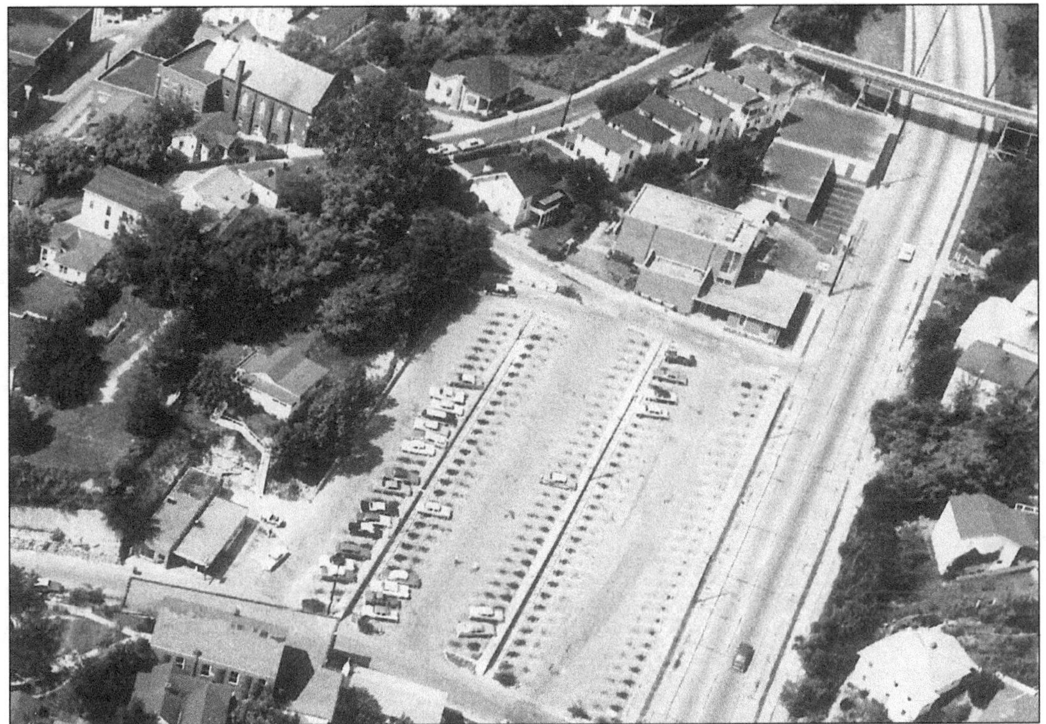

An aerial photograph of the parking lot on the old Hazard By-Pass shows oil-stained spaces left by parked cars before environmental awareness. The spaces farther away from town, where fewer cars parked, have fainter stains. The location beside the lot was chosen by the General Telephone Company for its facility.

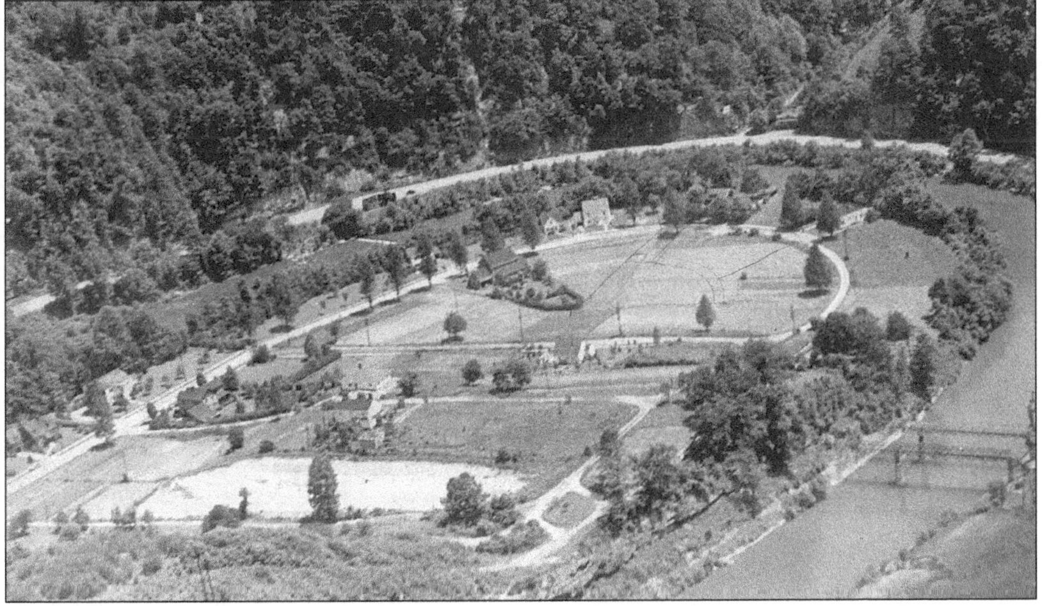

Woodland Park was open farmland before development. The bridge on the right is a spray bridge for the Kentucky Power Company plant in Lothair. Steam was piped from the power plant to the spray bridge to cool.

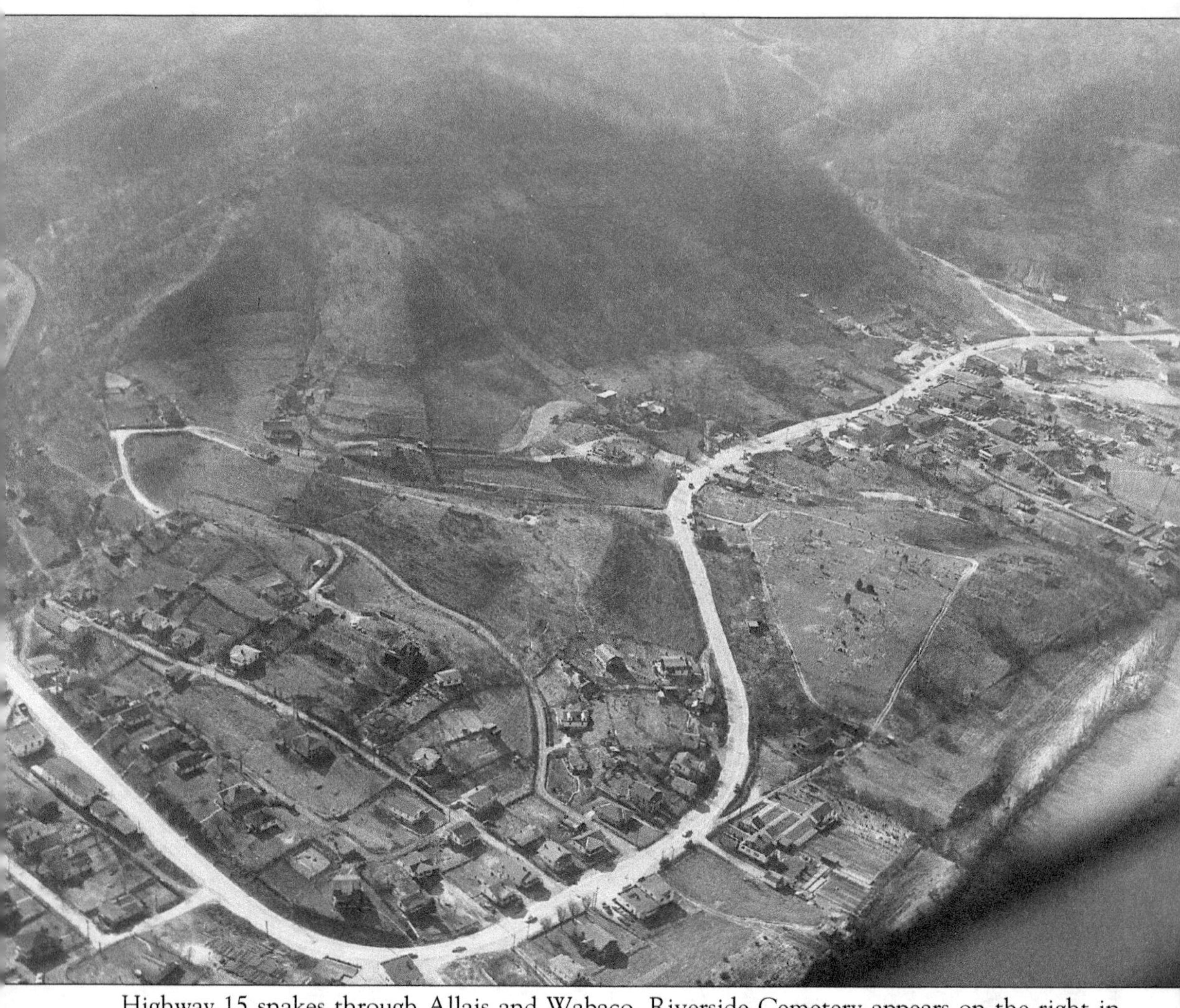

Highway 15 snakes through Allais and Wabaco. Riverside Cemetery appears on the right in the shape of a triangle, between the road and the river. Since the early 1960s this section has become densely developed.

Five

Floods

Floods provided important milestones in the development of Perry County. The most noteworthy floods, causing extensive damages and then the incentive to rebuild, occurred in the years 1927, 1957, and 1963. Each flood was unique. The 1927 flood was a "flash flood," killing 62 people, who were swept away without any warning. In 1957 the waters crested at 39 feet (flood stage is 20 feet). The flood of 1957 was the worst flood ever recorded in the area. Hazard was isolated, causing thousands of people to feel trapped and hopeless. The 1963 flood, cresting at 37 feet, was actually two floods. Soon after clean-up efforts were underway for the first flood, the river rose again to 24 feet.

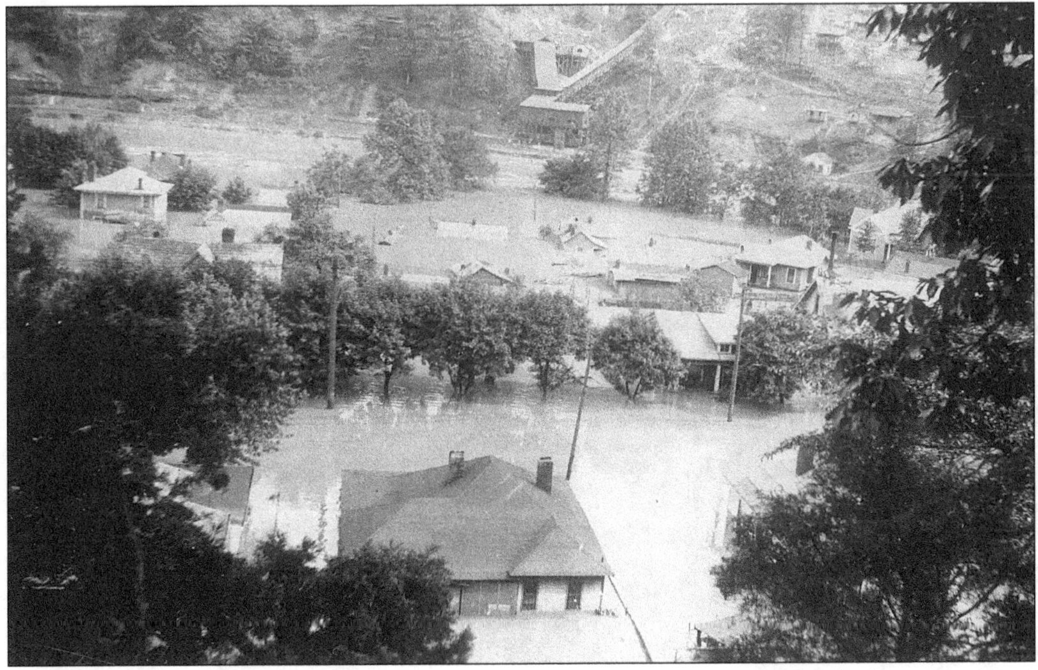

This shot of the 1927 floodwater shows the Big Bottom section of Hazard along East Main Street. The old Hazard Coal Company coal tipple is visible across the river.

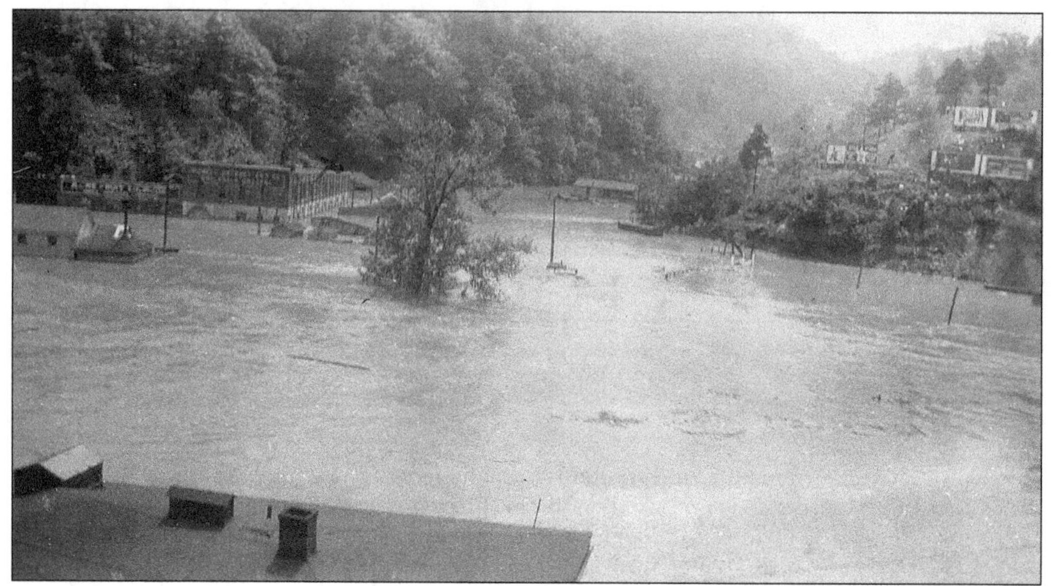

This photo was taken looking toward Bluegrass Hollow in 1927. The warehouse in the background belonged to the Powell Hackney Wholesale Company. The billboards on the hillside are in a cemetery.

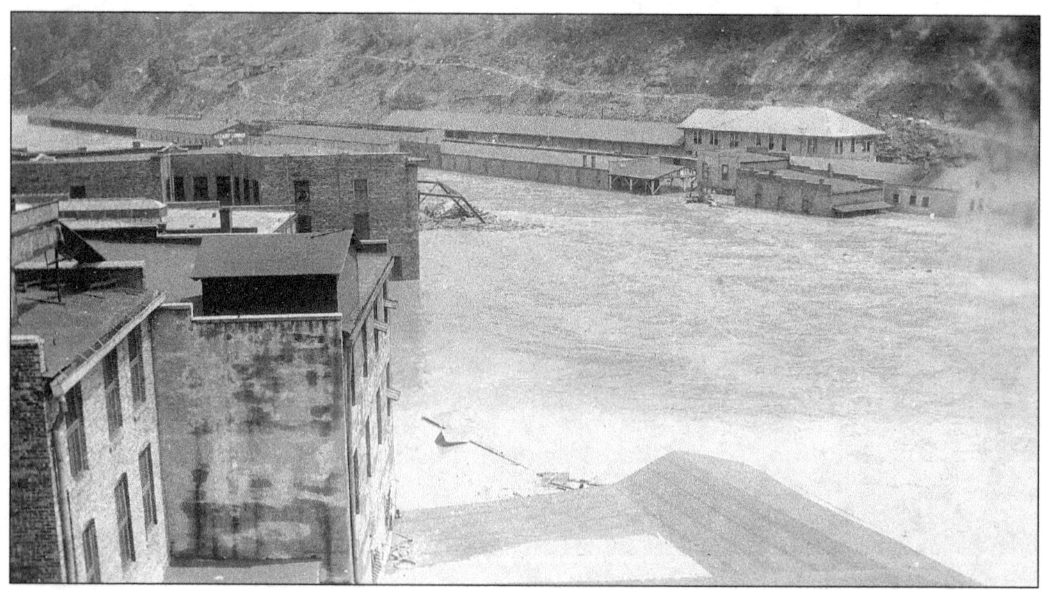

This view, in the direction of Home Lumber Co., shows the destruction of the Town Bridge as a result of the 1927 flood.

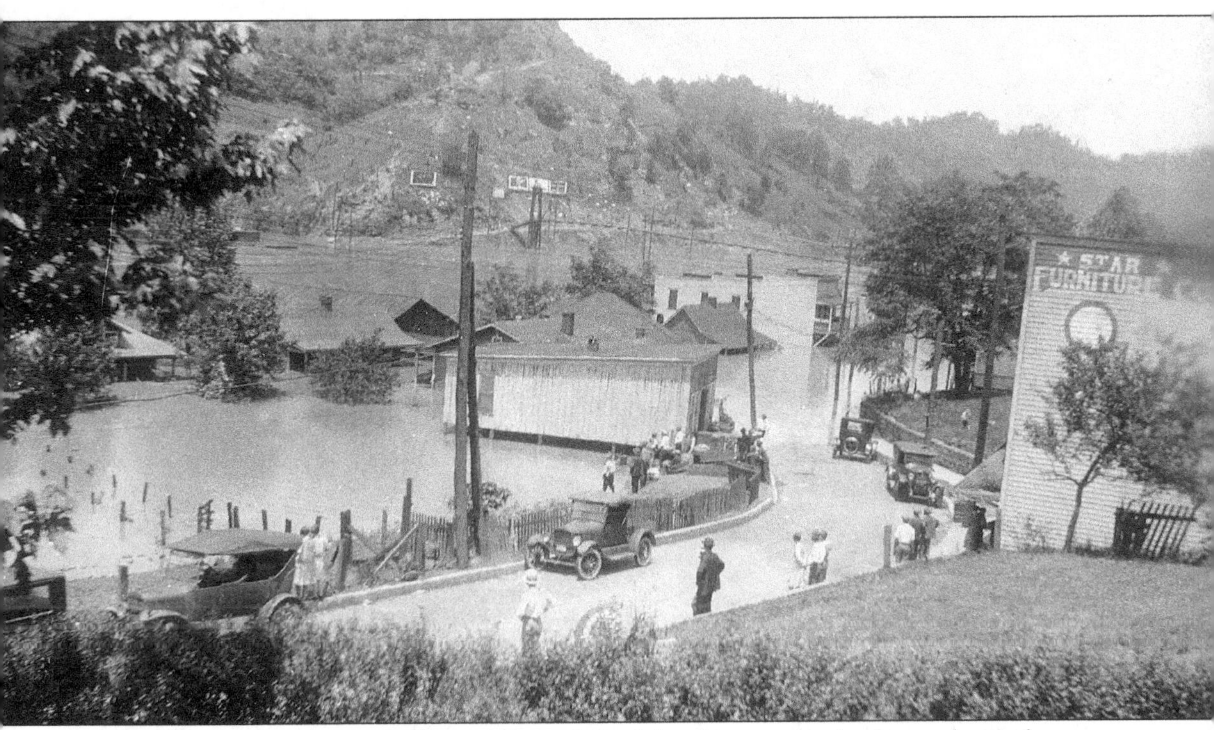

The north end of town was equally waterlogged. Luckily, the swinging bridge to the yards was still standing due to its elevation.

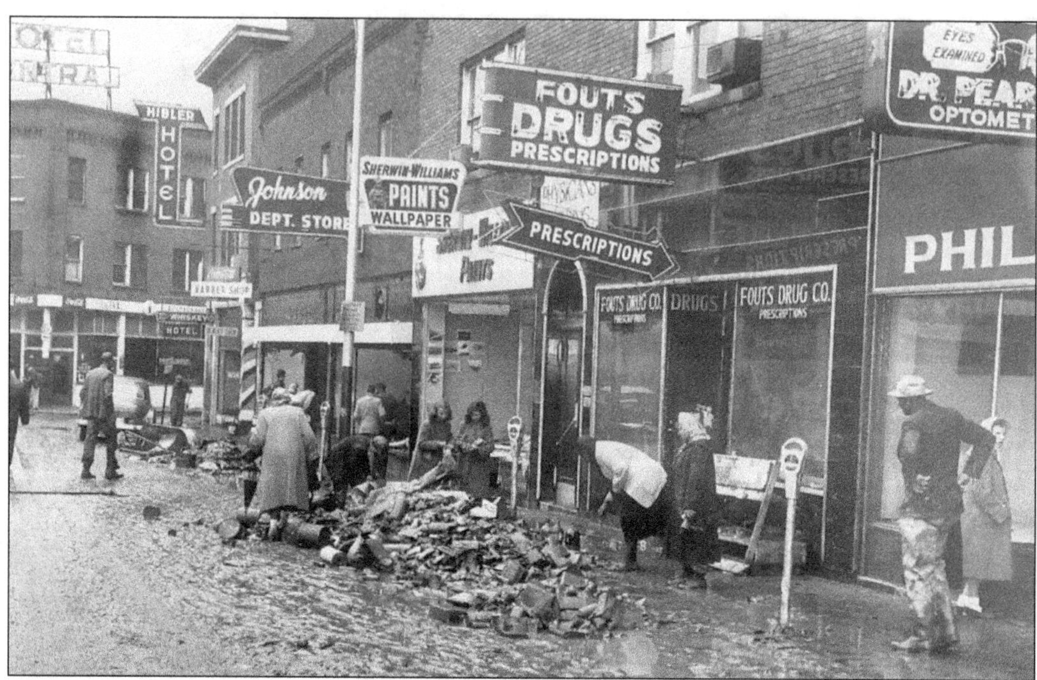

Owners of Fouts Drug were accustomed to the process of moving their merchandise with the threat of a flood. Clyde Baumgardner and Leighton Abshear, pharmacists of Fouts Drug, moved the stock to the second floor. The flood waters rose to the ceiling of the first floor.

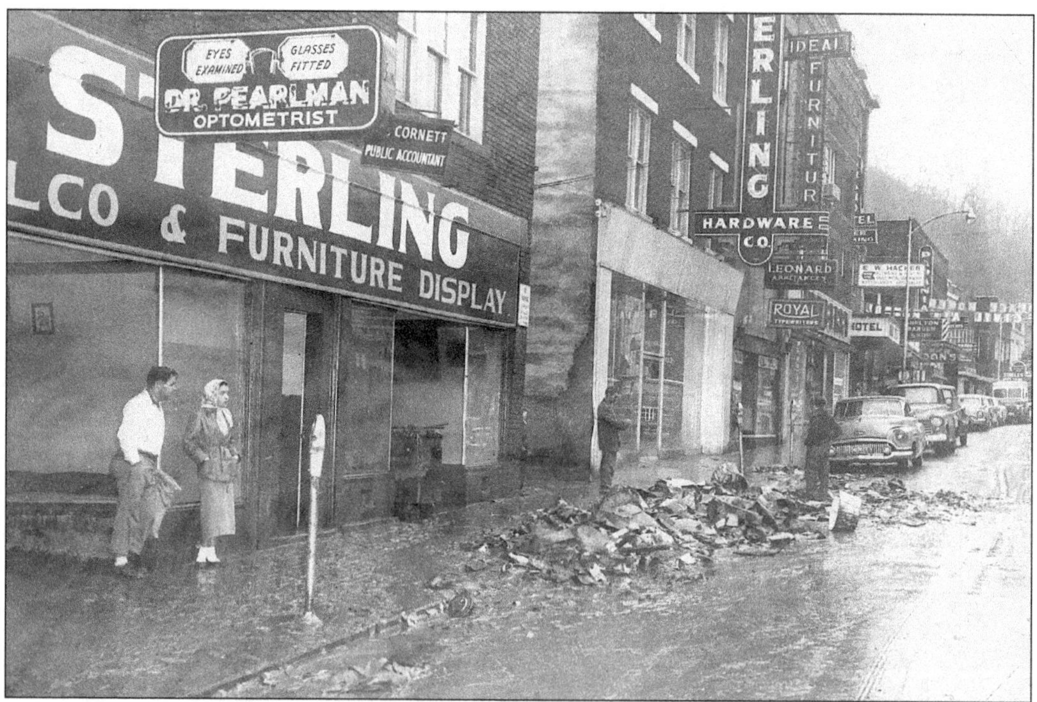

In the aftermath of the flood, shopkeepers threw sodden and ruined merchandise in the streets. Army and state trucks picked up the debris and took it to the dump.

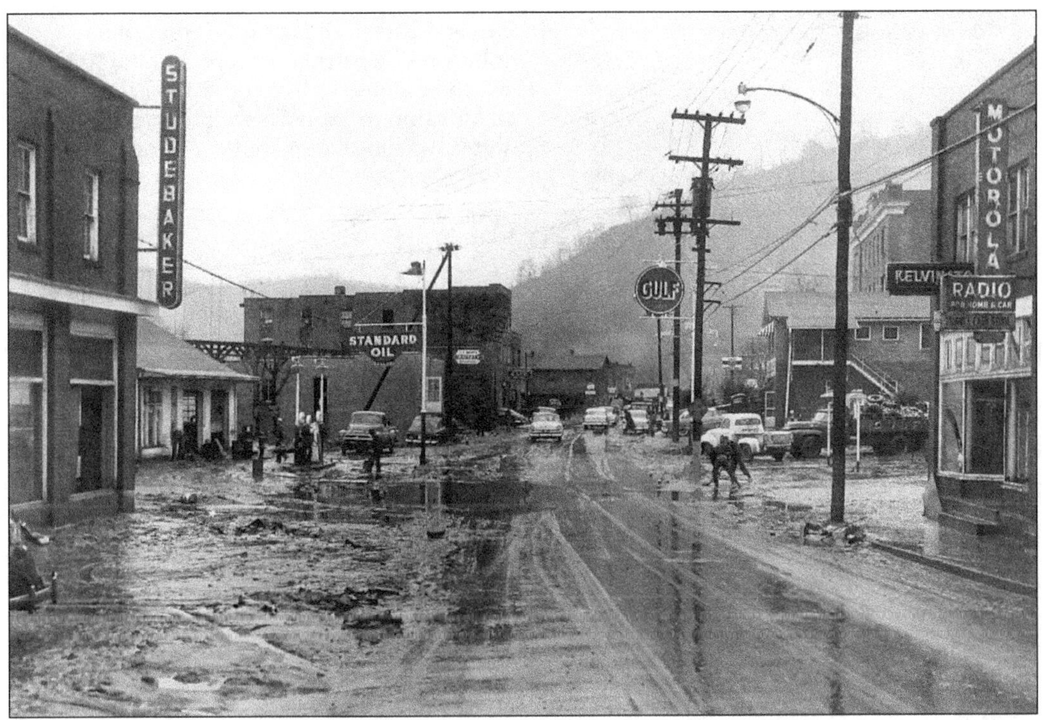

After flood waters receded in 1957, mud was deep on North Main Street.

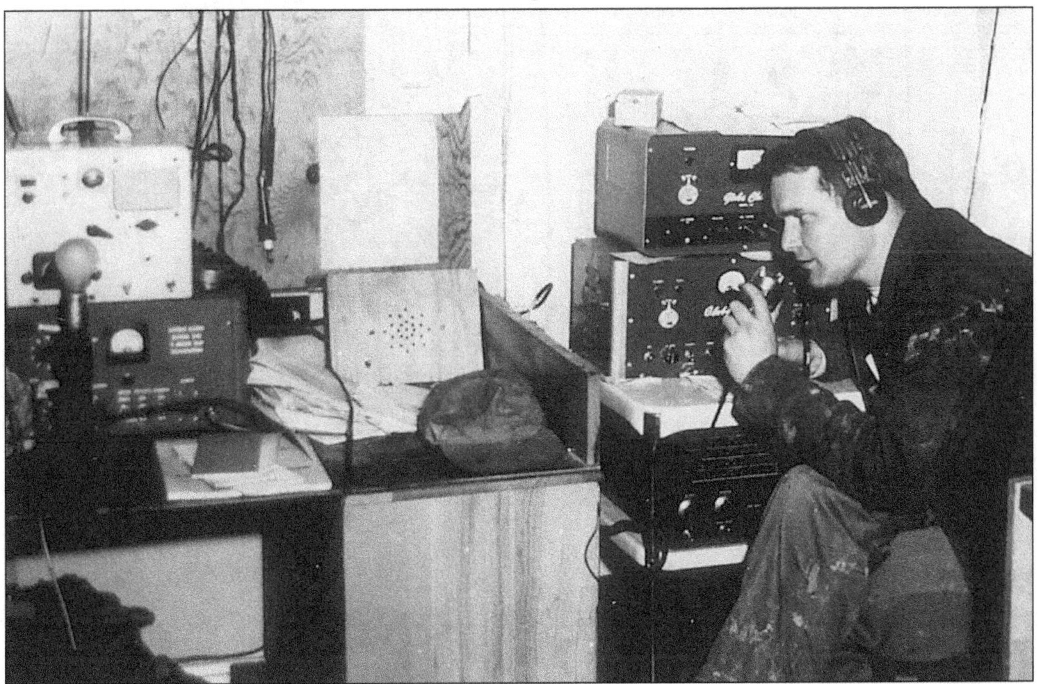

In 1957, floodwaters cut off all communication between Hazard and the outside. Electricity was off, telephone lines were down, and the roads were covered with water and mud. Bill Roll's amateur "ham" radio provided the only contact for 30 hours. Help came when the Civilian Air Patrol airlifted medicines and other emergency equipment into Hazard.

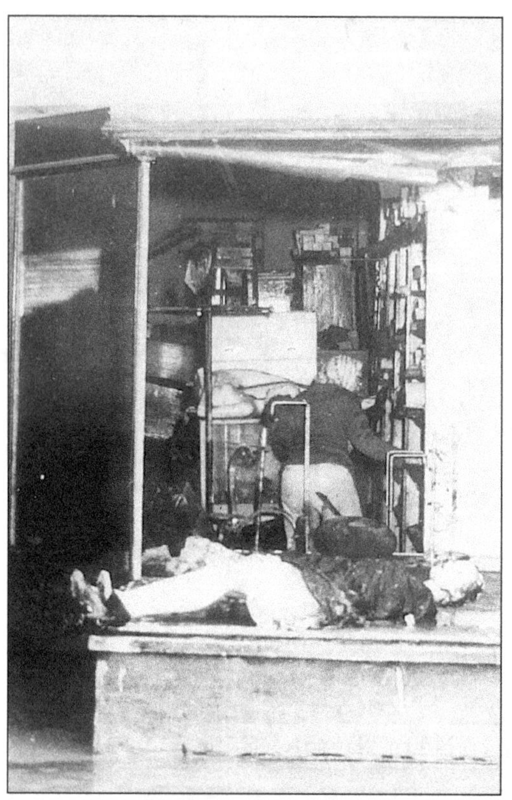

Mr. and Mrs. J.O. Harper, owners of Johnson's Department Store, lost $50,000 worth of merchandise in the 1957 flood. This mannequin in Johnson's window, after the water receded, caused quite a furor.

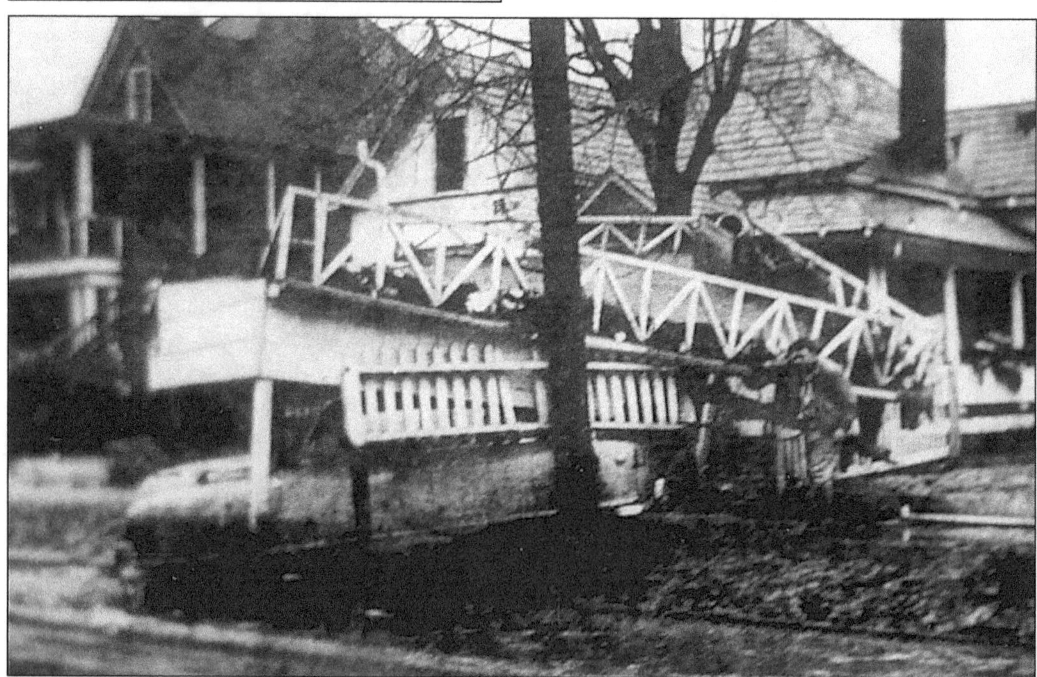

During the days of the 1957 flood, weariness and despair prevailed, but it was tempered with the hope that the town would rebuild itself better than before. After Mayor Doug C. Combs toured the flood-drenched city, he returned to the damages of his own home in Big Bottom.

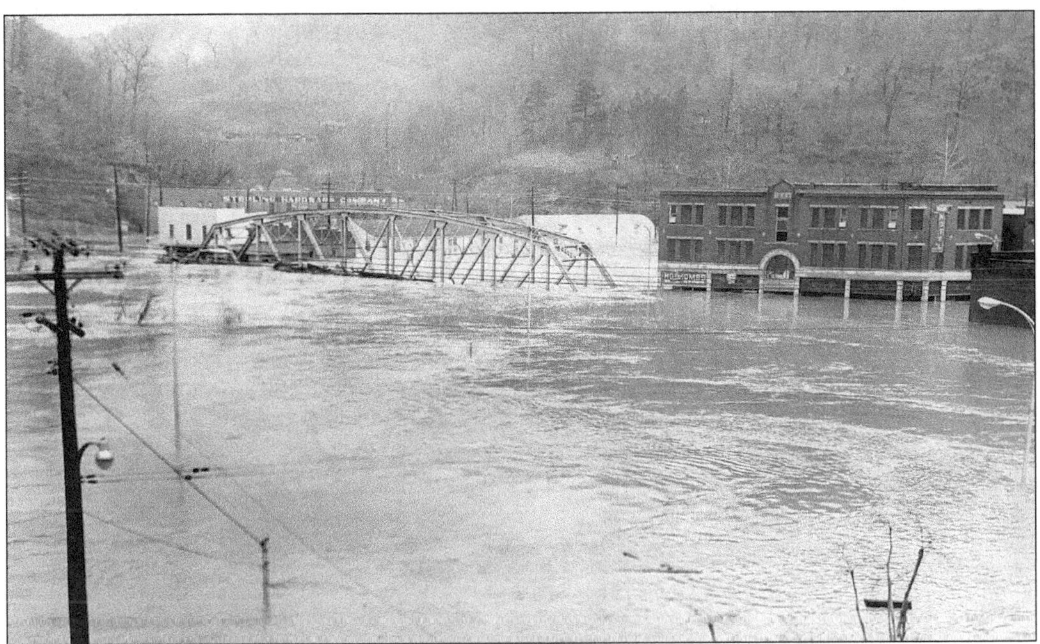

This photograph was taken in 1963, on the corner of Baker Hill, looking toward the Hibler Hotel (on the right) and the Sterling Hardware warehouse (on the left). The river crested at 37 feet, 2 feet less than in 1957.

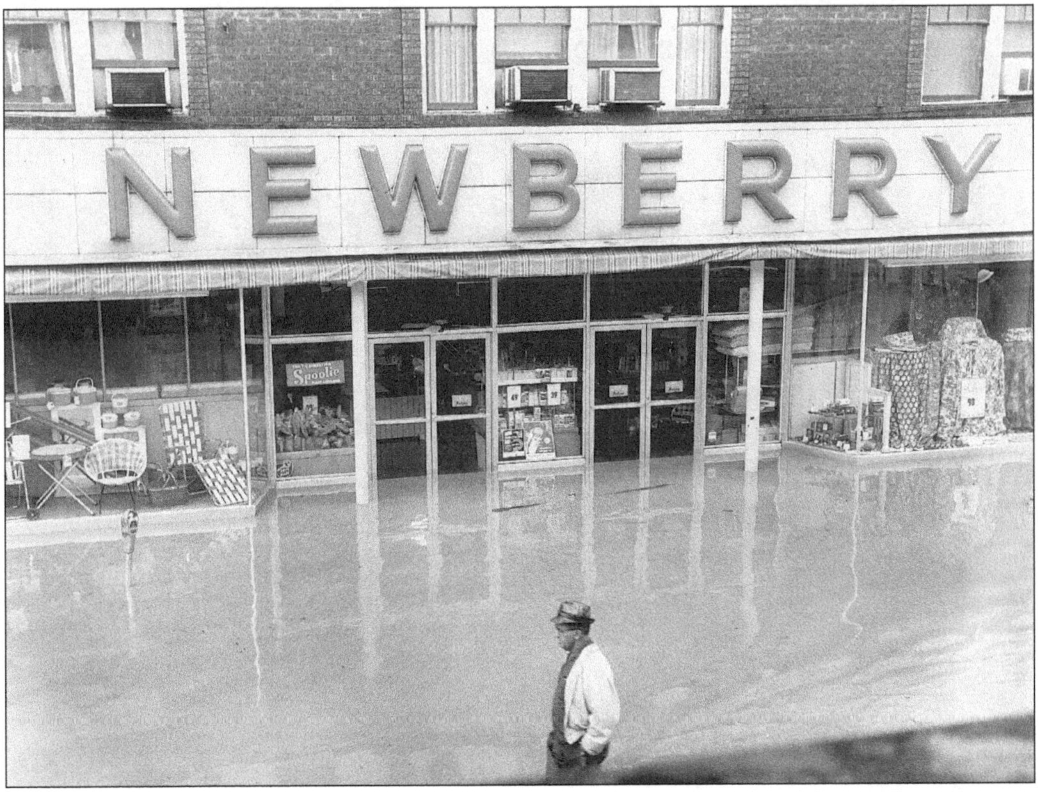

Chester Stevens strolls through the waters of the 1963 flood. Six inches fell in 24 hours.

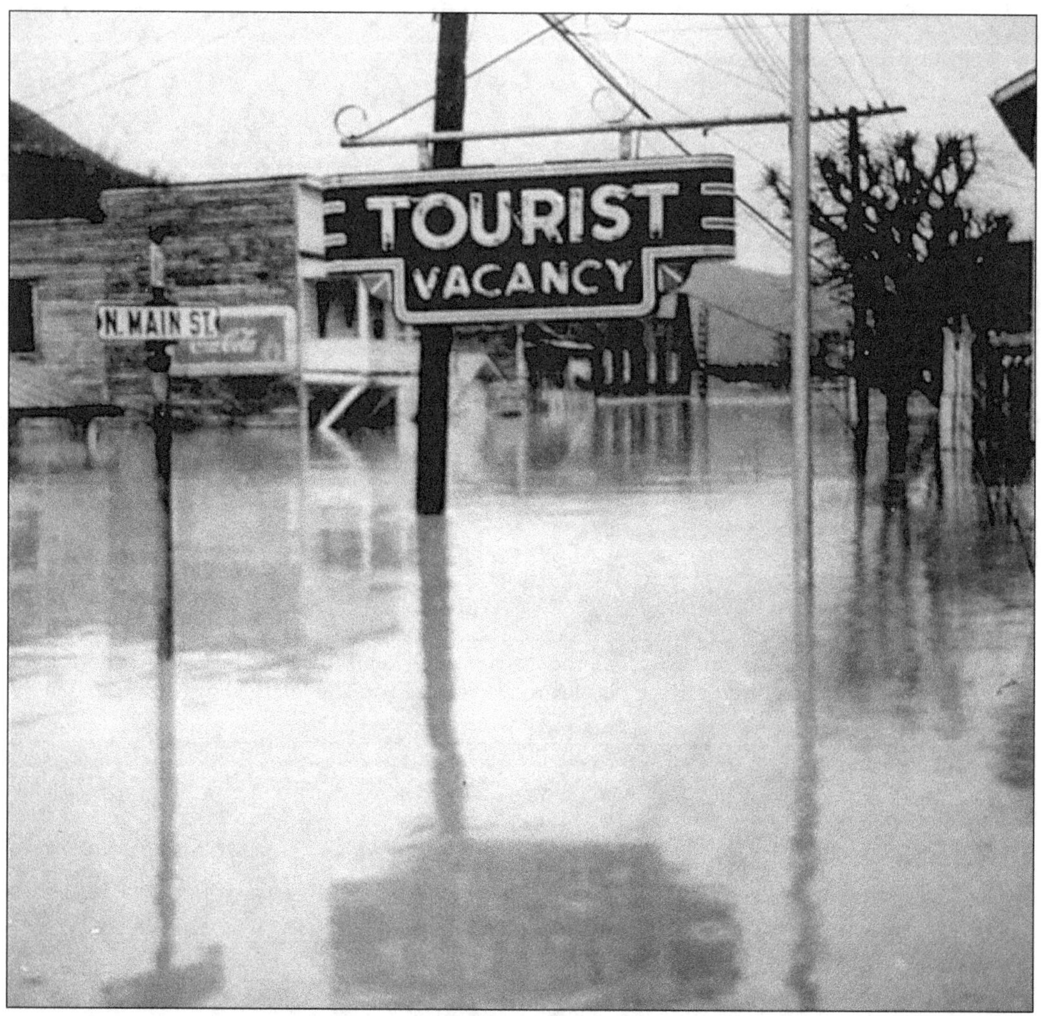

Tourism came to a temporary halt in 1963, during the two devastating floods that drenched Eastern Kentucky and four other states in the Appalachian chain. After the waters ebbed, a second flood came within six days. The newspaper called it a "baby flood." Although it was not as serious as the first flood, cleanup was slowed, and in some instances had to be started over.

Six

Around the Town

Hazard reflected the abundance and privation of the country through eras of the coal boom, the Depression, World War II, and the years after the war. It seemed at times that the town was isolated and insulated enough to withstand the desperation of other locales. As when the stock market collapsed, Hazard banks advertised that they were strong against the effects of the crash.

New construction and street improvements occurred all over Hazard in the 1950s. This impetus for growth and development was ongoing and continues to the present.

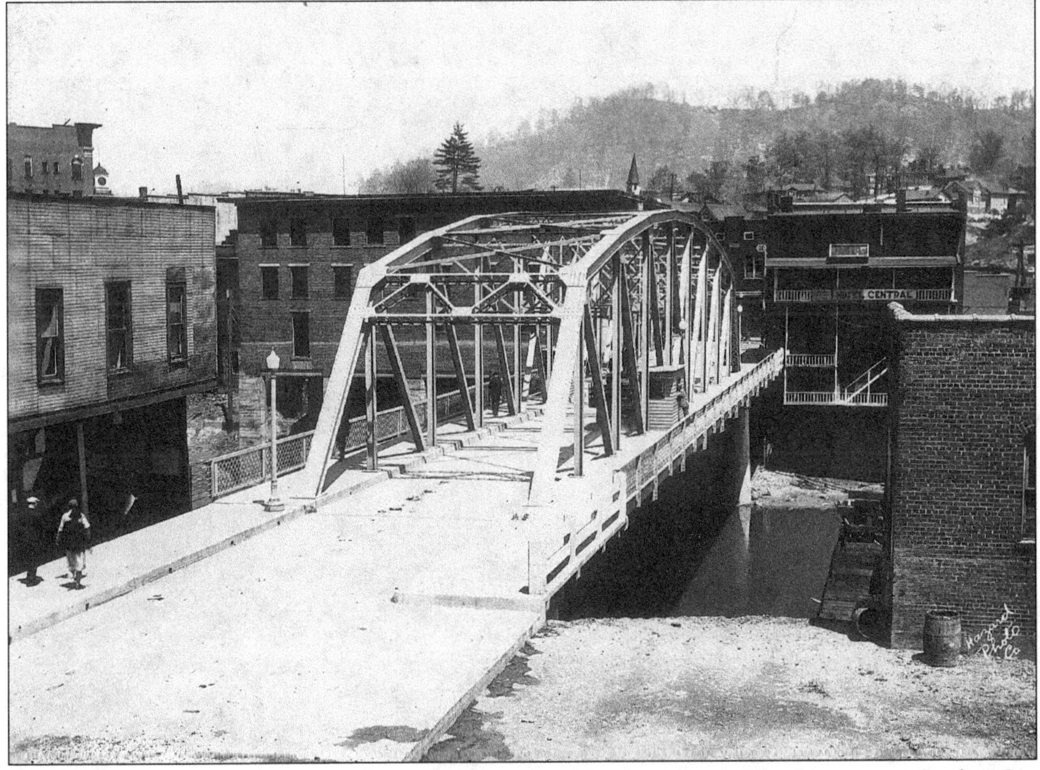

The original "Penny Bridge" was washed away in the 1927 flood. The Vincennes Bridge Co. built this one for $63,000; it opened in January 1928 as a toll bridge. After July 26, 1937, the toll was removed.

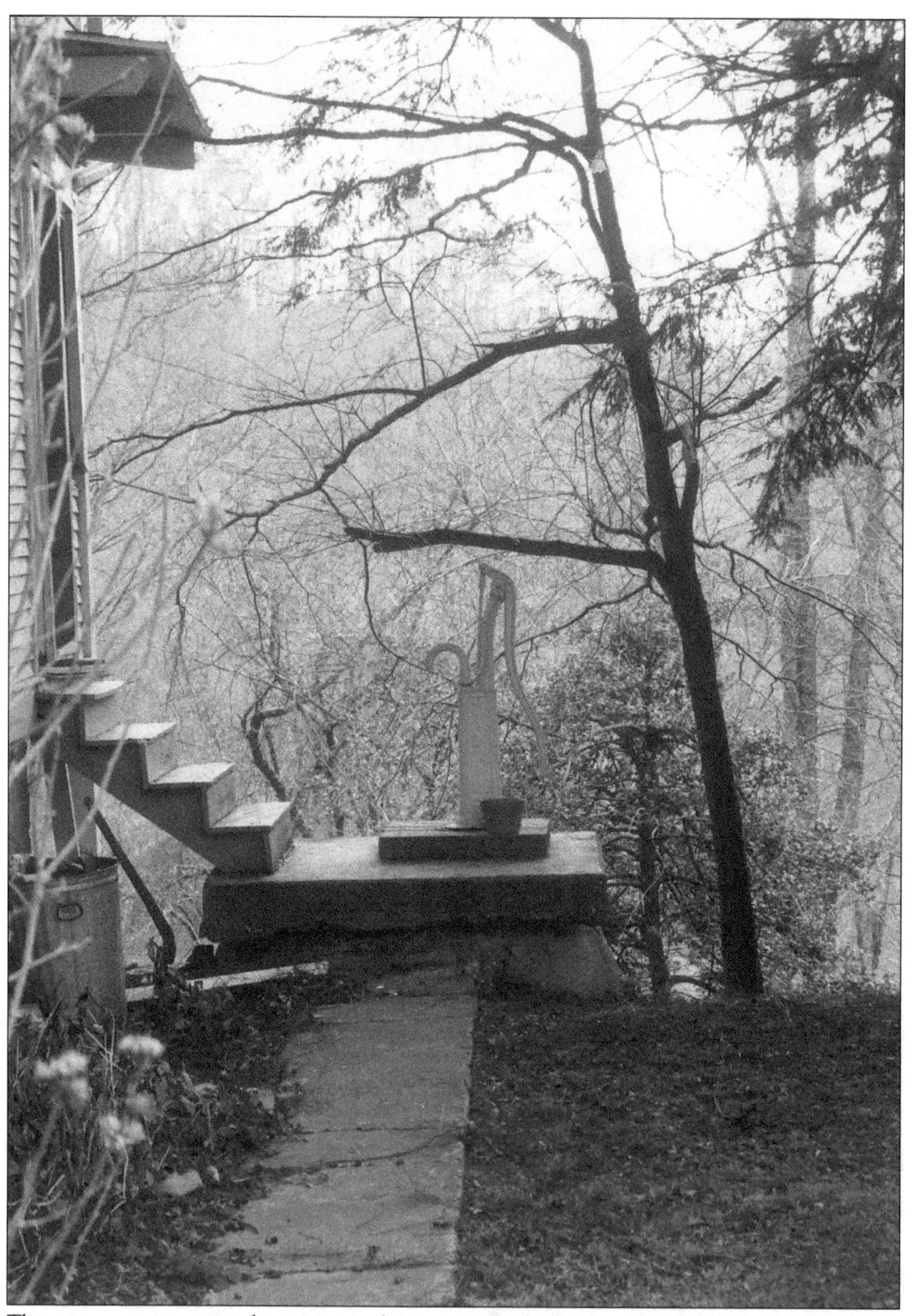

This water pump remained in its original spot, outside the kitchen door of a house on Oakhurst Street, as late as 1988. The sight of it was a reminder of simpler times.

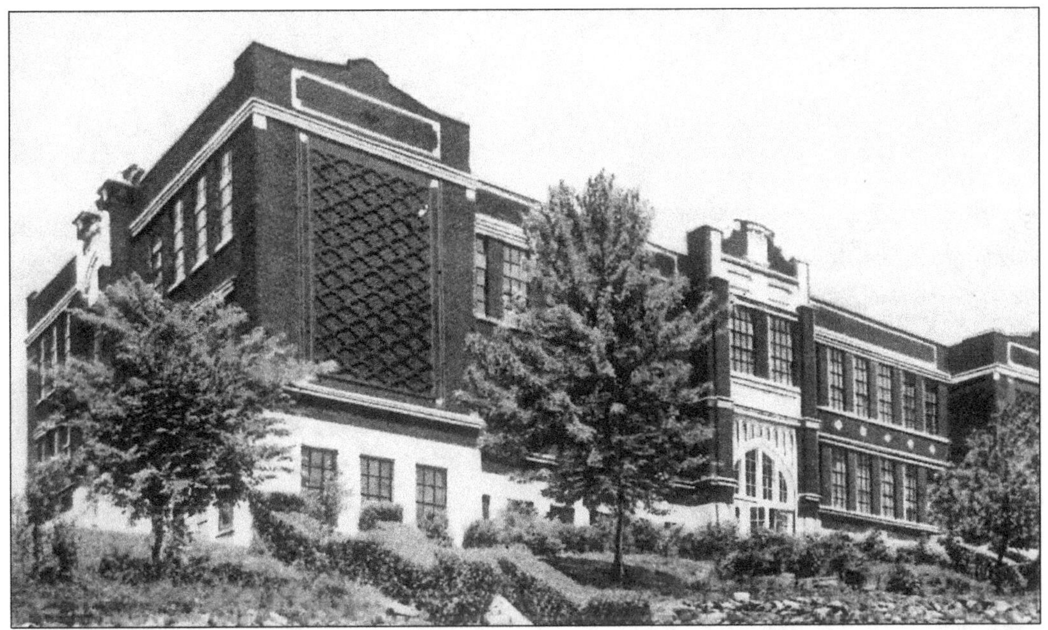

The Hazard High School on Baker Street (sometimes called Baker Hill) was finished in 1924 at a cost of $140,000. It was completed just in time for the steady increase of enrollment during the 1920s. At this time attendance in Hazard schools was growing more rapidly than in any other town in the state of Kentucky.

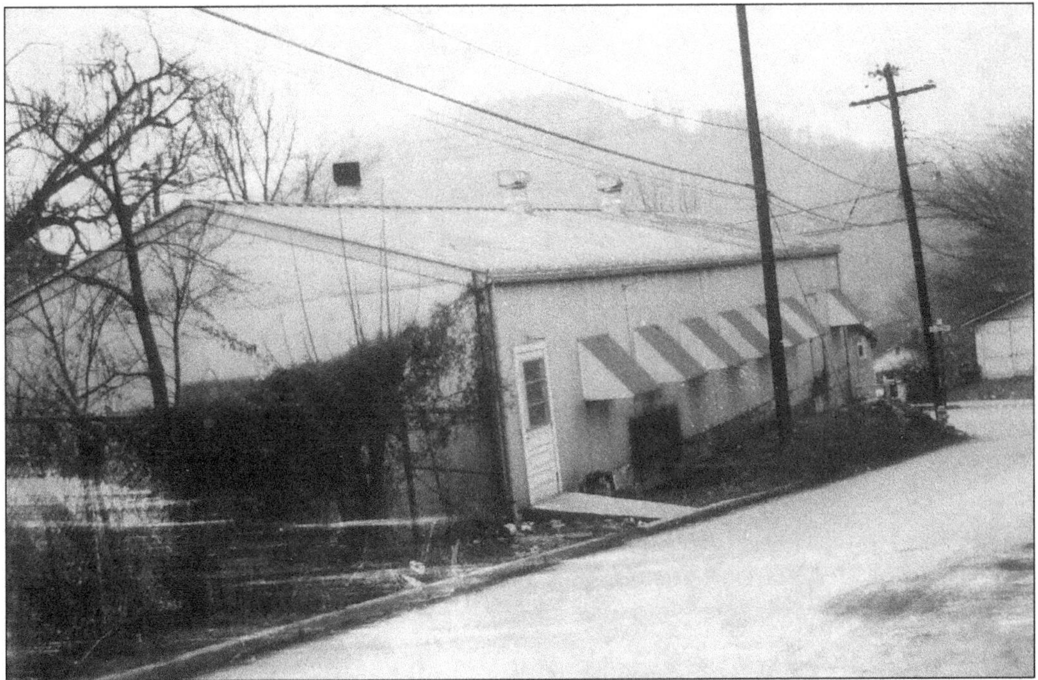

The popular name for this building was "The Rec." It was officially the Hazard Recreation Building. Located in the corner of Collins Field, at Broadway and College Streets, it was remodeled in 1959 to be a school for mentally handicapped children. The building was removed when the Hazard Pavilion was built in 1988.

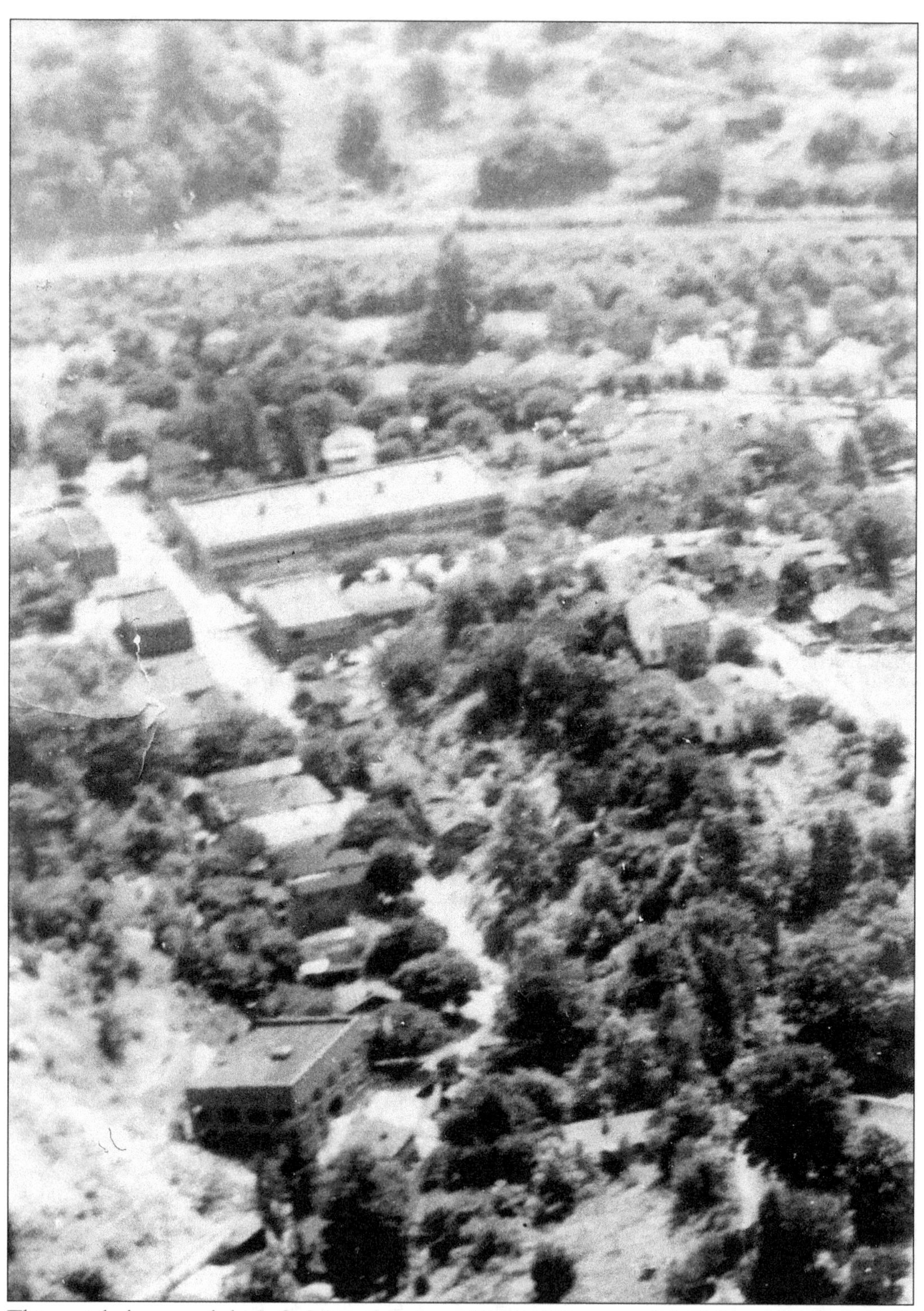

This aerial photograph by L.O. Davis is a view of Liberty Street and the Liberty Street School. It is one of the few pictures of this street and building. The school is on the left, where Liberty Street makes a slight curve. The street joins East Main Street at the top.

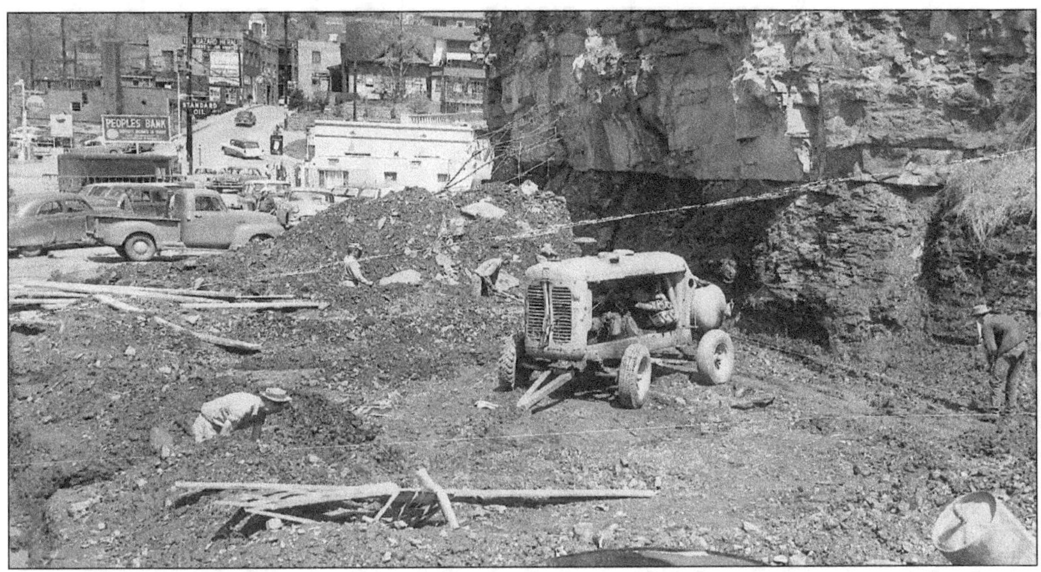

The site of this excavation is beside the Hazard Fire Department. The white building in the background is the Standard Oil Service Station. The Hazard Herald office is farther up on High Street, opposite the Mount Mary Hospital. Civic pride and the Perry County Development Association promoted urban renewal in the early 1950s.

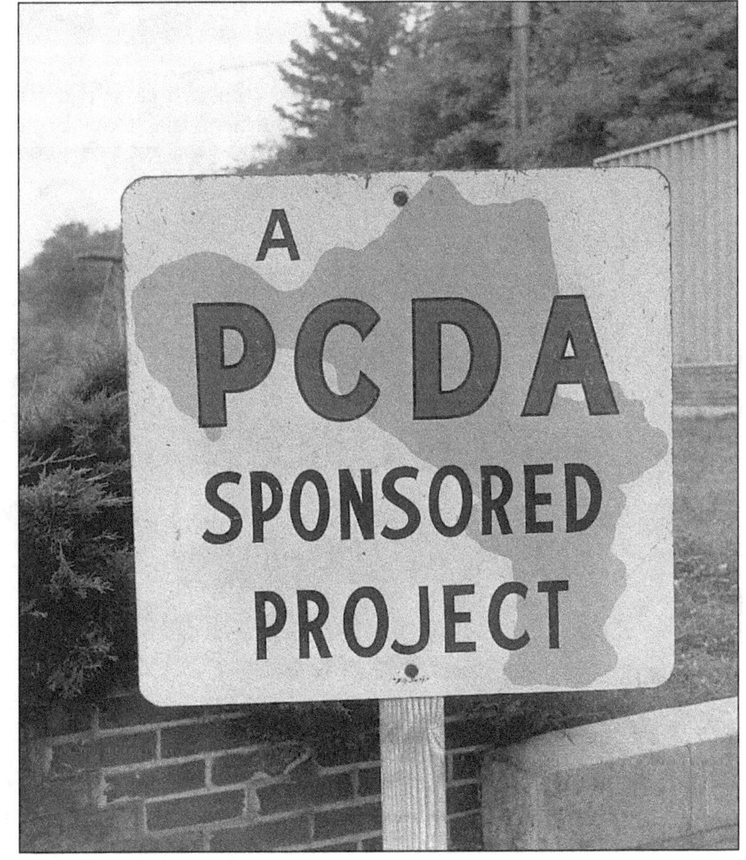

The Perry County Development Association (PCDA), founded in 1954, used the slogan "People Can Do Anything." Within the first year, the members developed a list of 100 objectives. The PCDA assisted and encouraged businesses in renovation, aided clean-up projects, and promoted enterprise in Hazard and Perry County. These signs were seen frequently in front of reconstruction sites. In 1959, the PCDA joined with the Hazard Chamber of Commerce.

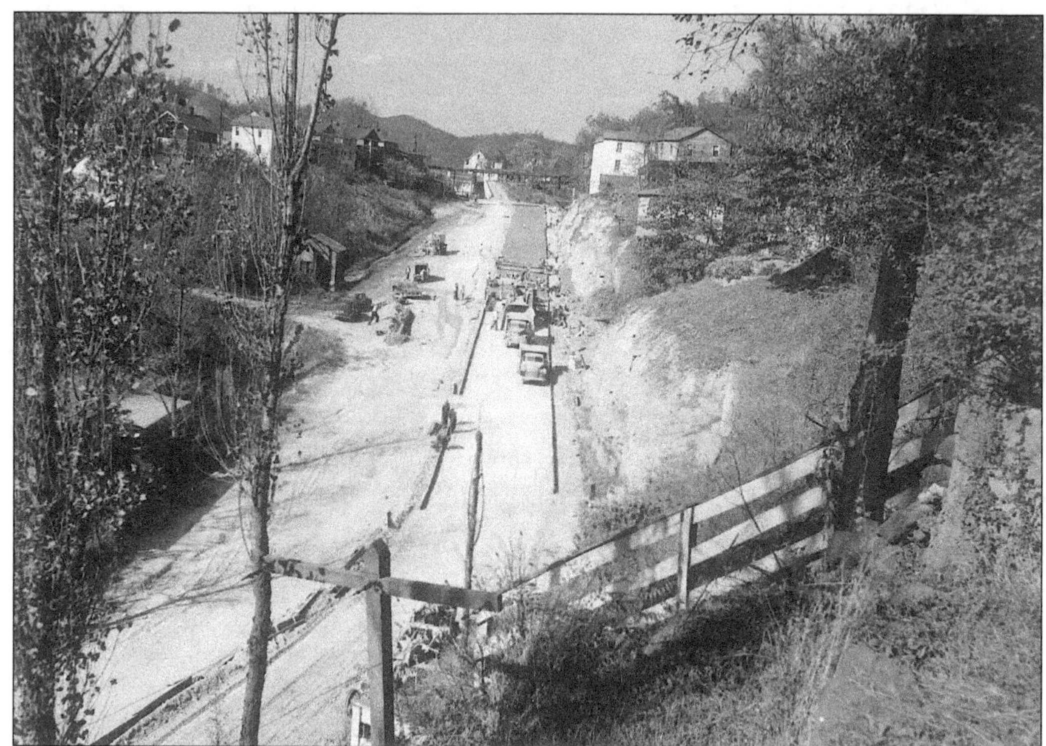

The new Relief Route was dedicated July 12, 1951. A section of it follows the old Town Branch. Large culverts were laid under the By-Pass that still carry the waters of Town Branch to the river. The opening is a short distance upriver from the "Perry Bridge."

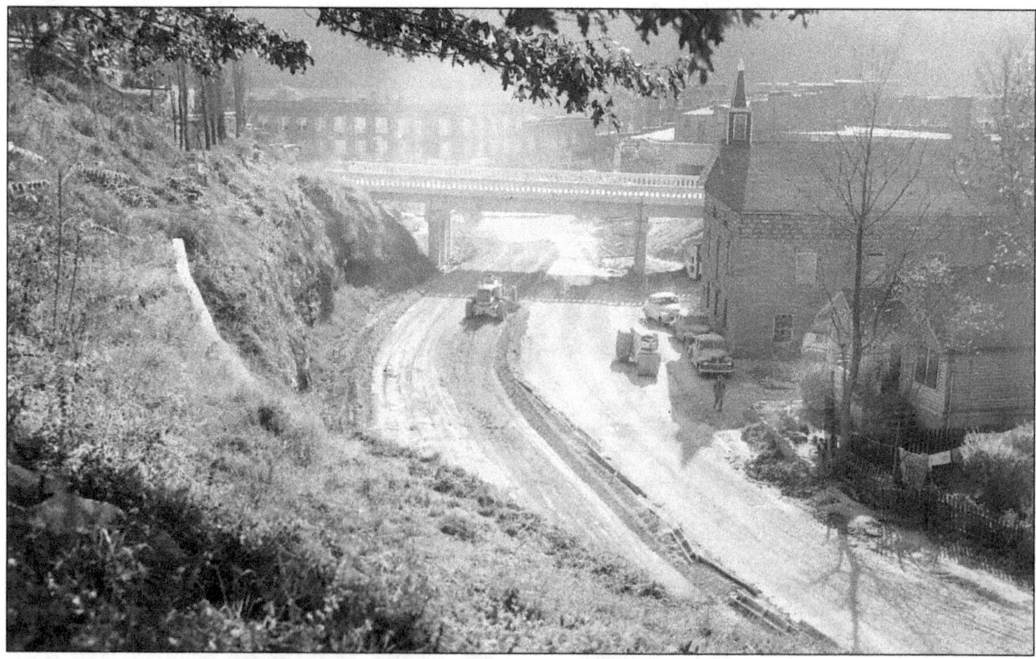

The south entrance to the By-Pass travels under the bridge at the bottom of Baker Hill. A bridge was first built at this location by Barney Baker in 1927.

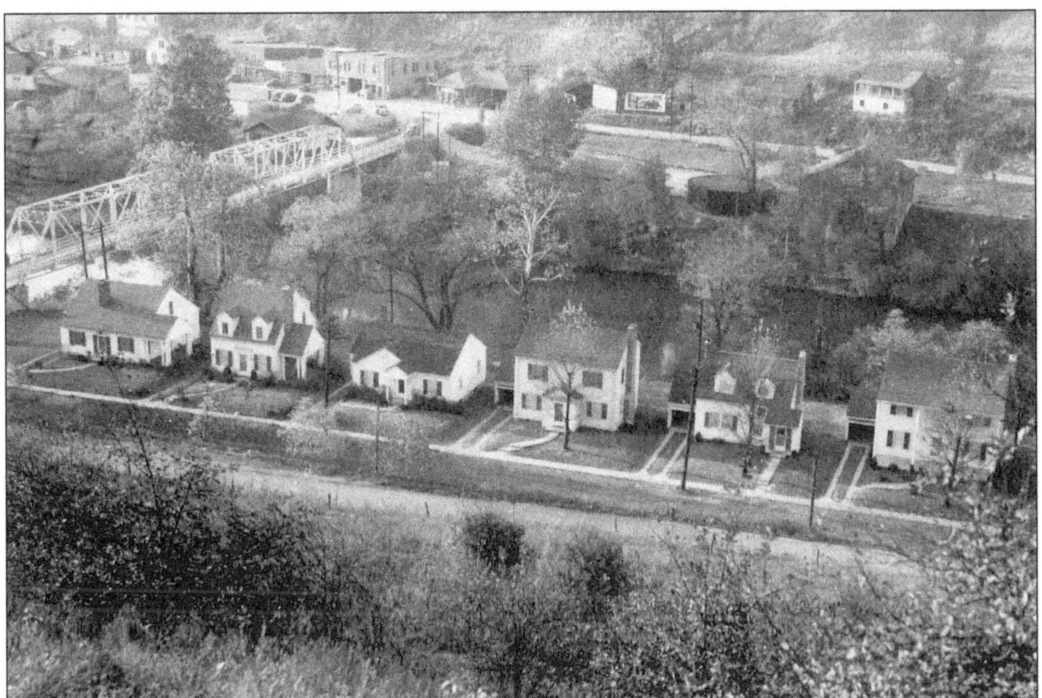

Located in Woodland Park, beside the North Fork of the Kentucky River, these six houses are pictured in the late 1940s. They were in one of the high water sections. Since the last major flood in 1963, most of them have been raised above the flood line.

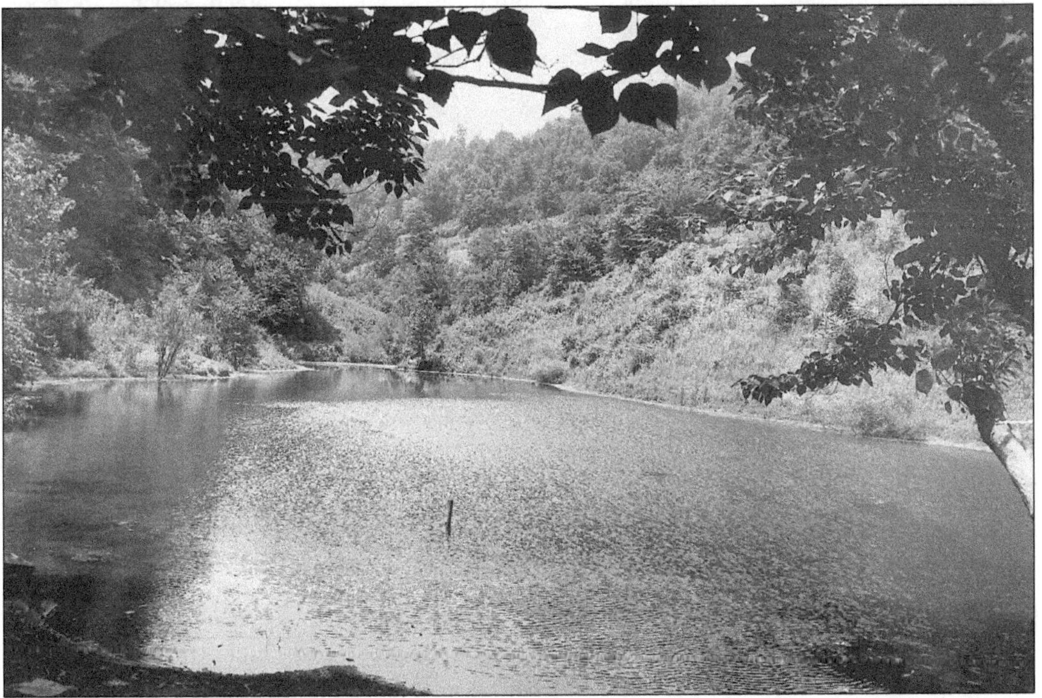

Happy Hollow, a serene fishing pond, was drained to become the site of the Hazard High School in 1976.

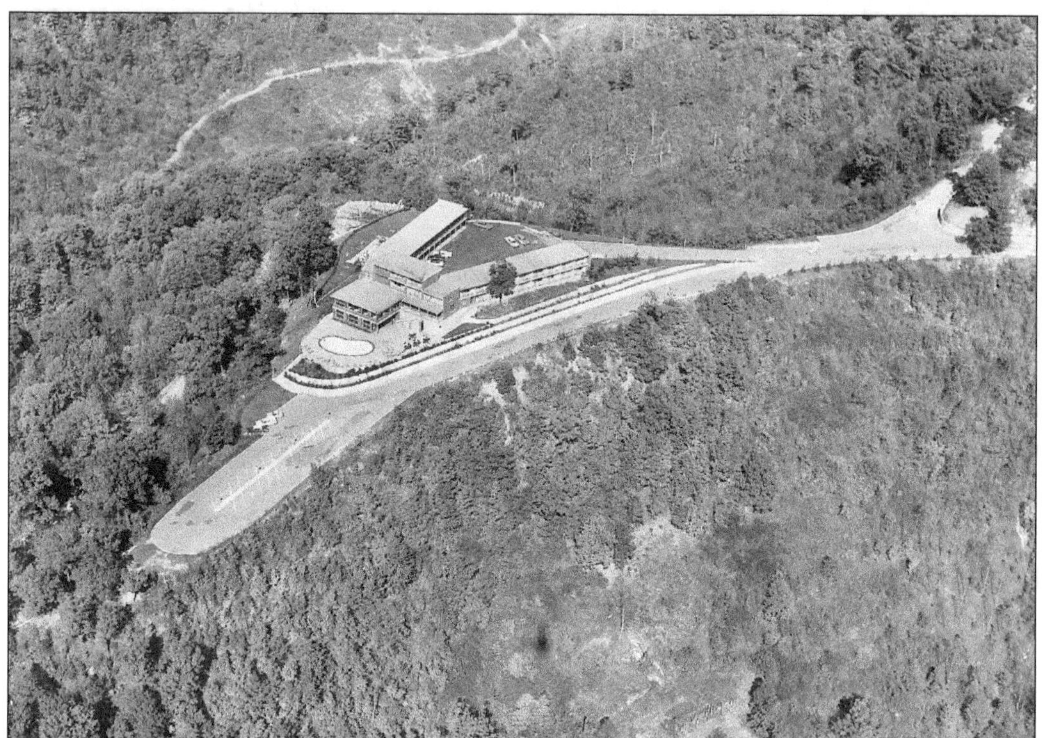

Attracted by the resort motel overlooking the valley, thousands of tourists came to Hazard. Horse-riding trails were opened around the mountain. A small putting green, a swimming pool, and "dining above the clouds" provided so much to do that when visitors made the meandering drive up the mountain they would stay for days without leaving.

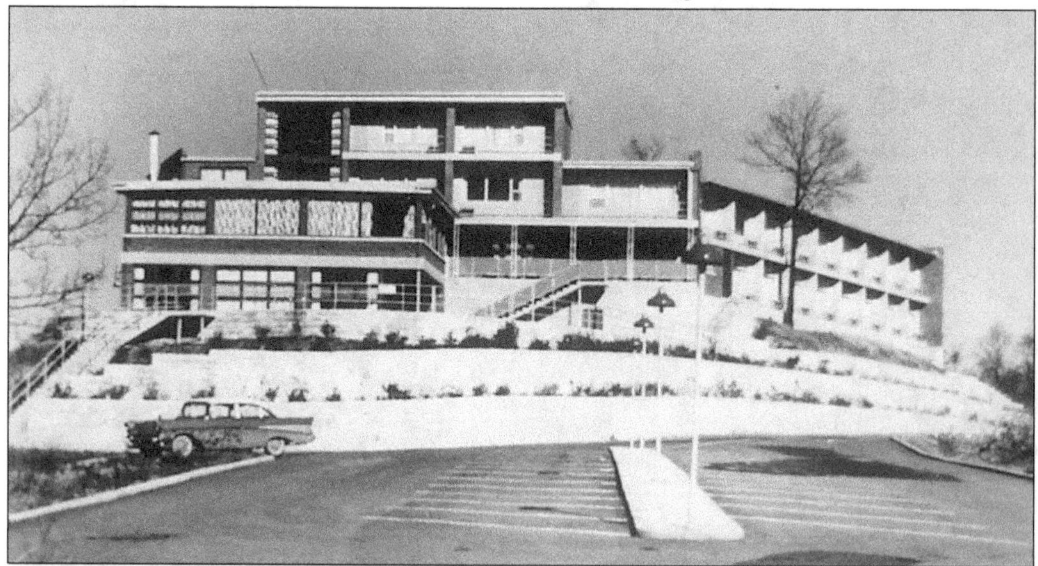

La Citadelle, completed in 1958 by Lawrence Davis, was positioned on the point of a mountain overlooking the town. Its openness to sun from all angles gave it the feeling of a Caribbean resort. The rooms on the top were suites. Every room had a balcony with a breathtaking view of mountains and the town of Hazard.

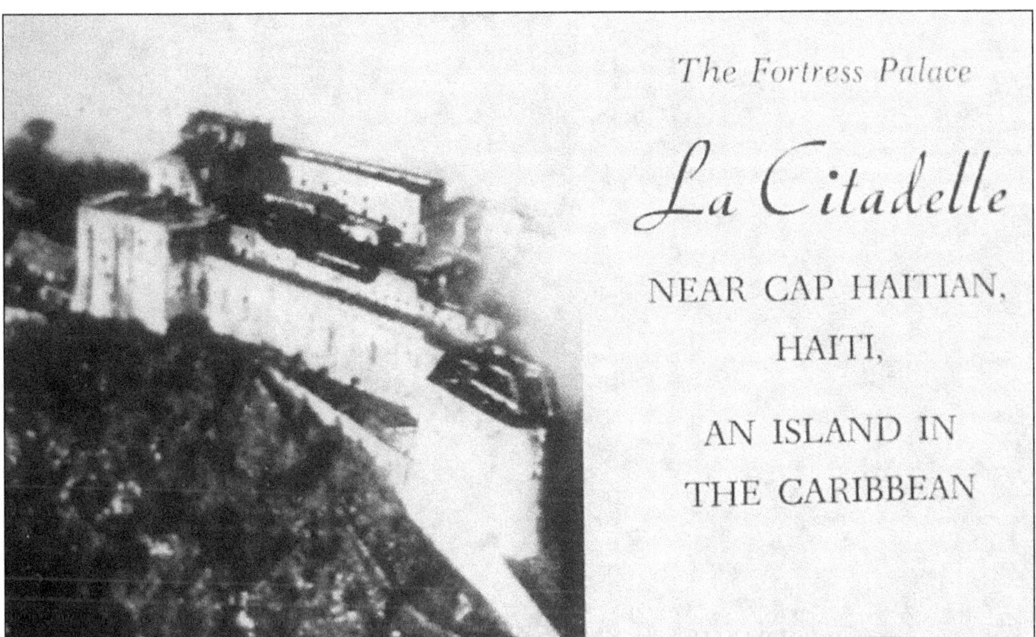

Mr. Davis once visited this fortress on the island of Haiti. It provided his inspiration for the design and name of La Citadelle.

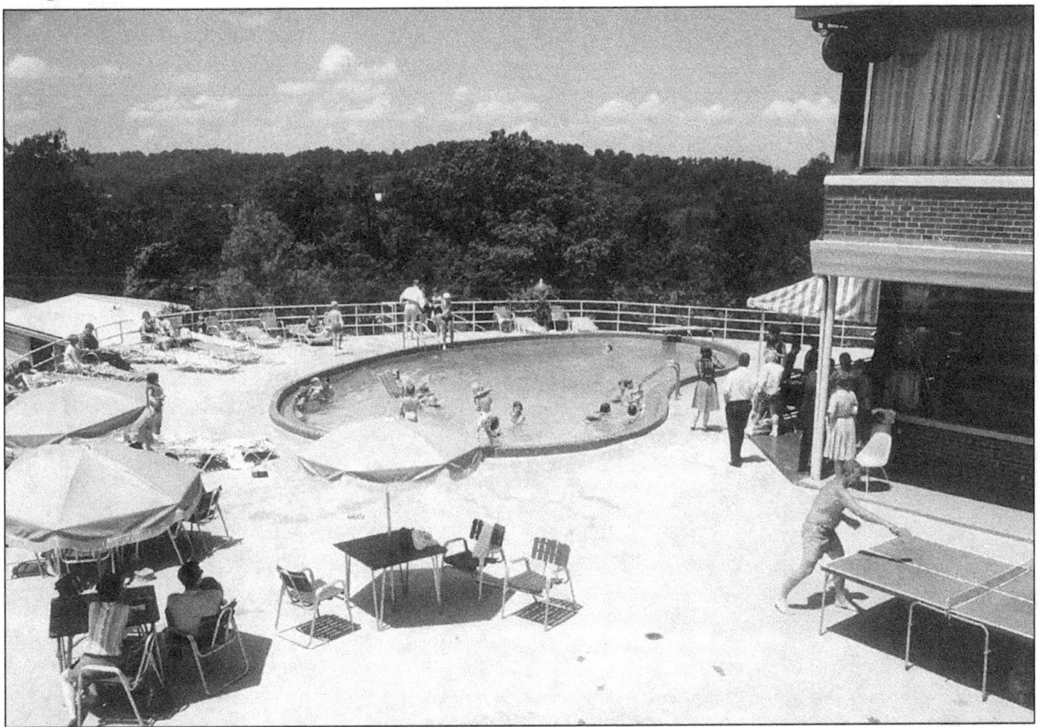

The atmosphere of relaxation brought many people back to stay at La Citadelle. This summer scene, in 1960, displays the beautiful surroundings. On most mornings in the summertime fog blanketed the valleys and the light of sunrise, shining over the clouds, created an unforgettable vista.

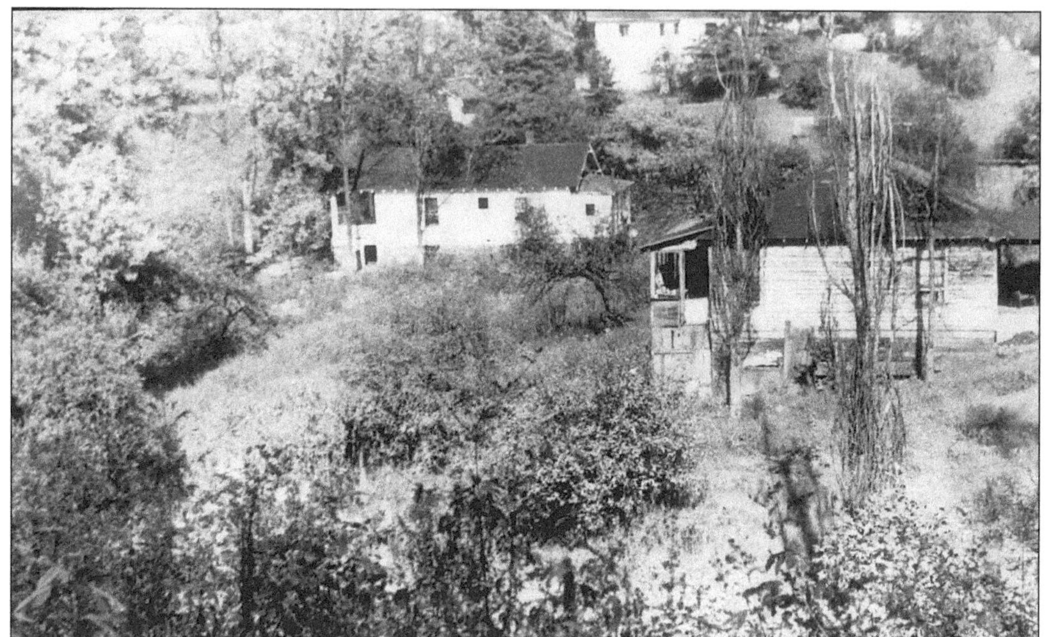

Ground was broken on this site for the Memorial Gymnasium in October 1949. Money that remained from the Civilian Defense Council, after the war, was used to start fund-raising for the project. Dr. R.L. Collins donated a portion of the land. The committee chose this property because of its proximity to the Hazard High School. It was on a block bordered by Oakhurst, Craig, and Laurel Streets.

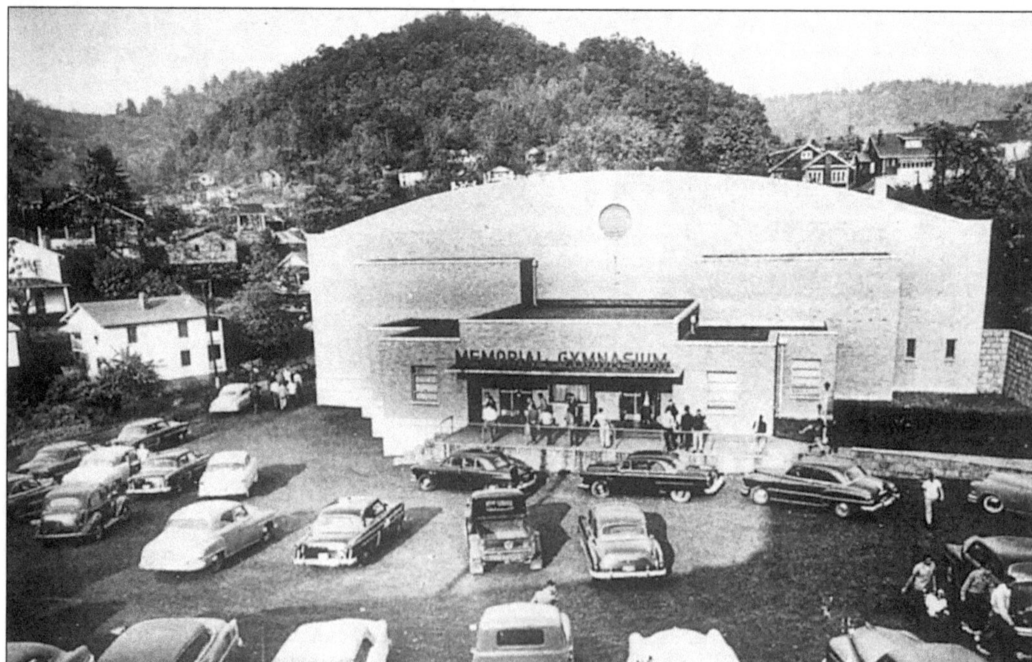

The Memorial Gymnasium construction project was spearheaded by L.O. Davis, president of the Civilian Defense Council and secretary of the Hazard Chamber of Commerce. The building was completed in late 1951.

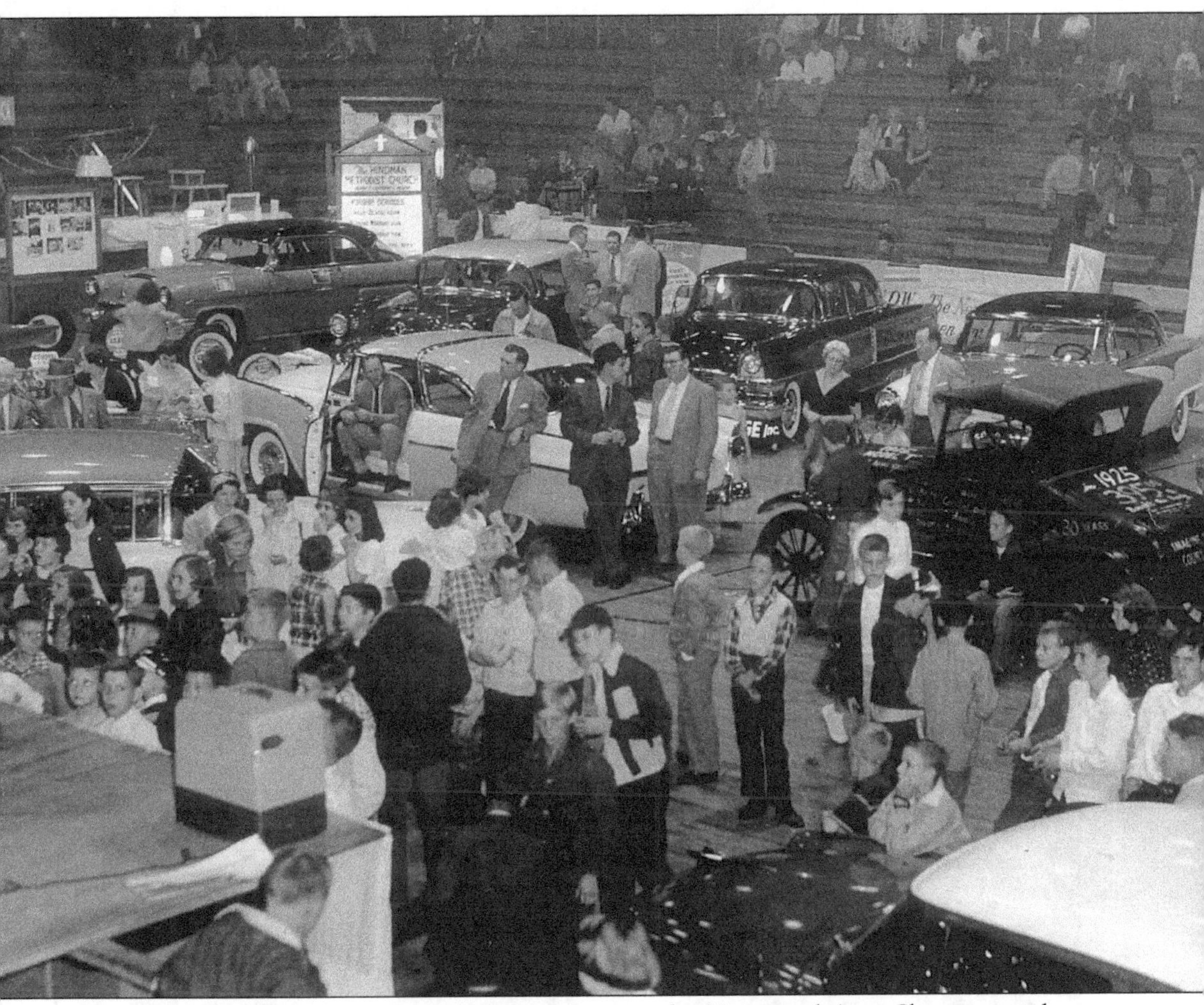

The first event held in the Memorial Gymnasium was the Home and Auto Show, created to celebrate progress in Eastern Kentucky. A woman, brought to the exhibition by Home Office Supply, could type 133 words per minute on her Royal typewriter. During the first show, 13 appliance dealers exhibited their lines and 10 car dealers parked their autos on the gym floor. This picture is from one of the Home and Auto Shows from the early 1950s.

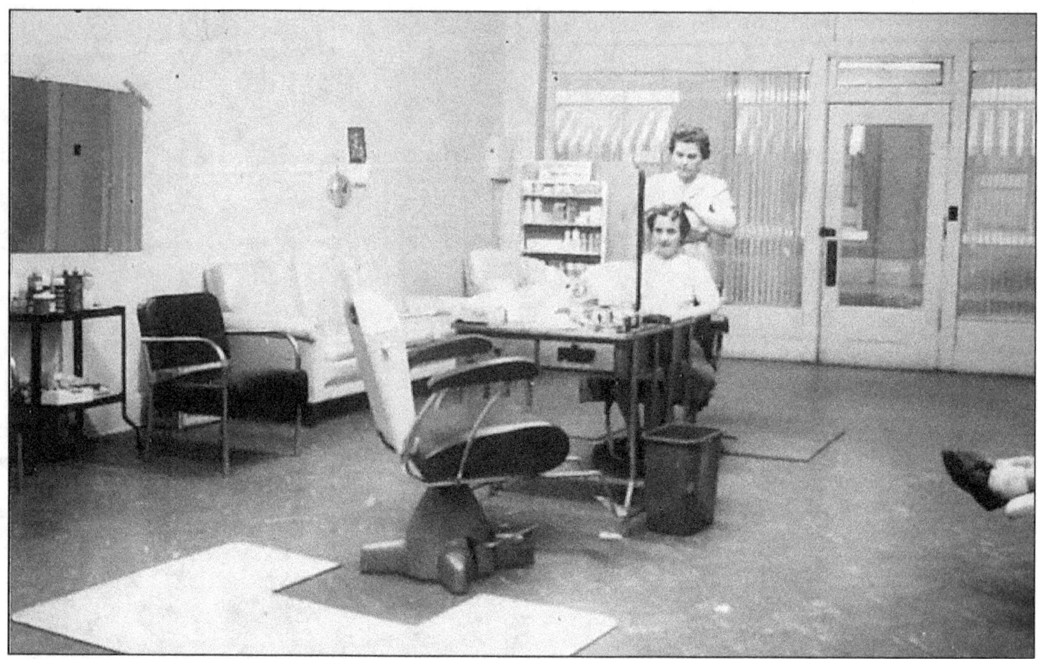

This 1953 photograph shows the Isabella Beauty Shop, owned and operated by Mrs. Isabella Suttles on High Street across from Mount Mary Hospital. Mrs. Suttles had previously owned Isabella's Beauty Shop in Blue Diamond for 26 years.

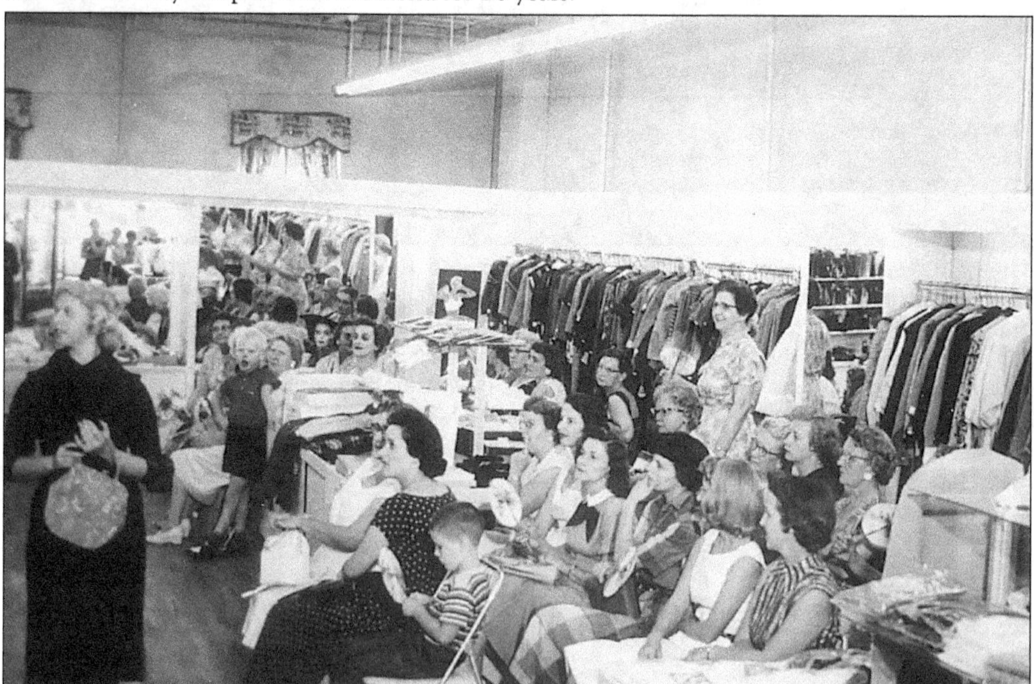

Following the 1957 flood, Johnson's Department Store opened with an all new interior, including fluorescent lights, and walls painted pastel gray and chartreuse. Mr. and Mrs. Harper invited their customers to a style show. The seamstress in the rear of the store was always available for alterations.

Seven

Early Mining Days

Members of the Hazard Chamber of Commerce at the February 19, 1926 meeting heard that the county could not depend on the mines alone for a thriving economy. Still, on July 11, 1927, Engles, a store on Main Street, took in $1,107.40 in one day. It is easy to see why no one believed that the end of the coal boom was near. In 1939, during the whole month of July, customers at Engles paid a total of $714.35 for merchandise and charged $2,119.02. By the end of World War II, receipts in the same store only averaged $383.90 a day, during July.

The great migration to Ohio and points north for jobs meant the separation of families. On weekends, streams of cars loaded with Kentuckians crowded the highways. Gradually, East Kentuckians left and made their homes in Ohio, Indiana, and Michigan, and their children grew up there. The migration was complete.

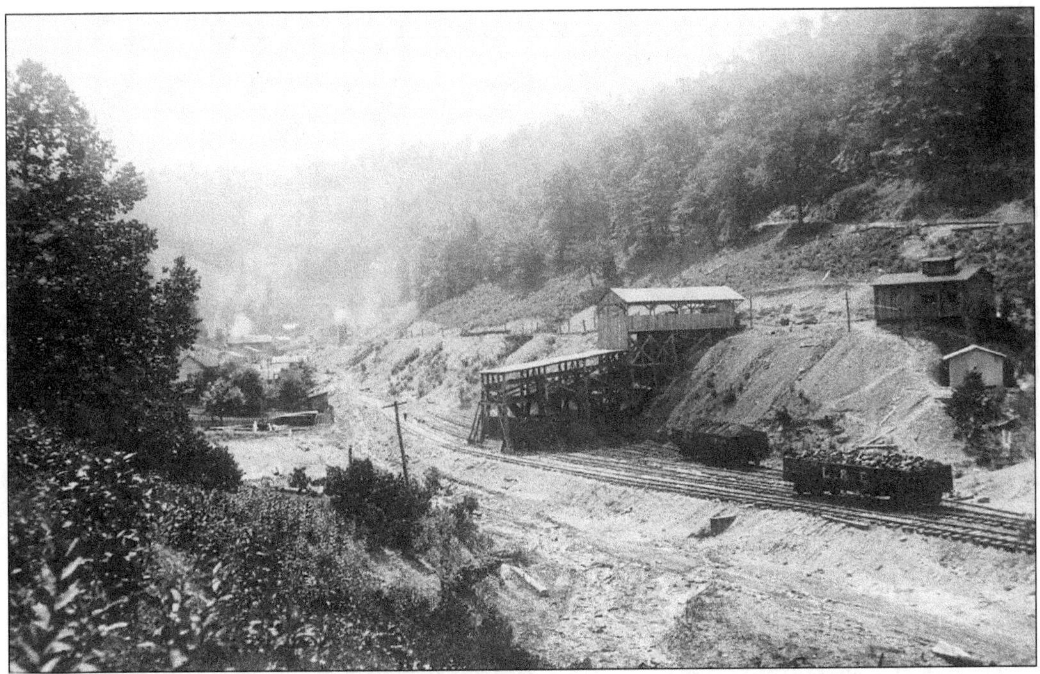

The Hazard Coal Company, the third mine to ship coal out on the railroad, was the first mine in the Hazard field operated with electricity. It was located just across the river from the east end of Hazard. The superintendent was Perry Gorman, and the general manager was W.G. Polk.

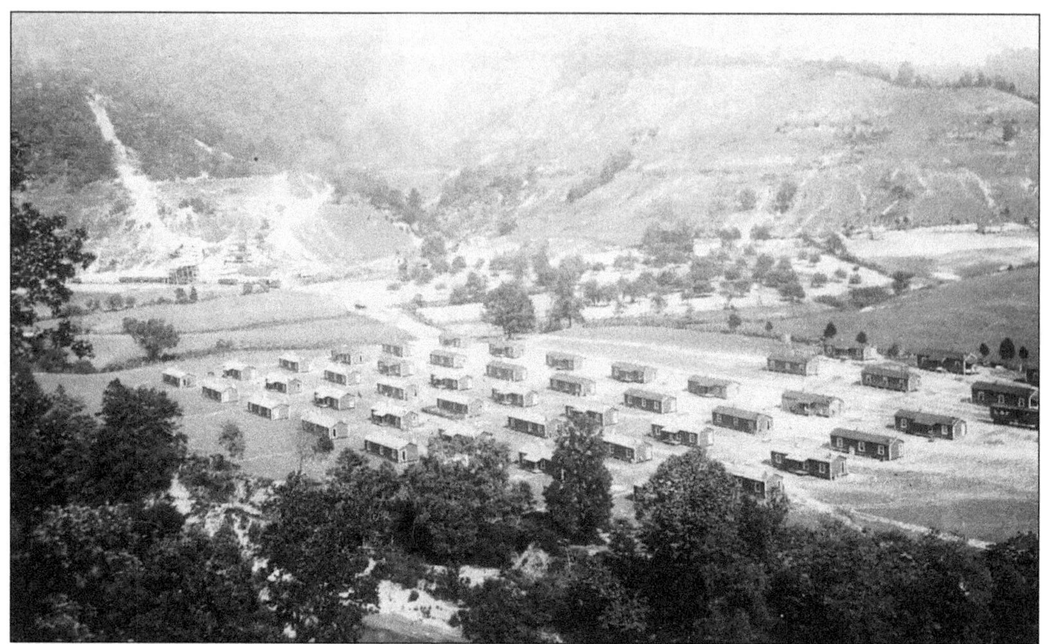

The Kentucky Jewel Coal Company (KJCC), shown here in 1916, shipped coal for the first time in October 1913. It was the fourth mine to start shipping coal from the Hazard field. The first load was about 30 cars. In 1915, KJCC produced the greatest amount of coal of all the mines in Perry County. In 1917, the mine changed its name to the Algoma Block Coal Company.

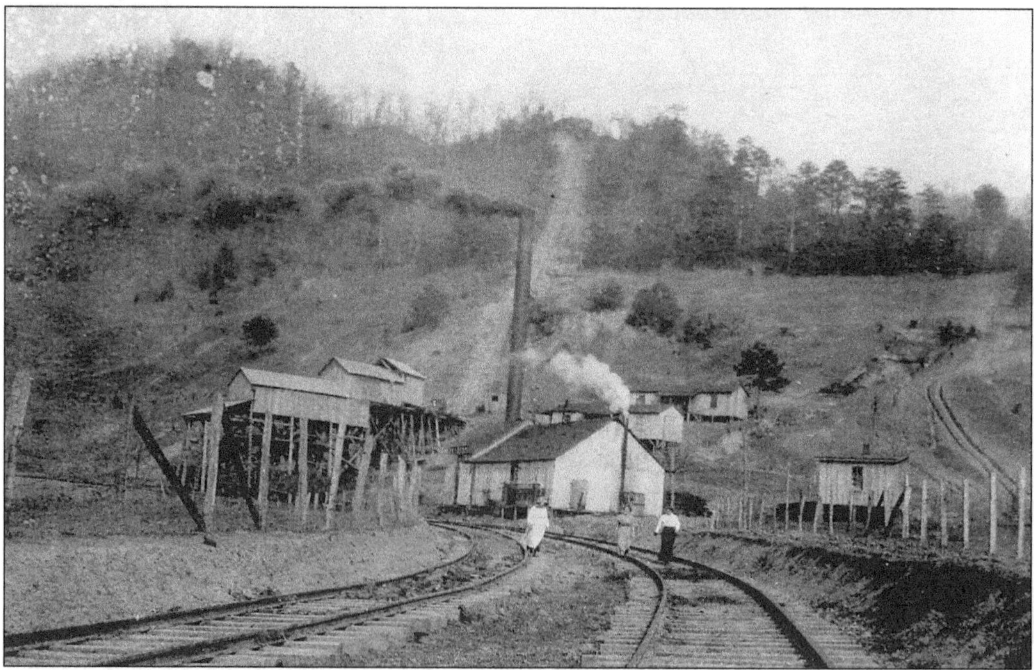

John Kinner took this *c.* 1913 photograph of the Kentucky Jewel Coal Company in Lothair. This is the site of the old Hazard Light and Power Company and now the Kentucky Power Company.

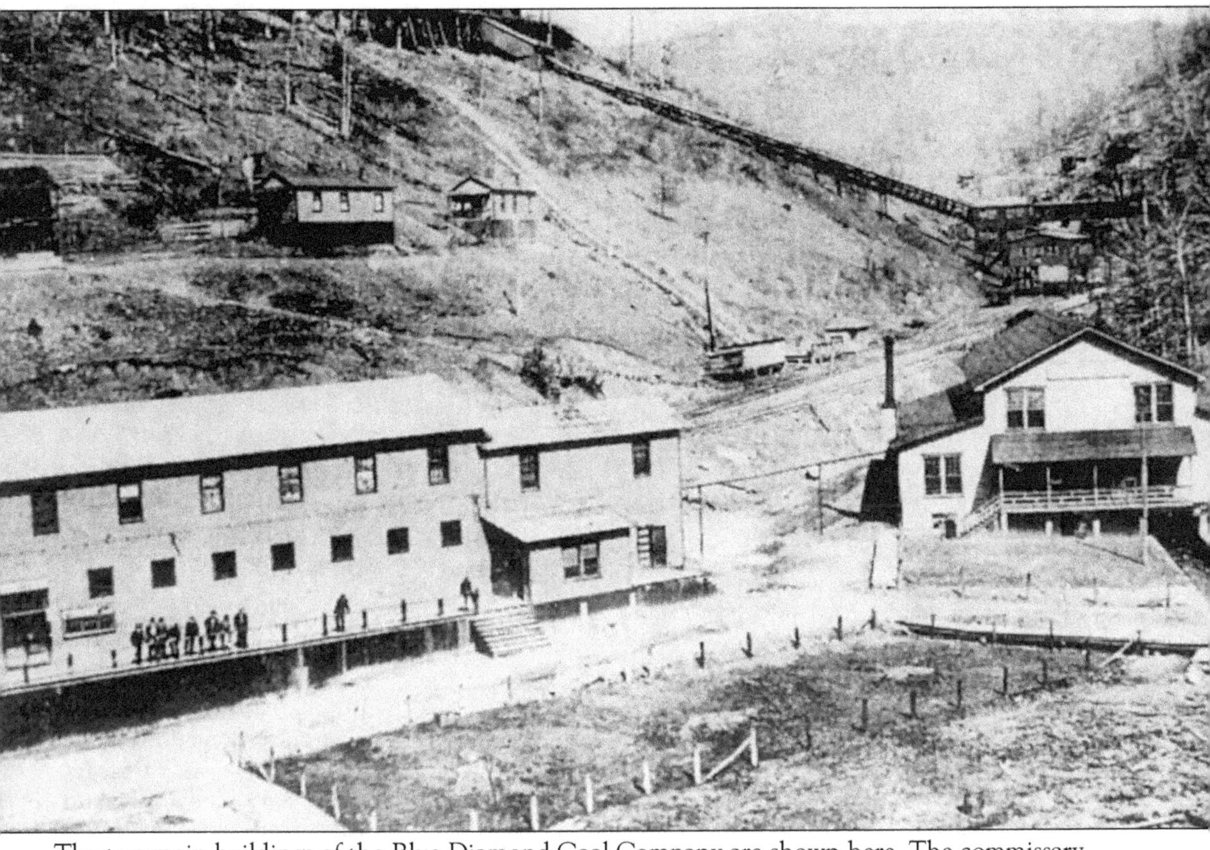

The two main buildings of the Blue Diamond Coal Company are shown here. The commissary is on the left and the YMCA and boardinghouse are on the right.

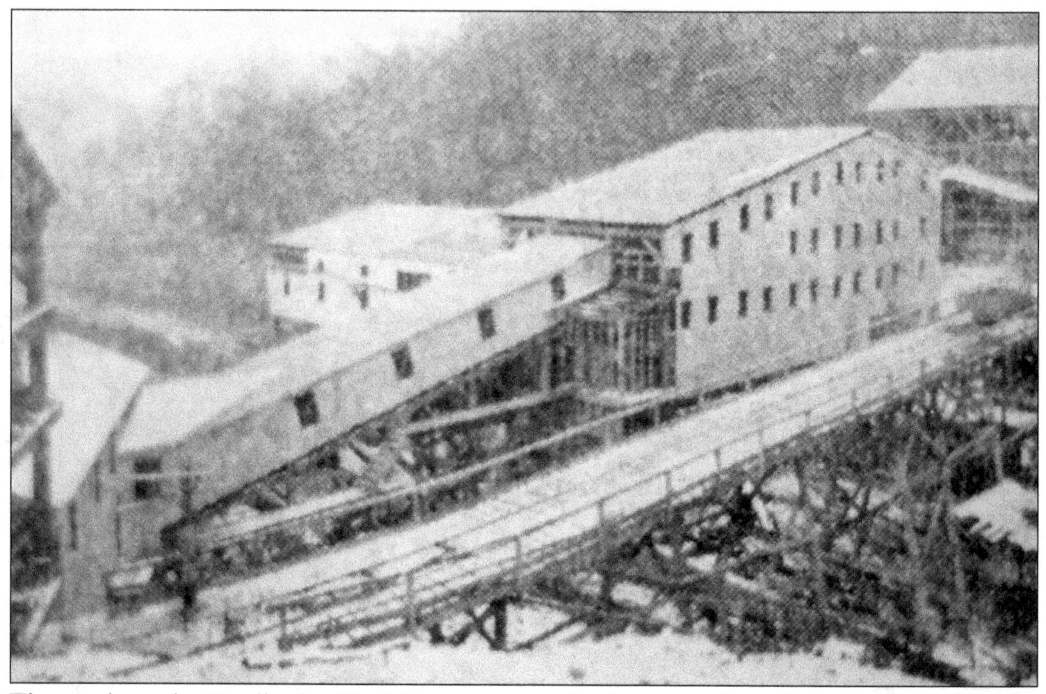

The tipple at the Hardburley Coal Company was the largest coal tipple built of wood in the world. Coal tipples not only deliver coal to railroad cars and coal trucks, they also enclose the machinery that crushes coal to the size ordered by customers. On October 19, 1962, fire destroyed the Hardburley coal tipple owned by William B. Sturgill and R.H. Kelly of Hazard. The newspaper reported that the alarm could not be called in to the Hazard Fire Department because the party-line was busy. The tipple had been hit by two previous fires.

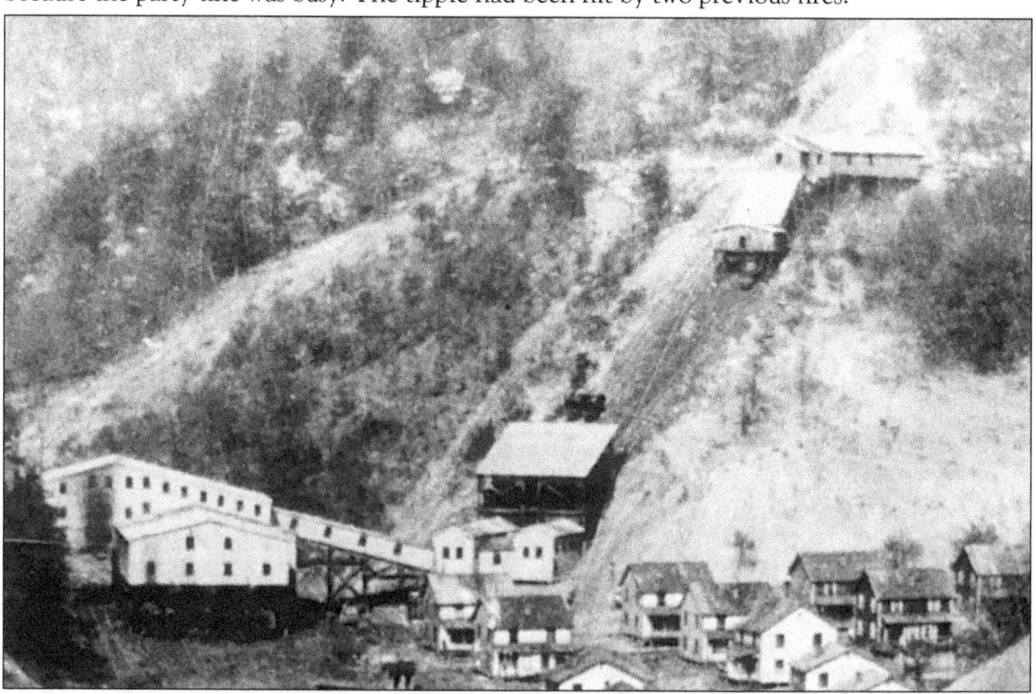

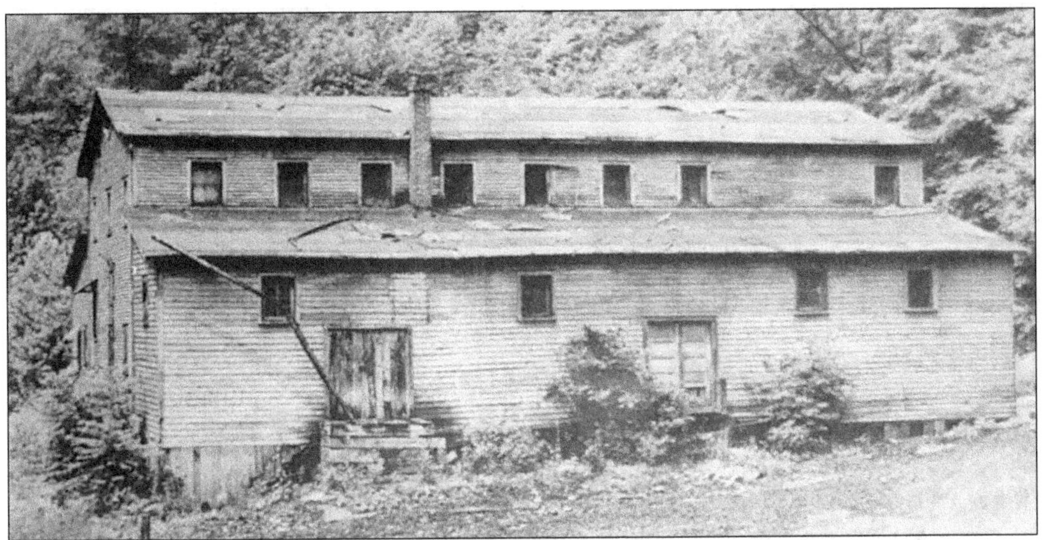

The Kenmont Coal Company store at Jeff once served hundreds of miners and their families in the Kenmont coal camp. This image, taken in 1974 of the empty commissary building, is representative of the entire hollow after its decline.

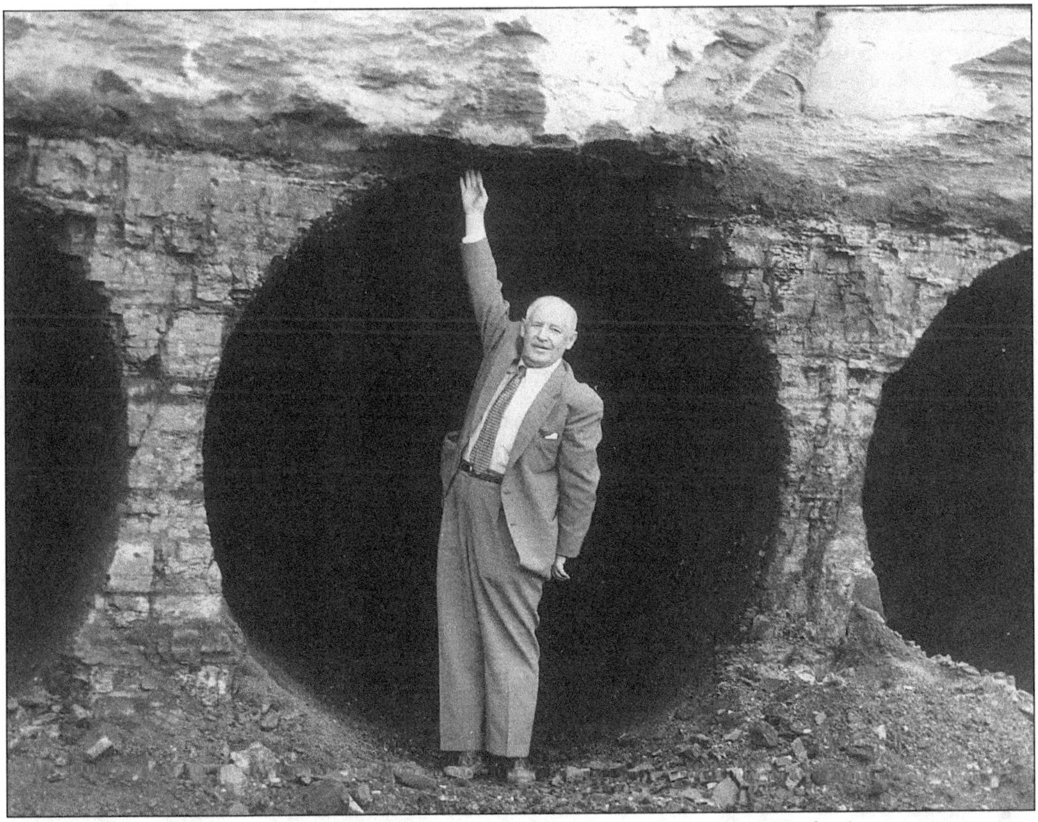

Lawrence O. Davis stands in an auger hole 7 feet in diameter at Carrs Fork. Auger mining was developed in the early 1950s.

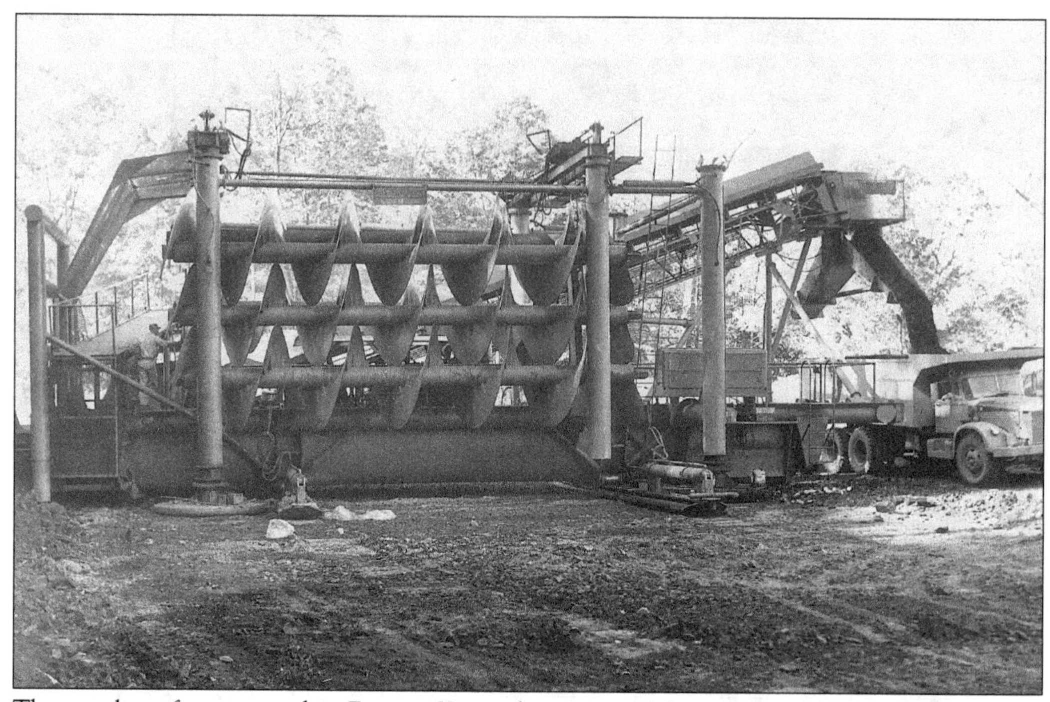

The number of augers used in Eastern Kentucky increased from 15 in 1954 to 58 in 1957. In those years the total net tons produced by auger mining tripled. Operators used augers in limited conditions, such as on the faces of seams. Coal, extracted by the enormous bore, is lifted directly into a coal truck. Augers permitted utilization of "thin underground seams that break through close to the surface of the steep slopes of mountains." (Mary Jean Bowman and Warren Haynes, *Resources and People of Eastern Kentucky*, Baltimore, MD: Hopkins Press, 1963.)

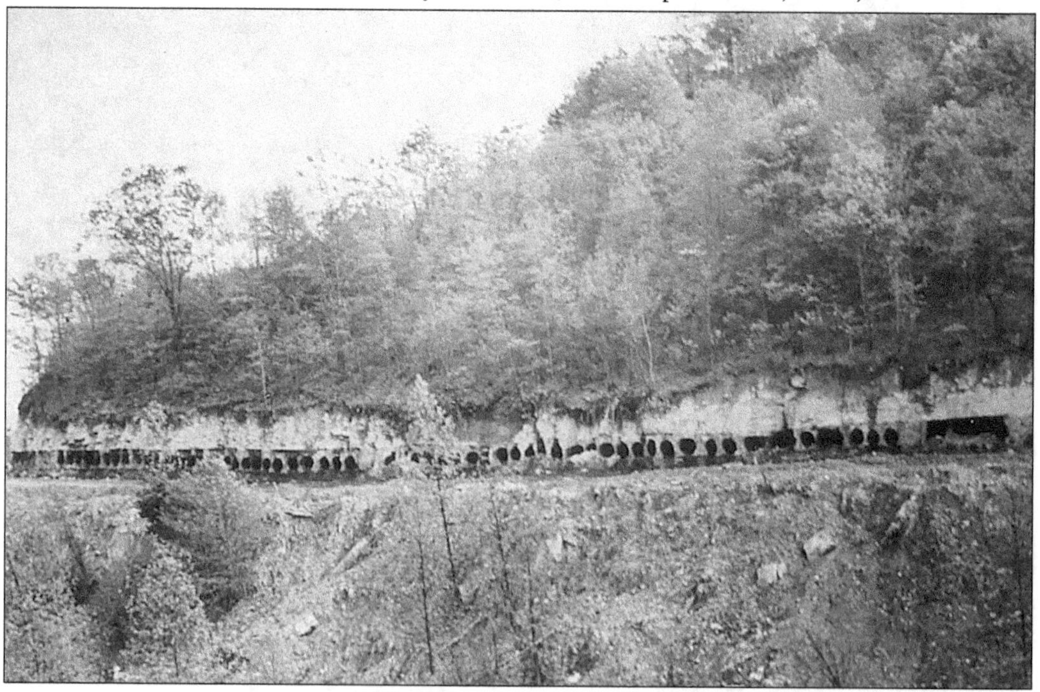

Eight

Perry County Scenes

Perry County was the center of culture and business in Eastern Kentucky and remains so today. People from the surrounding counties travel to Perry County for employment, health care, shopping, and education. This tradition began when Perry County encompassed a large area, reaching all the way to Estill County. The founding father, Elijah Combs, urged Perry Countians to build roads all during his public life.

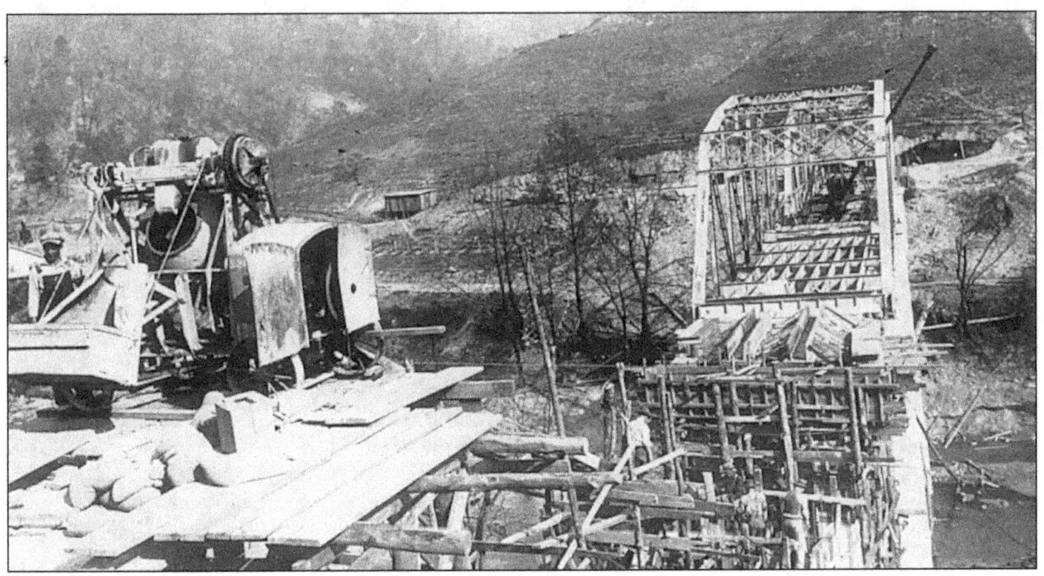

The state planned a road to Virginia in the early 1920s. The bridge at Glomawr, which was part of this plan, was finished in 1926.

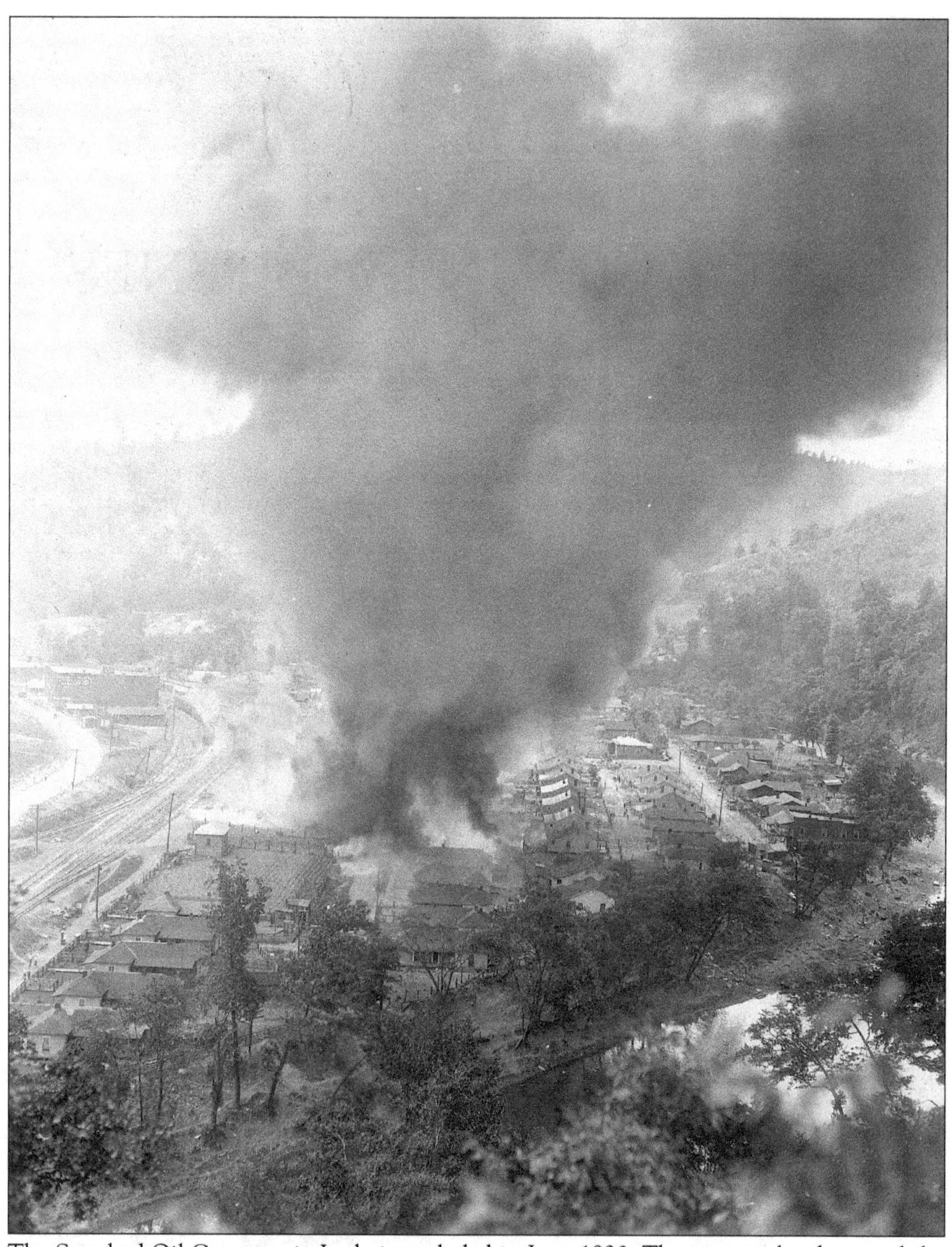

The Standard Oil Company in Lothair exploded in June 1930. The impact also destroyed the Bowman Watts Wholesale Grocery Company.

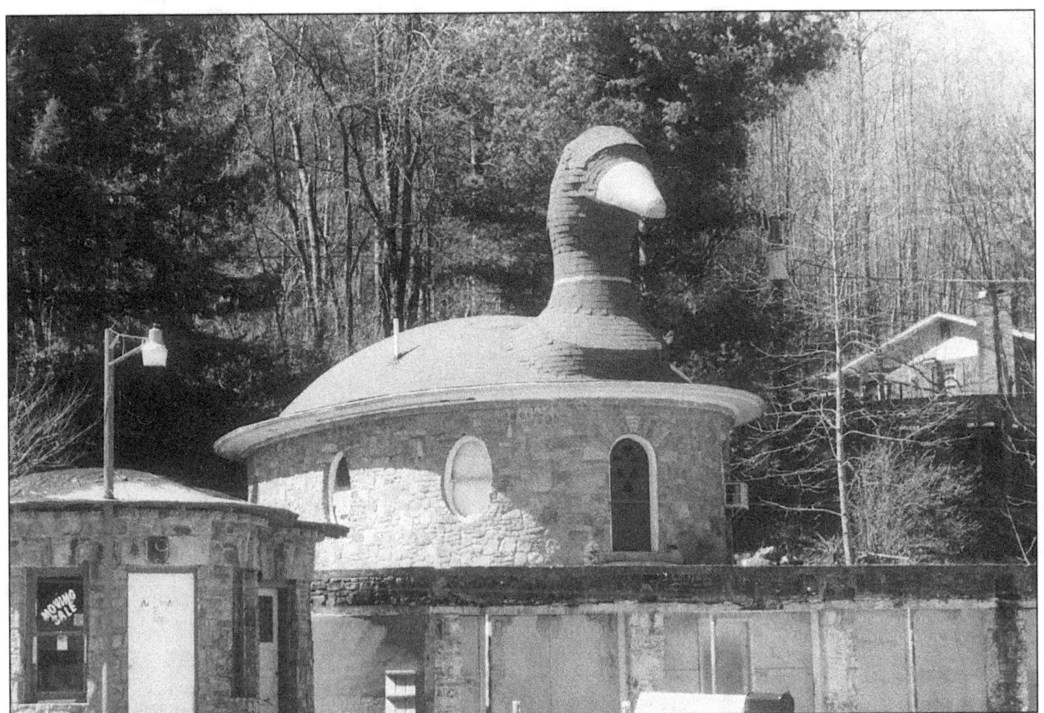

In 1936 George Stacy shot a goose, cooked it, and removed the meat. Then he studied the carcass as a model for his new house. In 1940, Stacy finished his house. It looked just like a goose. Stacy's home is located on Highway 476 in Wabaco. In 1999, "The Goose" was on an Oprah Winfrey show that featured unusual architecture.

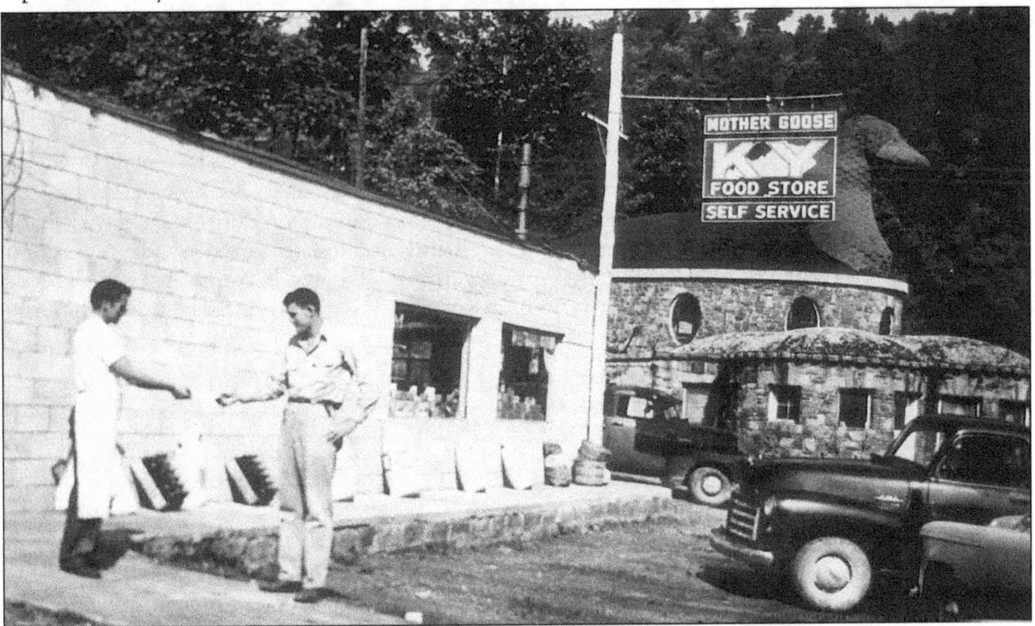

The Mother Goose Market expanded from the original stone structure to a fresh, busy supermarket, with ample parking space, in 1955. The fast-growing business provided a stunning tourist attraction from the time it was built. Today, "The Goose" is still occupied as a home.

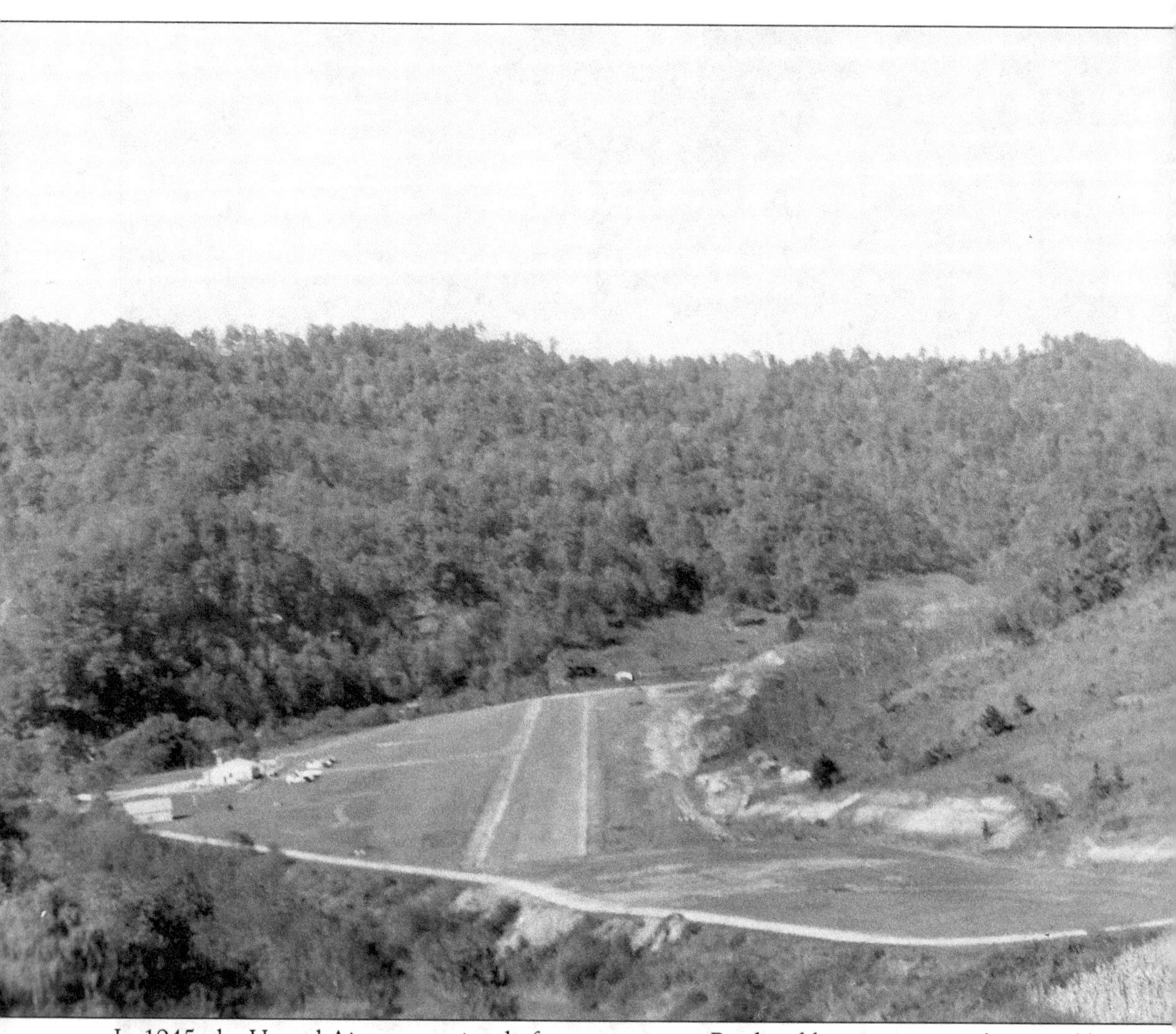

In 1945, the Hazard Airport consisted of a grass runway. Bordered by mountains, obstructed by transmission lines, and sustaining unpredictable crosswinds and fog, the airport had a reputation for danger. In 1987, the doors of the Hazard Airport terminal, located between Airport Gardens and Combs, closed. Air service moved to the East Kentucky Regional Airport, now called the Wendell H. Ford Airport.

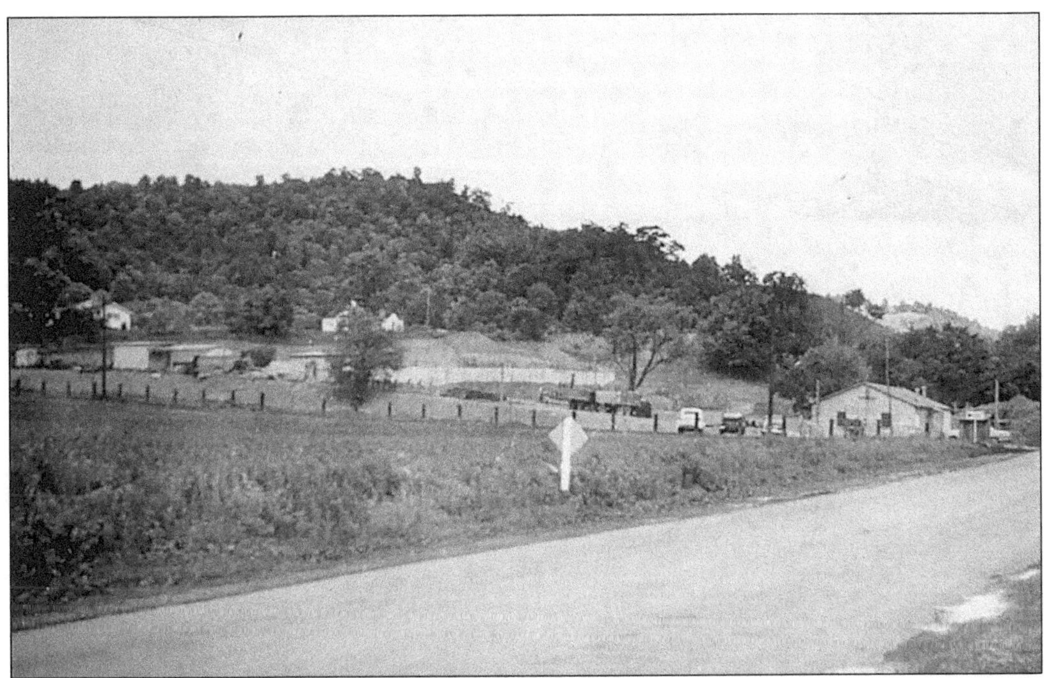

This photograph shows the countryside in Airport Gardens before the ground-breaking of the UMW Miners Memorial Hospital.

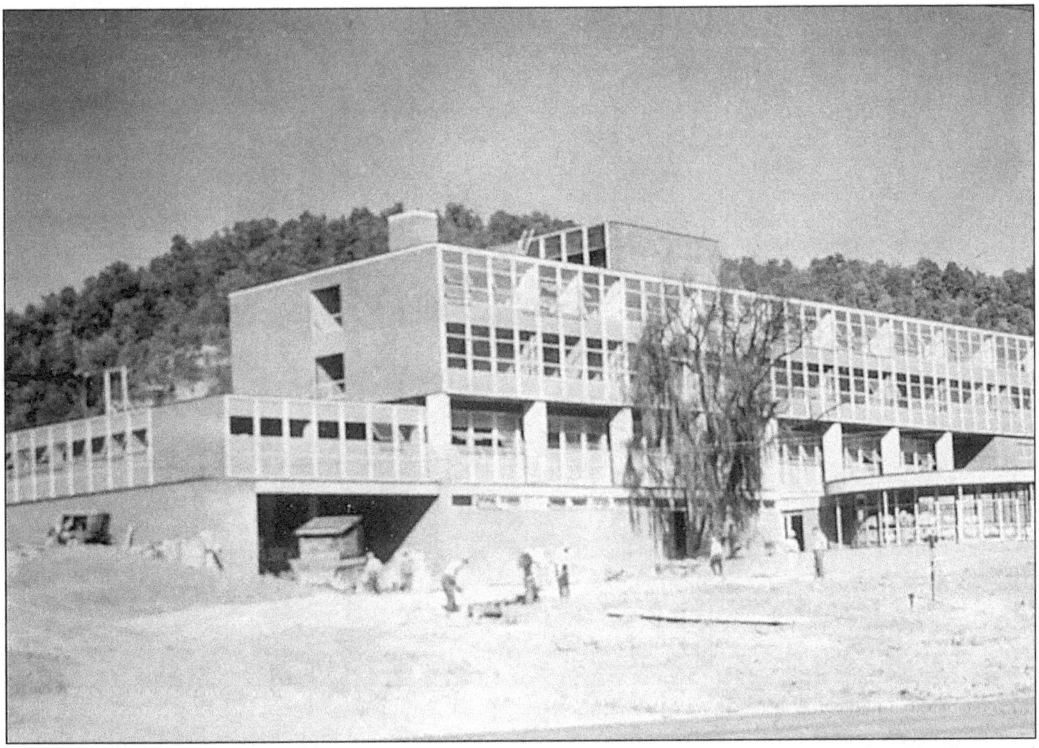

This is a picture of the UMW Miners Memorial Hospital while under construction. The hospital was dedicated June 1, 1956.

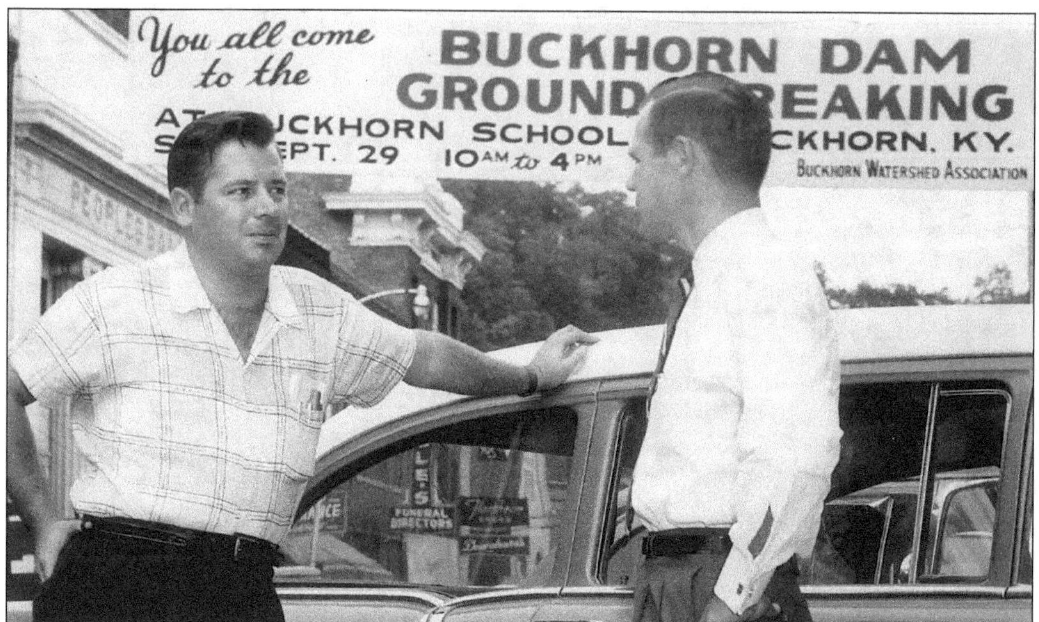

After three years of intense work to get the dam at Buckhorn the great day finally arrived. The House of Representatives approved the building of the Buckhorn Dam in June 1956. The celebration for the ground-breaking at Buckhorn took place at the dam site. Bill Gorman and Vernon Cooper discuss the big event in front of a banner across Main Street in Hazard.

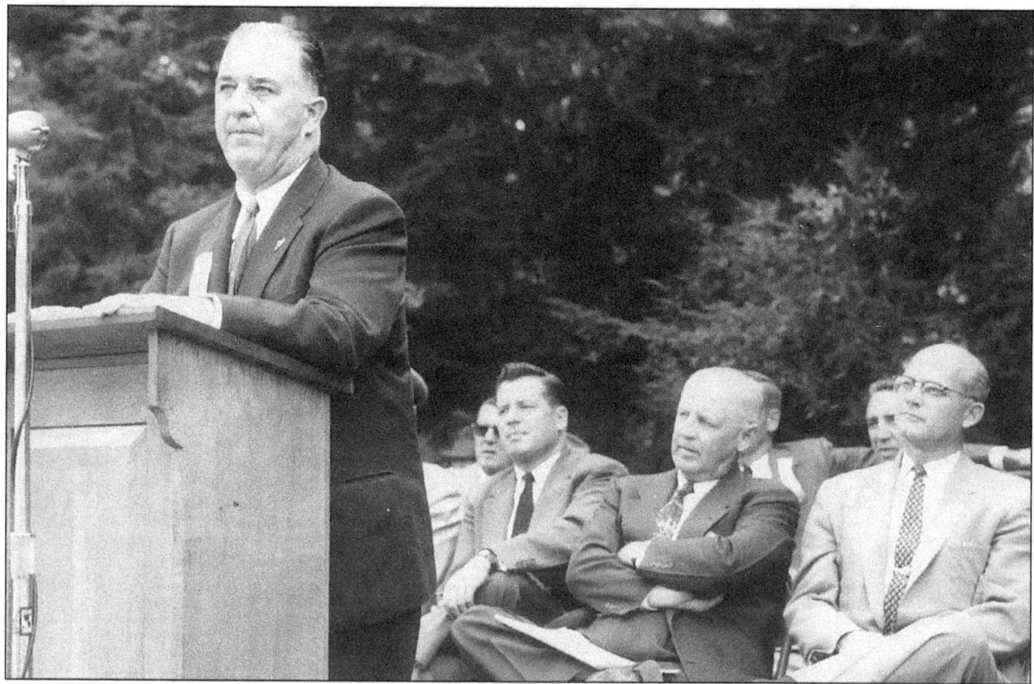

After rallies, petitions, and public hearings, the day of the ground-breaking finally arrived. Bill Gorman, L.O. Davis, and Arlie Barber listen as Governor "Happy" Chandler speaks on the importance of the event. Everyone believed that the lake and the new state park would provide a magnet for tourism.

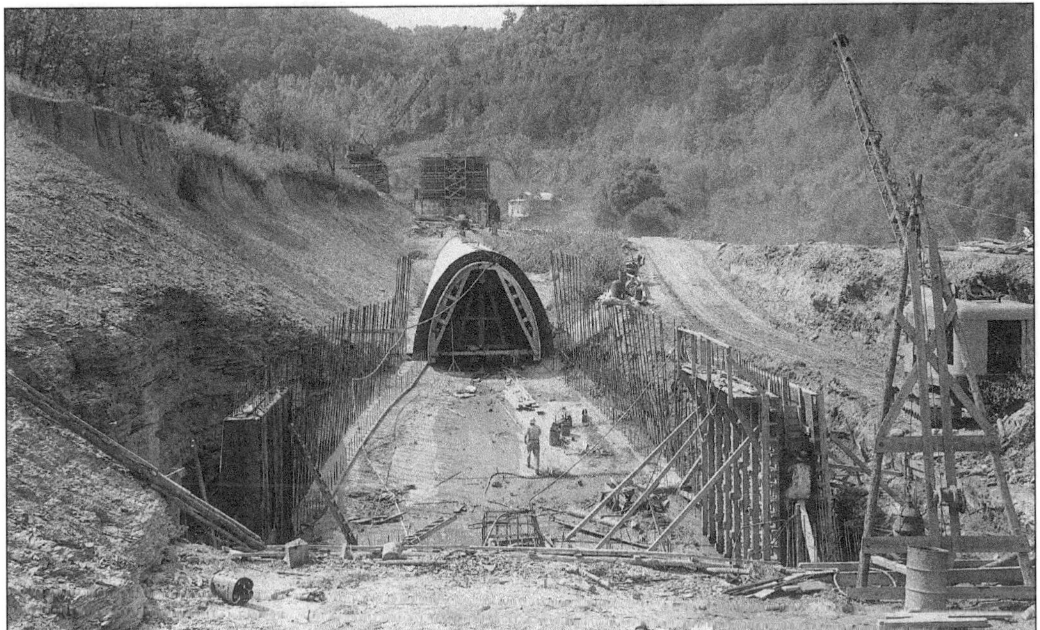

This September 2, 1957 photograph (taken by the Louisville District, Corps of Engineers, U.S. Army) shows the construction of the outlet works on the Buckhorn Dam, looking upstream at the stilling basin and the conduit. Lewis Construction Associates, Inc. of Goldsboro, NC, did the work.

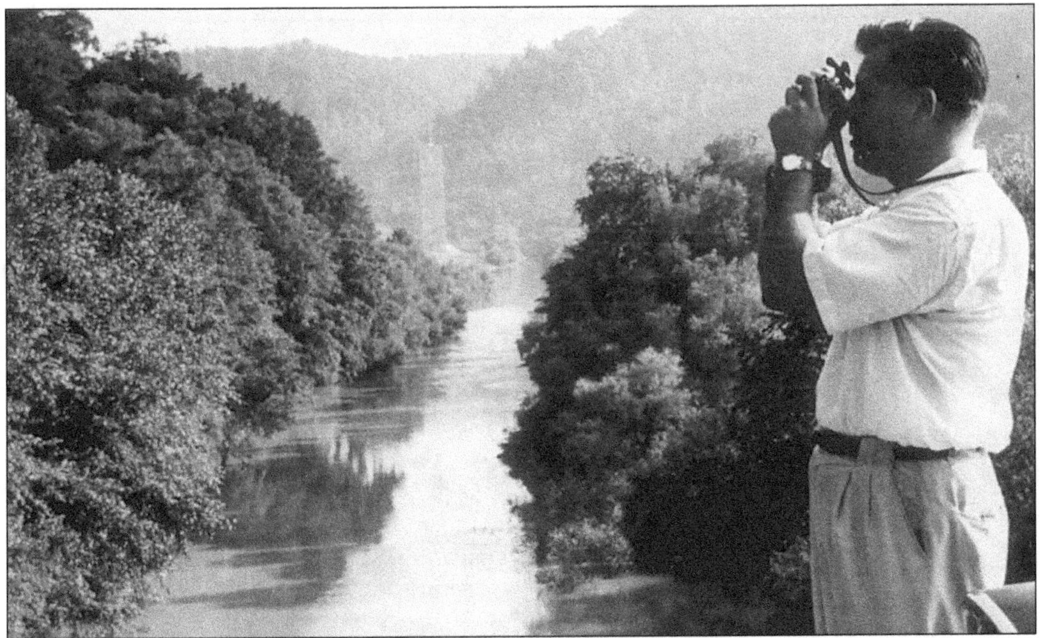

Bill Gorman (shown here), president of the Buckhorn Watershed Association, took up the crusade for the dam at Buckhorn. A flood control act, passed by Congress on June 2, 1938, was not actively promoted. At one point, Bill Gorman, Dan Mitchell, and Elmer Begley, judge executive of Leslie County, went to Washington, D.C. to ask for appropriations and were successful by 1956.

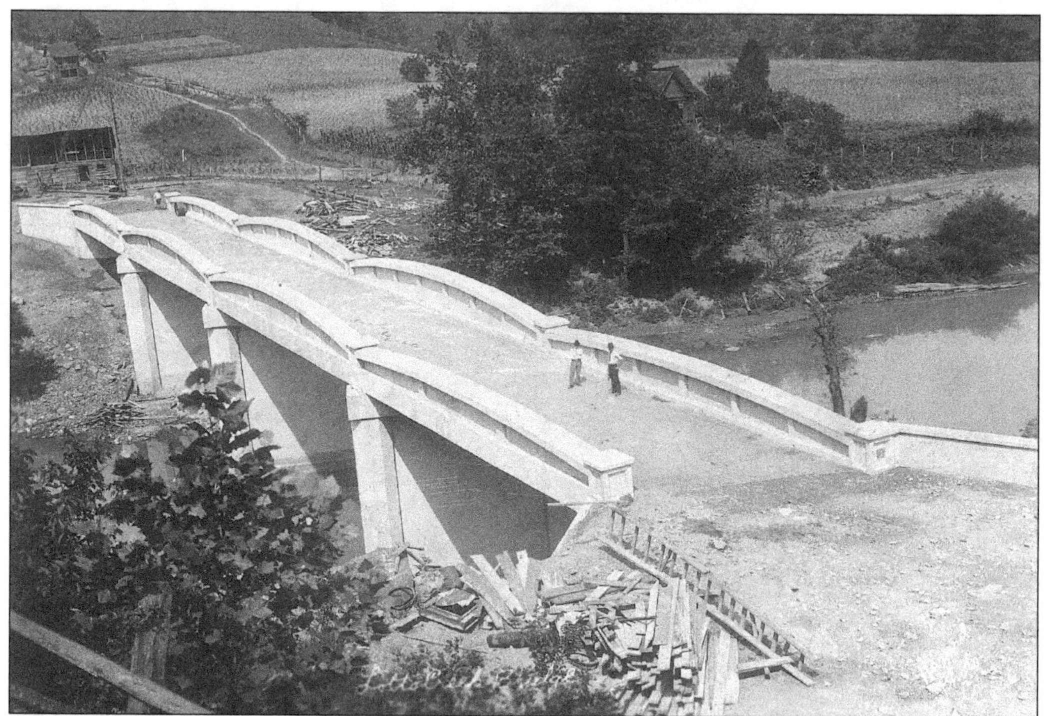

The state of Kentucky built the Lotts Creek Bridge, pictured here, in 1925. In 1995 the state replaced it with a wider bridge.

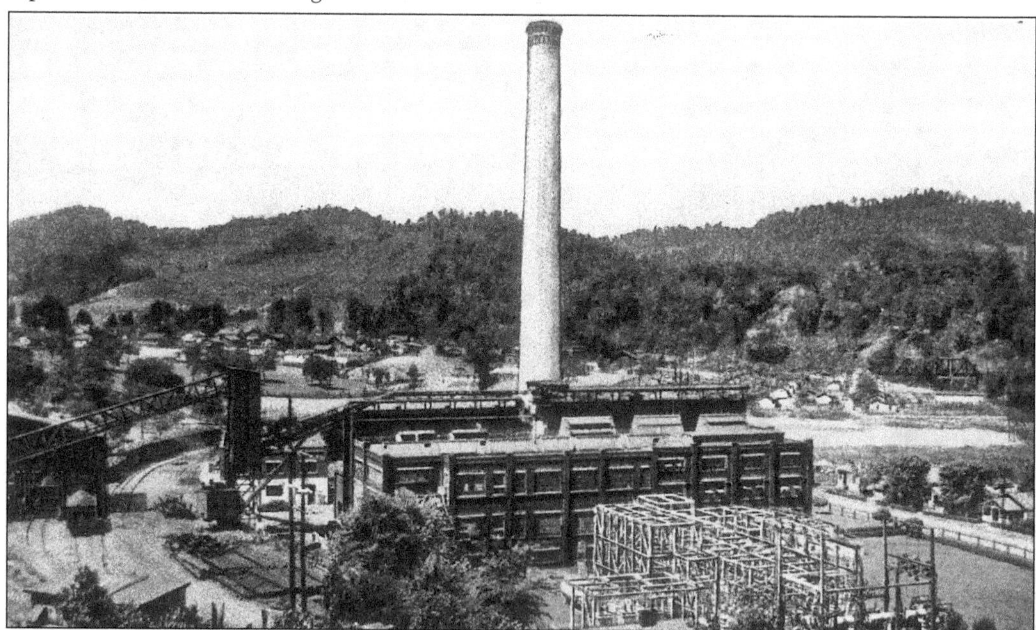

The Hazard plant of the Kentucky Power Company, in Lothair, was a veteran of over 40 years of service when it was retired in 1958 (refer to p. 90). The 250-foot-high stack replaced four smaller metal stacks in 1927. On a stand-by basis from 1954 to 1958, the plant was a familiar landmark in Eastern Kentucky and a pioneer in electrical generation. The Kentucky Power Company dismantled the stack in 1958.

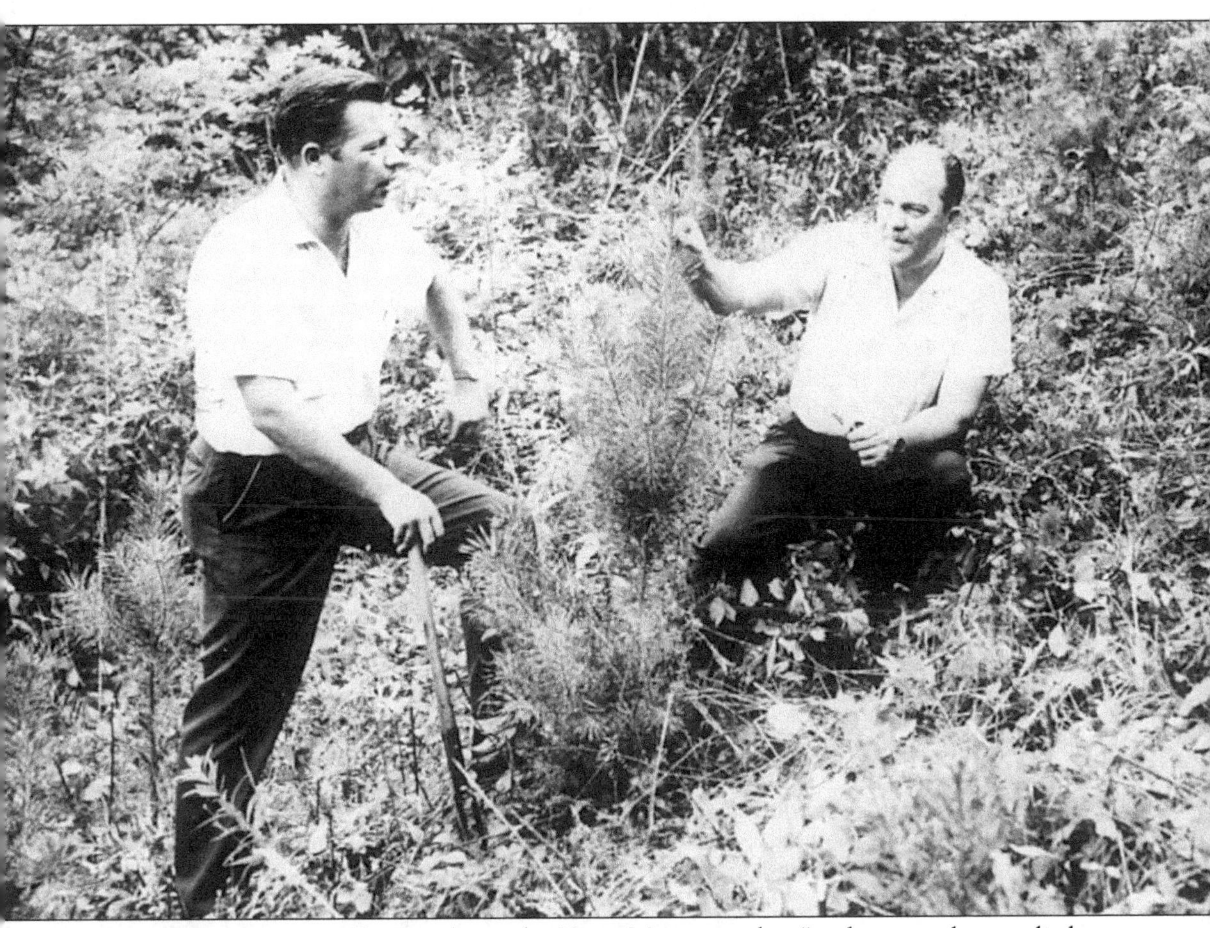

Lee Daniel wrote, in one of his articles in the *Union Messenger*, that "in days gone by very little attention was paid to conservation or crop rotation. They cleared the land and when it began to wash, it grew up with bushes and was often abandoned... the mountains have grown bald and lost their strength." In the early 1950s, Lee Daniel's son, Dewey Daniel, and grandson, William D. Gorman (son of Allie Daniel Gorman), became active in the reforestation of Perry County. Gorman poses here with Bill Morrill, the State Conservation Service forester. The work with the Soil Conservation Service, along with the Kentucky Division of Forestry, provided the present 50-year growth of trees.

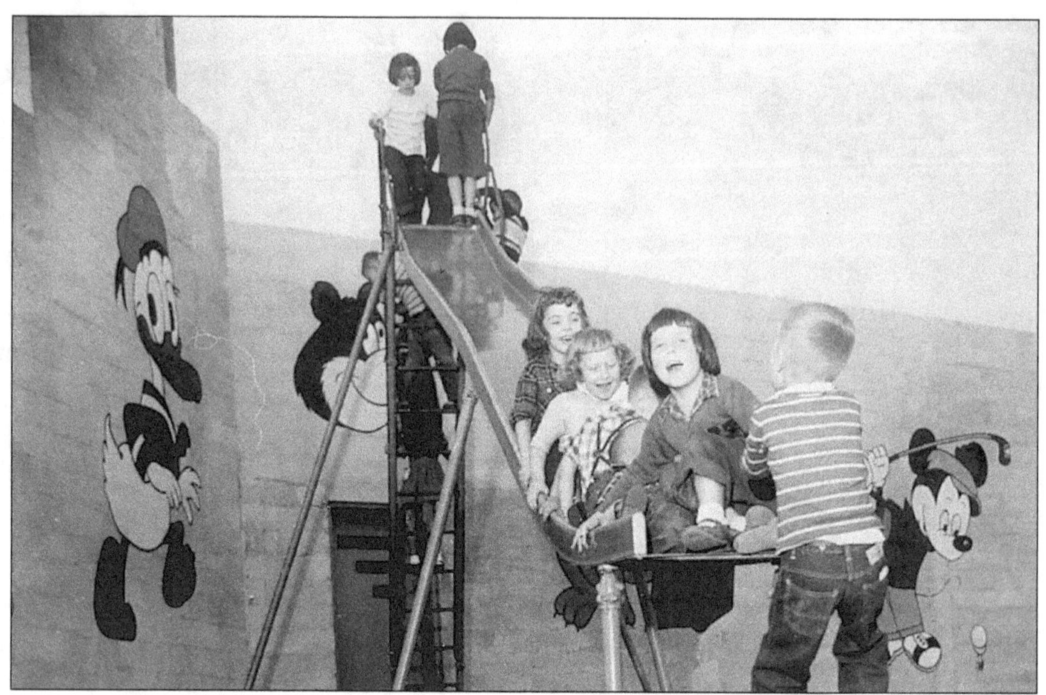

Before movies started at the Cinema Drive-In, children frolicked on the playground in front of the screen. The Cinema was a popular place for birthday parties. Movie-goers could watch the picture show from cars or, on warm evenings, sit in seats in front of the refreshment stand. It seems not many mosquitoes "bugged" the movie-goers at the Cinema, but the train came by every night, right in the best part of the movie. Perry Countians and those from miles around enjoyed hundreds of evenings at the Cinema Drive-In.

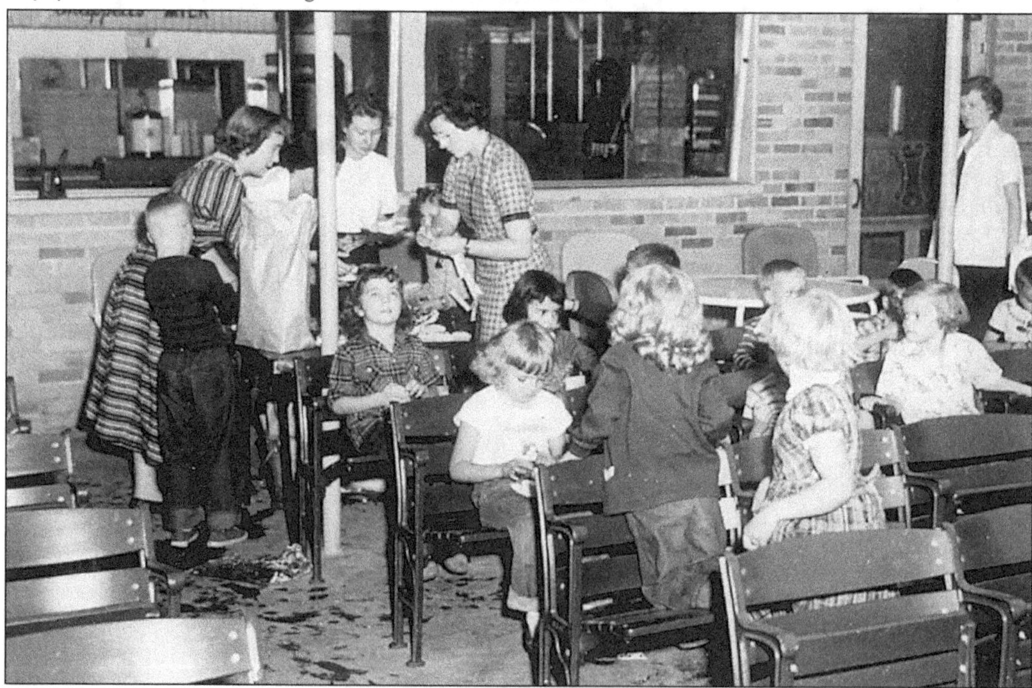

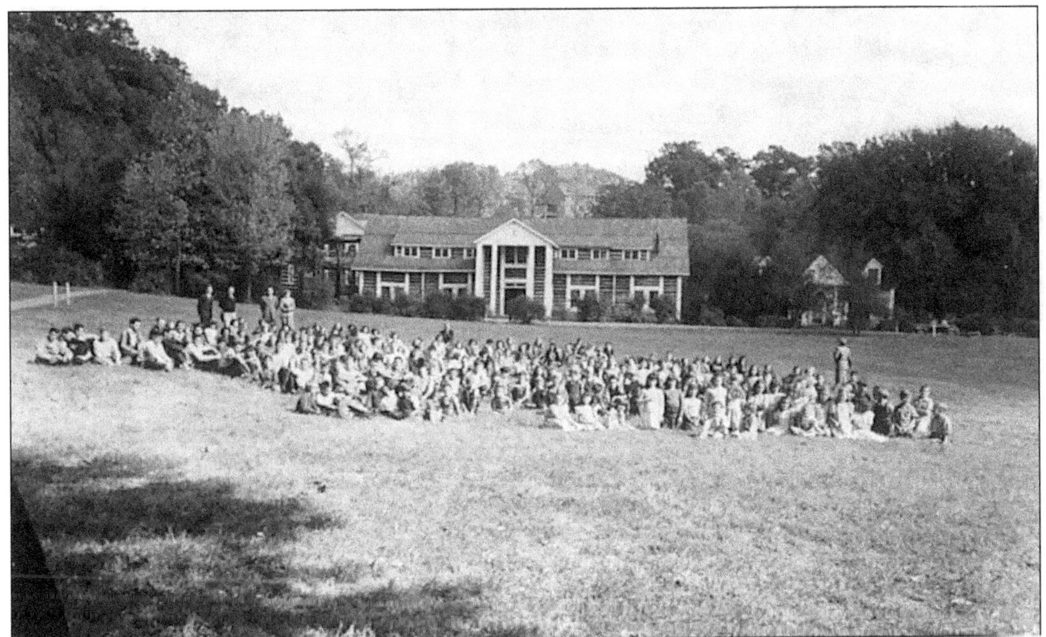

In 1902, Rev. Harvey Murdoch established the much-needed Witherspoon College, in Buckhorn. The school, named for the Presbyterian minister who signed the Declaration of Independence, educated children through 12th grade. McKenzie Hall, pictured here, housed the dining room.

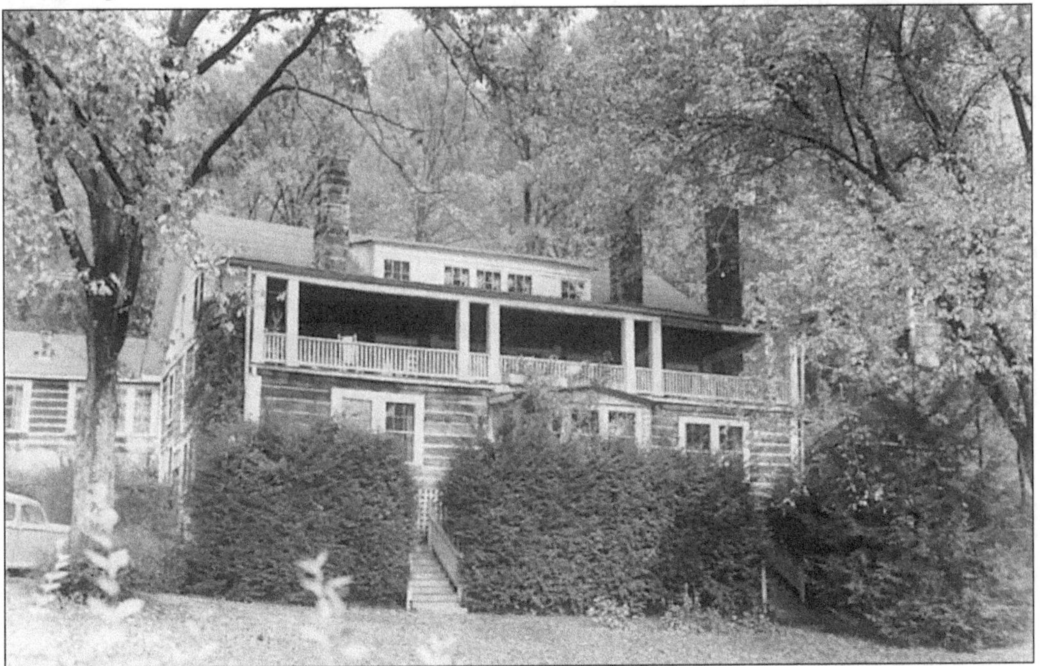

Murdoch realized that many of the children who attended the school were orphans and he raised funds for dormitories. The President's House, in this photo, was always open to the children. These are photographs from the early 1950s. Both buildings, as well as all the original ones, except the "Log Cathedral" (not pictured), have succumbed to fire.

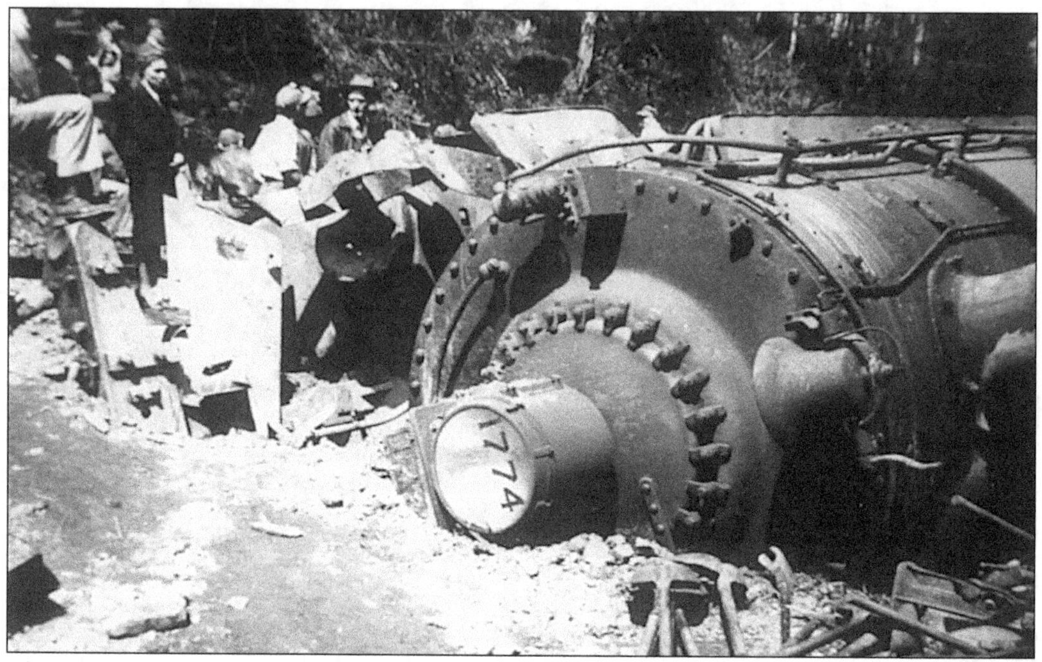

This tragic train wreck occurred on March 17, 1948, killing the brakeman and the fireman. Miller Cornet was the engineer.

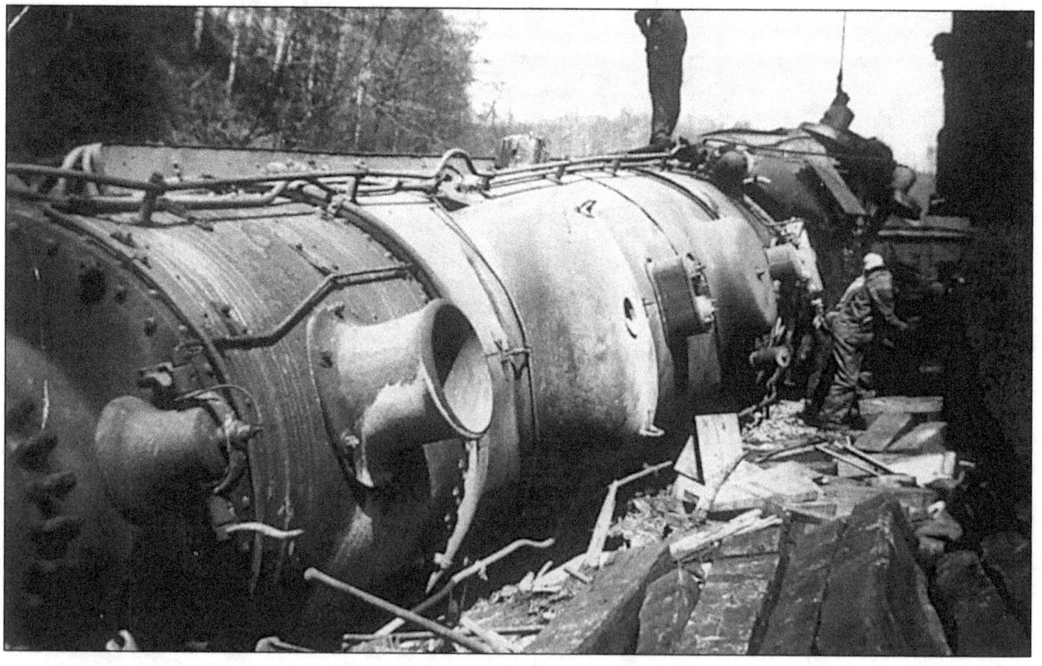

Nine

PERRY COUNTY PEOPLE

Are the people of Eastern Kentucky unique in the world? Perhaps they are not. There is the same goodness, anger, wealth, poverty, happiness, despair, creativity, and licentiousness in people everywhere. There is, however, one original quality: East Kentuckians, in particular, return home. If a mountaineer cannot come back home there always remains a longing. Visitors remark on the matchless welcoming spirit of mountain people. When looking for examples of "pride of place," East Kentuckians first come to mind.

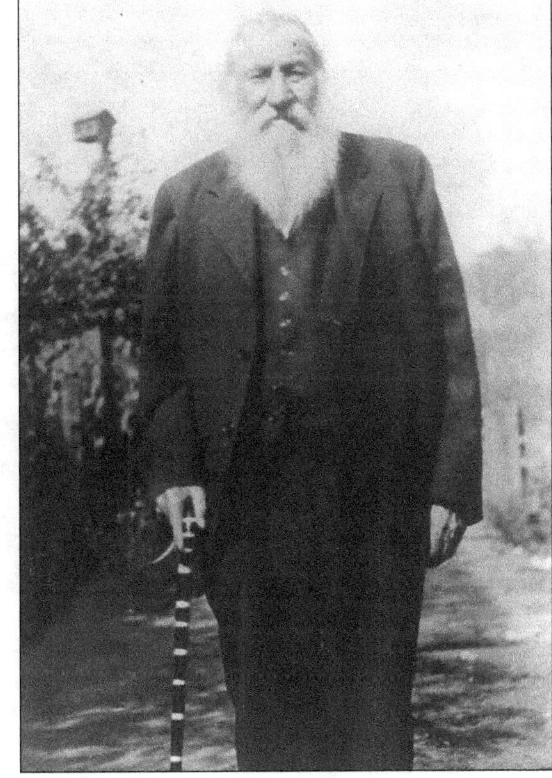

Ira Combs, "Uncle" to hundreds of Perry Countians, was born in 1844. Ordained in 1878, he performed many marriage ceremonies. He later said that of all the pairs he joined in holy matrimony, he only knew of three that broke up. During the Civil War he joined the Confederate side. Later, he changed to the Union forces. He died on April 8, 1934.

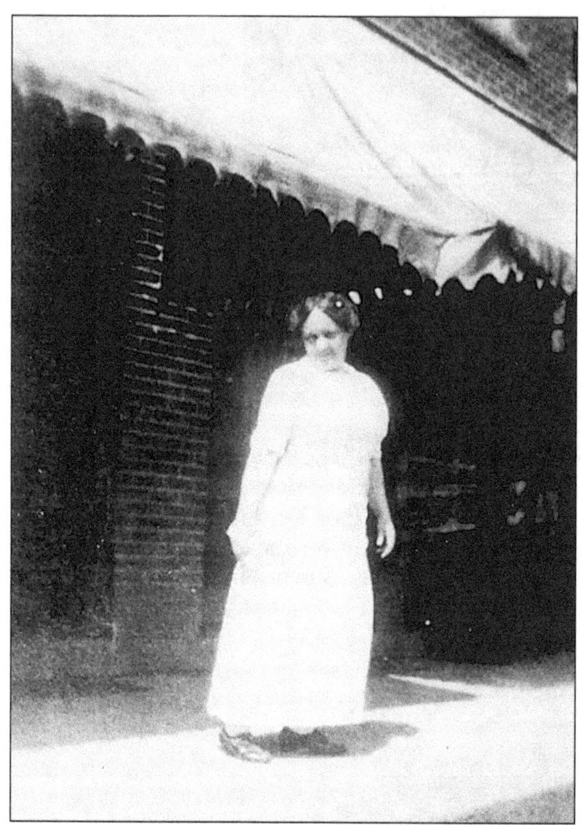

Mrs. Letha Hibler, or "Ma" Hibler, ran the Commercial Hotel on the Main Street end of the "Penny Bridge." During the flu epidemic in 1918, she made a section of her hotel into a hospital.

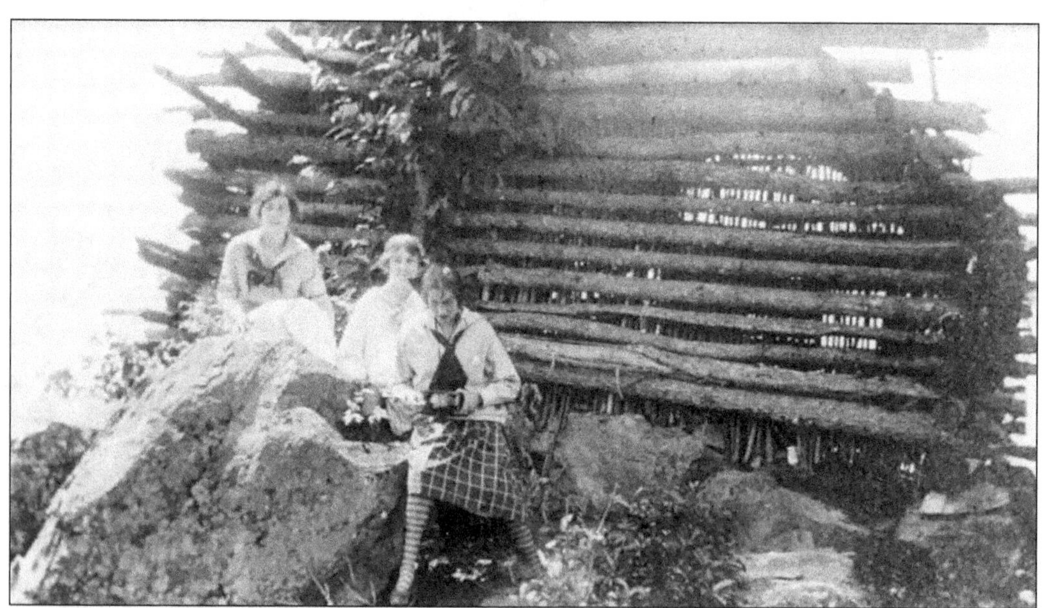

The Peterson girls and Katherine Megillen spend the afternoon at the Boy Scout cabin on Peter's Peak. The year was about 1917. It was a long climb that started in the backwoods at the water tank, but Hazard's young people always seemed to think the afternoon walk was worth the effort.

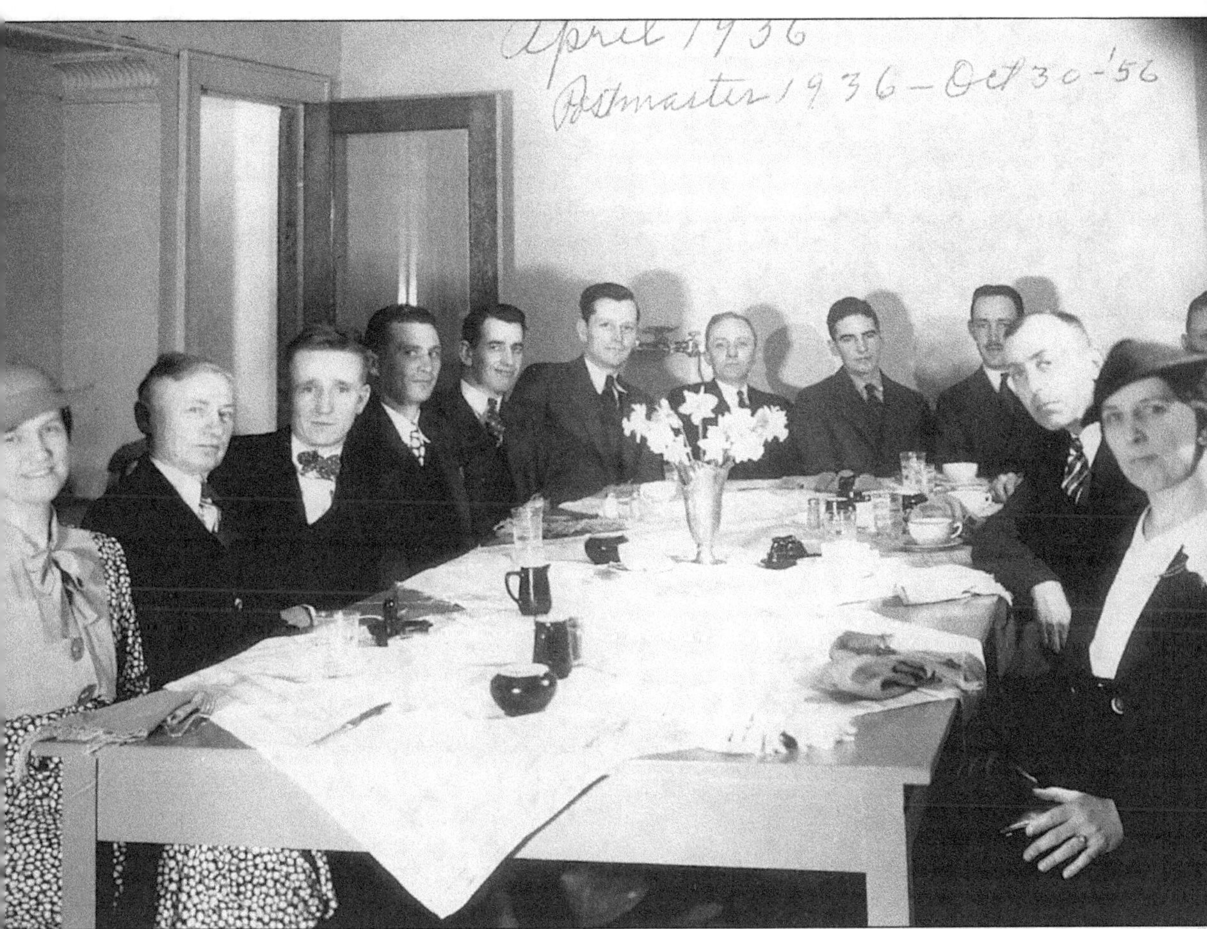

Dinner is served at the Grand Hotel in April 1936 to celebrate the appointment of Mrs. Anna Moore as postmaster of the Hazard Post Office. Diners are Mrs. Moore, Tom Moore, Jonah Daniel, Don Beams, Charles Nicholson, Dewey Daniel (former postmaster), E.B. Lovern (assistant postmaster), Warren ?, Roscoe Davis, Goodloe Combs, Edith Tatum, and Frank Baker.

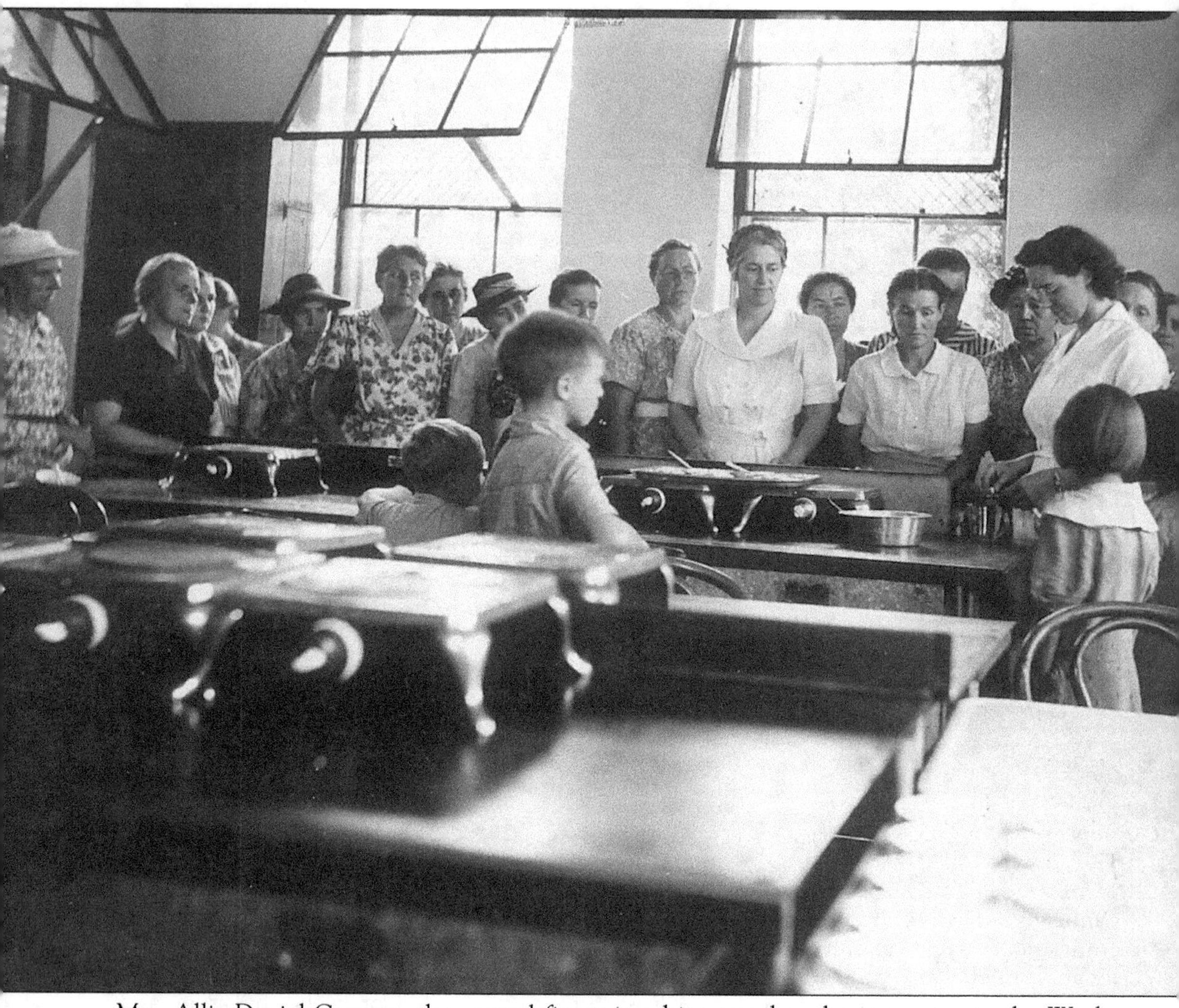

Mrs. Allie Daniel Gorman, the central figure in white, watches the instructor in the Works Progress Administration (WPA) cooking class at Hazard High School in 1940. The students learned nutrition and efficient housekeeping methods.

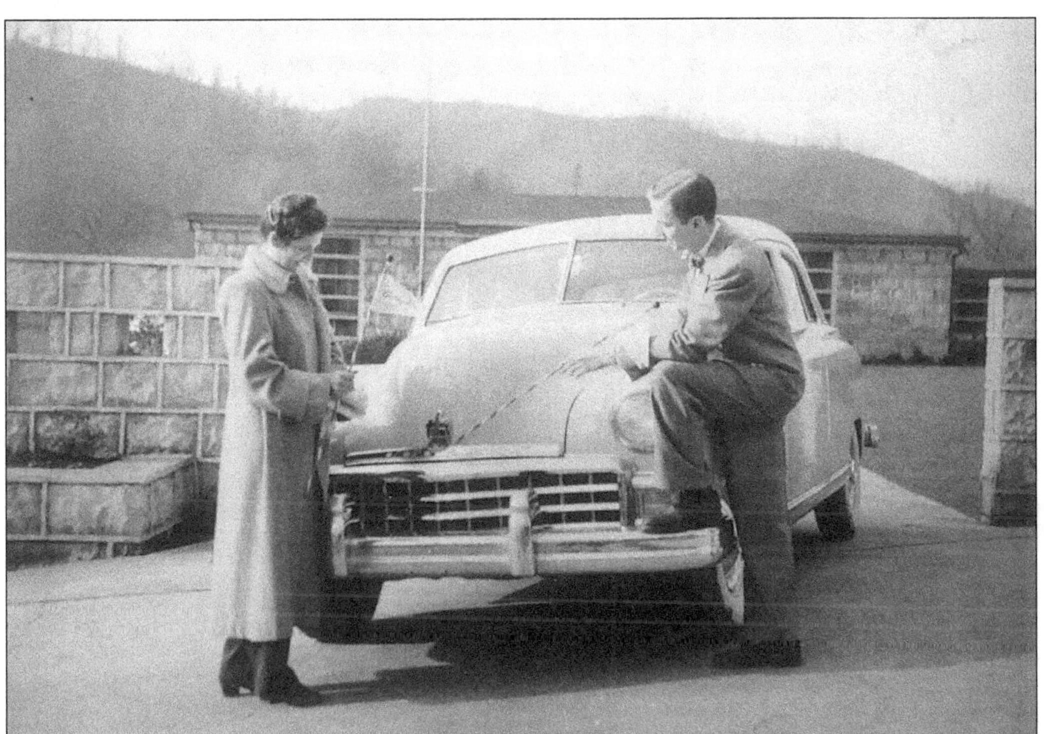

Betsy Francis came from California to visit Hazard. Her wish, to come to Hazard and see her parents, was granted by winning the radio game show "Queen for a Day." While in Hazard she drove a 1949 Frazier lent to her by the local Kaiser-Frazier car dealership. She is being interviewed by Hugh Dunbar of WKIC radio.

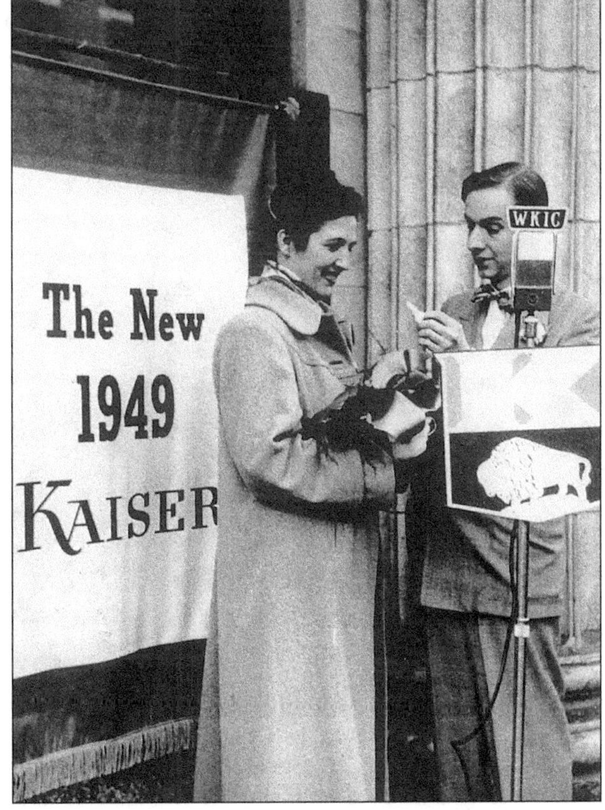

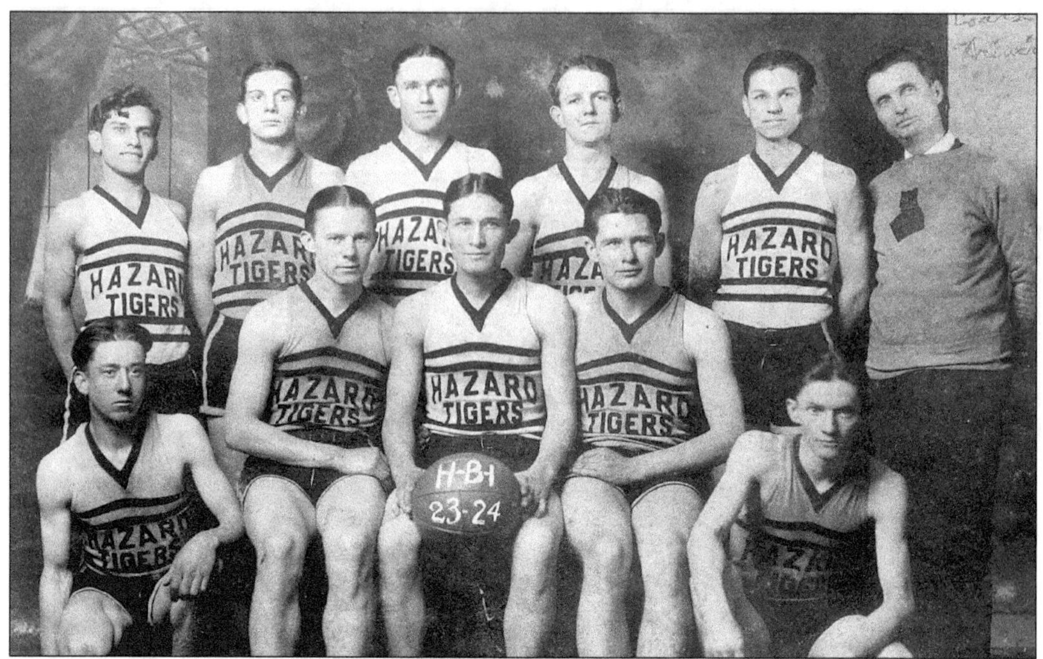

It is said basketball players from the mountains excel because they learn to control the basketball so they won't have to chase it down the hill. The following members of the 1923–1924 Hazard Baptist Institute Tigers are shown here from left to right: (front row) Billy Matthews, Mason Knuckles, Keiffer Strickland, Troy Baker, and Fred Burnett; (back row) unknown, Kelly Deaton, Sam Counts, ? Giles, Harvey Lusk, and Mr. Strickland.

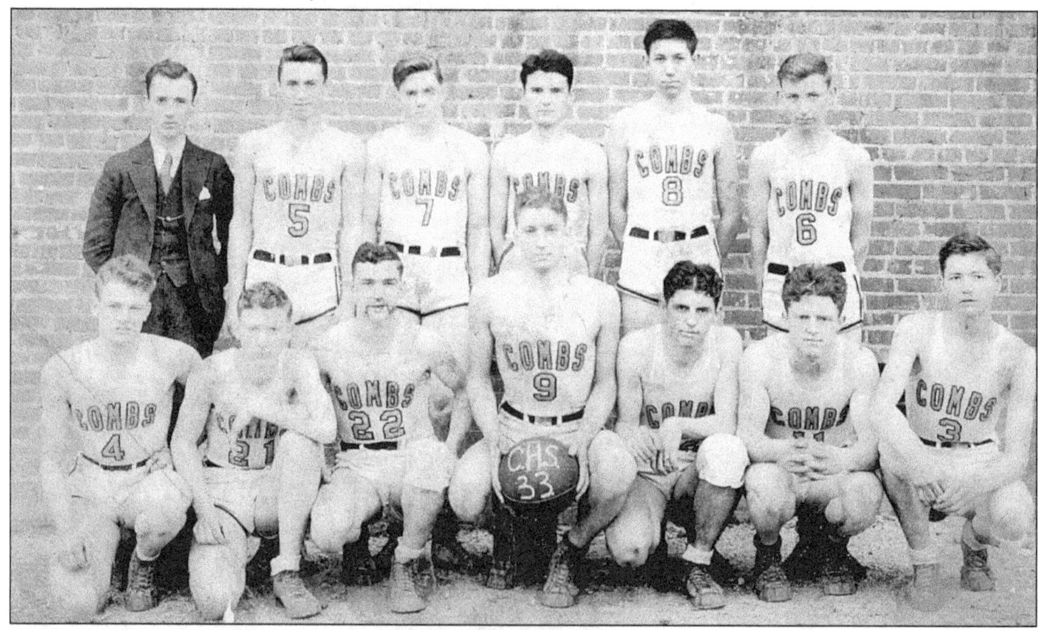

The 1933 basketball team of Combs High School included the following, from left to right: (front row) Clarence Woods, Doyle Leveridge, Pete Shicley (sic), Boyd Cecil, Buell Colwell, Red Wilson, and Gene Combs; (back row) Coach Adrian Ritchie, Clayton Smith, Ishmael Fields, John Goins, Noah Sellers, and Loyal Leveridge.

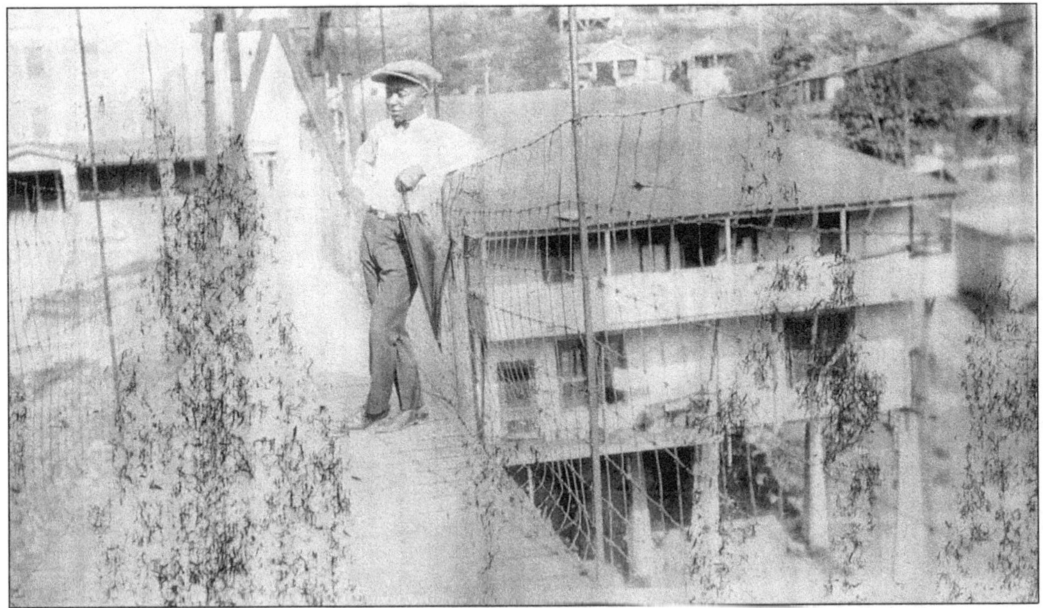

Ma Hibler hired Jess Richardson to come to Hazard as an employee in her hotel. In later years, he became a chef in great demand for social events in Hazard. Here he is pictured standing on the foot bridge, built in the early 1920s, which crossed to the railroad yards. The building on the left is the YMCA. On the right is Hyden Brewer's Store.

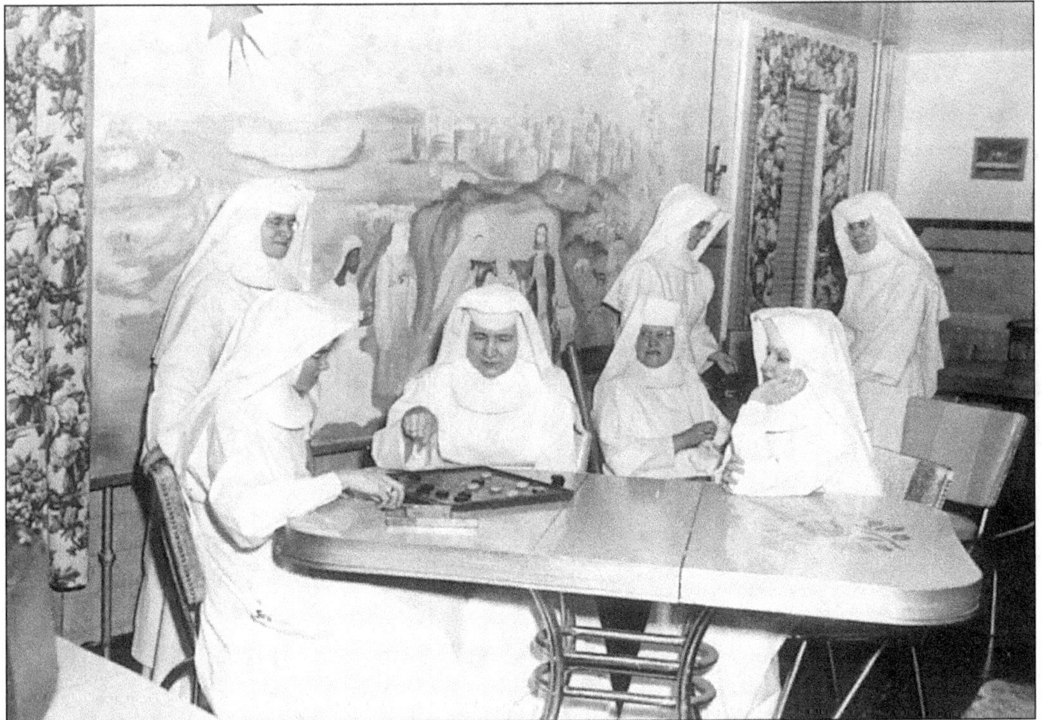

Sister Gabriel, standing on the left, began as the administrator of the Mount Mary Hospital in 1946. She left Hazard in 1963 to go to St. Henry High School in Erlanger, to be a teacher of Latin. This picture was taken in the recreation room of the hospital.

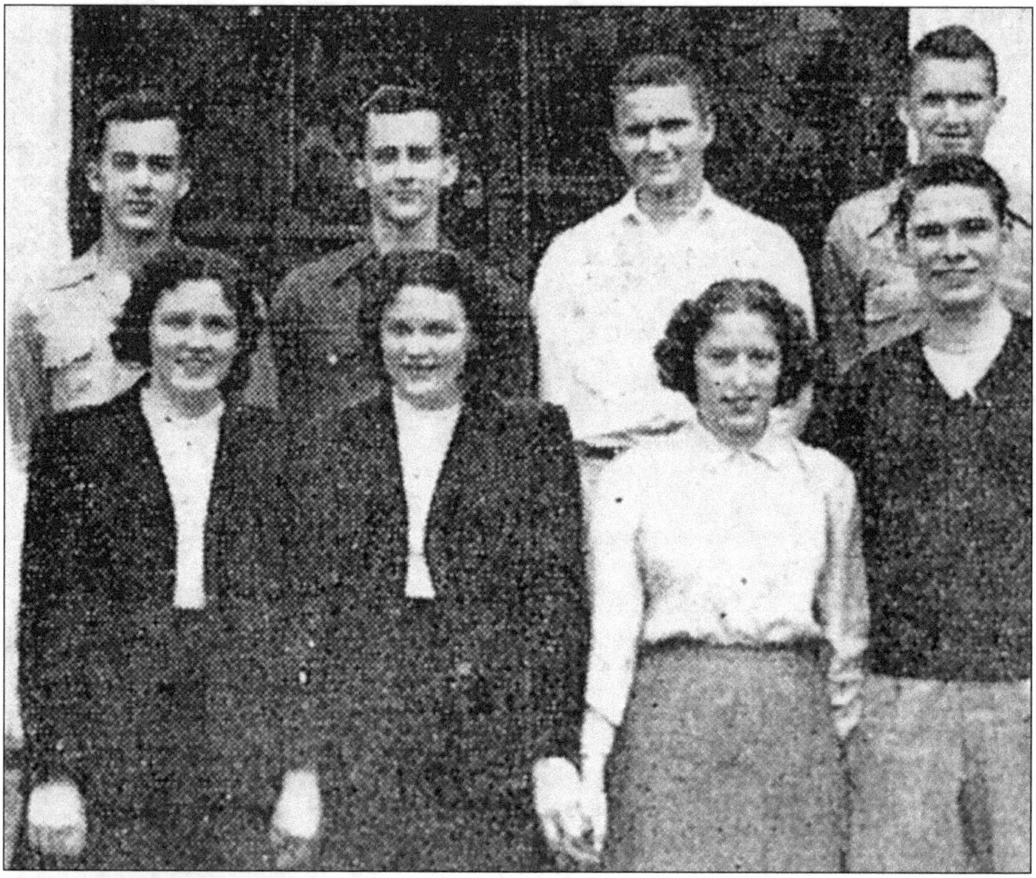

Four sets of twins graduated from Hazard High School in 1949. They are as follows, from left to right: (front row) Lorene and Colleen Branson, and Margaret and Joe Pat Gorman; (back row) George and John Green, and Bill and Ben Roll.

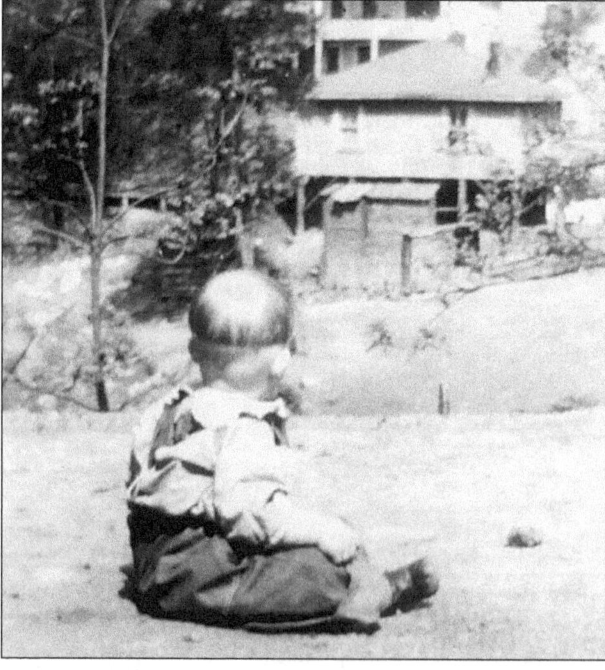

This little boy got his haircut around 1920. Today, boys still request this style from their barbers.

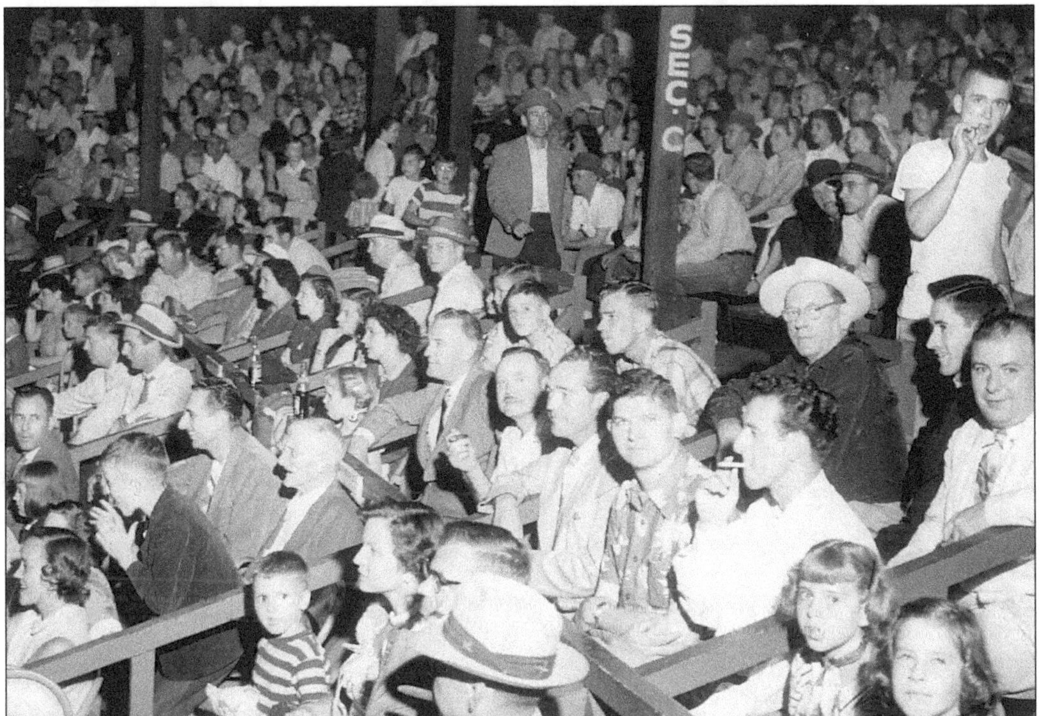

Baseball fans at Bomber Park in Wabaco cheer their heroes, the Hazard Bombers of the Mountain States League. Max Smith, with mustache, was the owner. Father Kraft, in white wide-brimmed hat, and Father Reimondo, priests at the Mother of Good Counsel Catholic Church, sit behind Mac Smith on the right. Vernon, Nell, and C.V. Cooper are in the foreground. The young girls in the lower right-hand corner looking at the camera are Linda Caudill and Sydney Hancock.

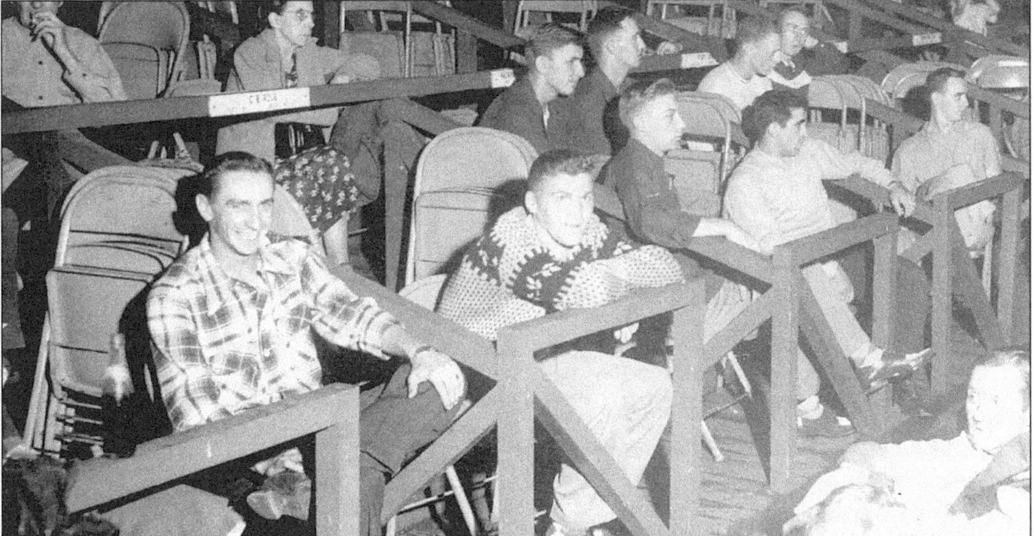

The Bomber's claim to fame was pitcher Johnny Podres. Podres went on to play with the Brooklyn Dodgers. He is shown here in the Bomber Park bleachers looking toward the field, third from the left.

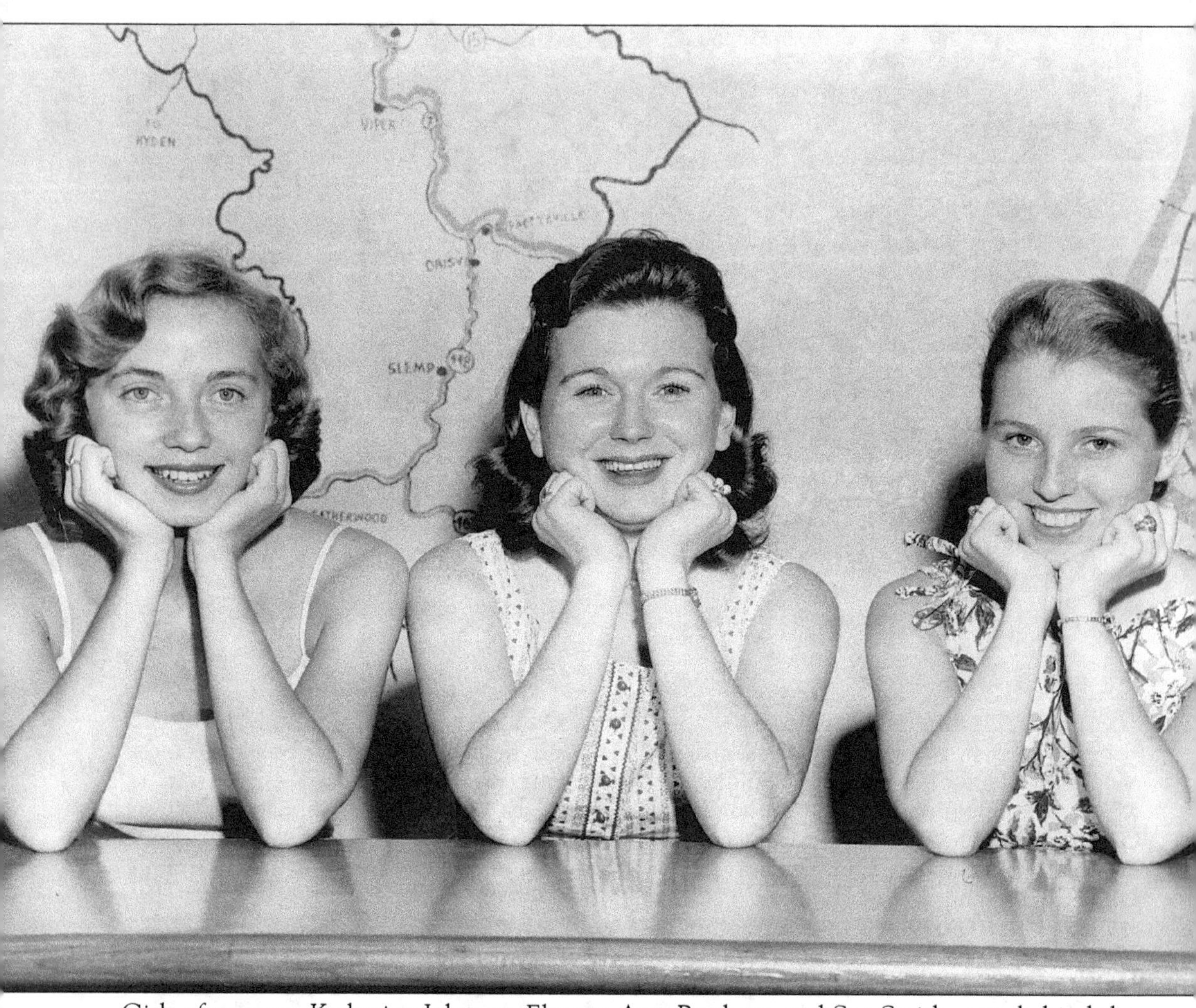

Girls of summer, Katherine Johnson, Eleanor Ann Brashear, and Sue Smith, pose behind the counter inside the PCDA building and Welcome Center on the corner of the "Old" By-Pass and Davis Street, *c.* 1955. The current orientation is now Memorial Drive and Lovern Street.

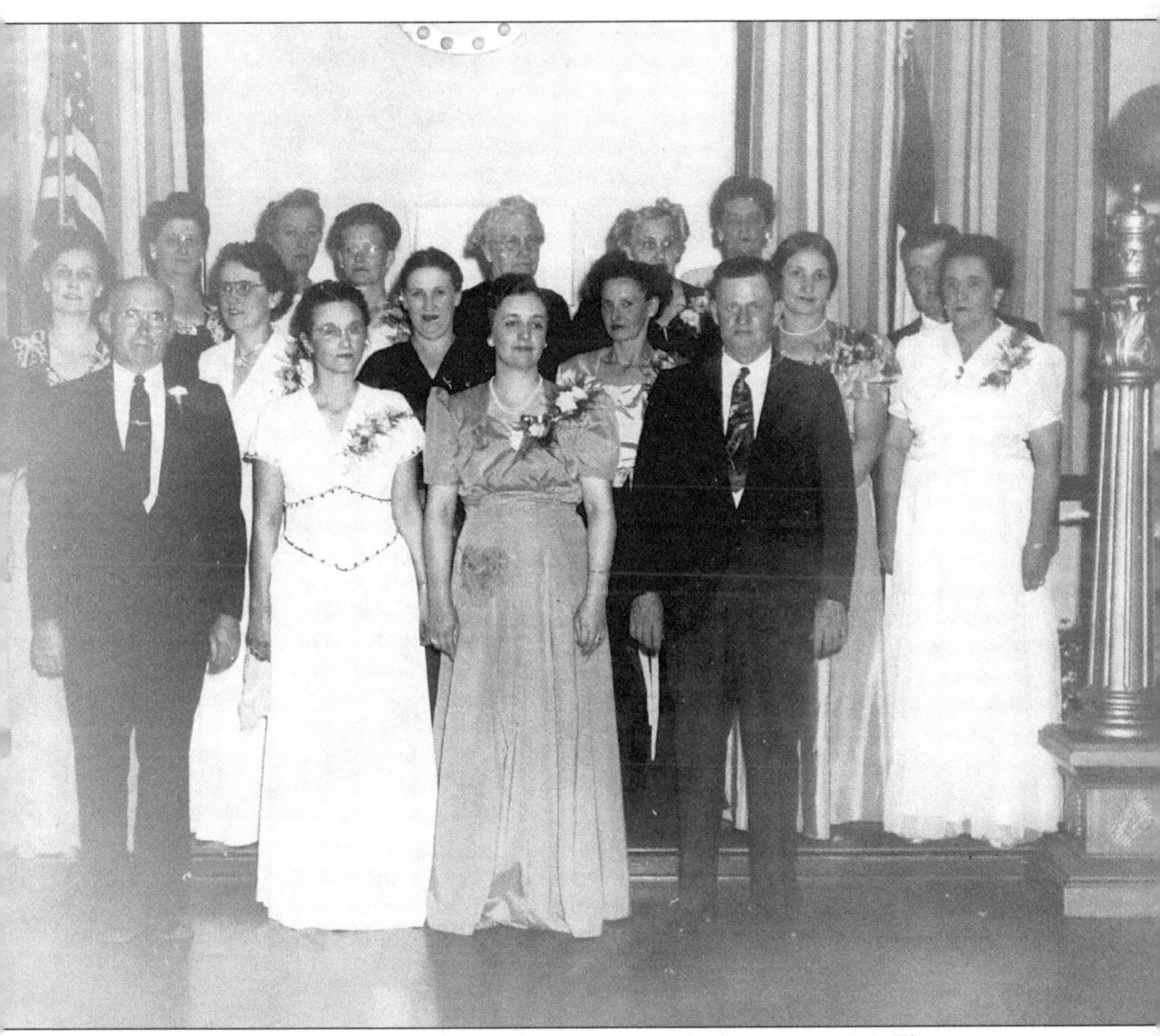

The Eastern Star is a woman's organization associated with the Freemasons. They promote patriotism, try to be honest in all things, and swear to help each other. The members in the 1940 group are as follows, from left to right: (front row) Bill Gay, Elma Gay, Mabel Smith, Bill Campbell, and Margaret Mitchell; (middle row) Minnie Campbell, Ila Caton, Pearl Combs, unknown, Nora Cornett, and Ernest Minnich; (back row) Pearl Brown, Alta Bonta, Cinda Feltner, Virgie Alexander, Cecile Bernard, and Flora Norman.

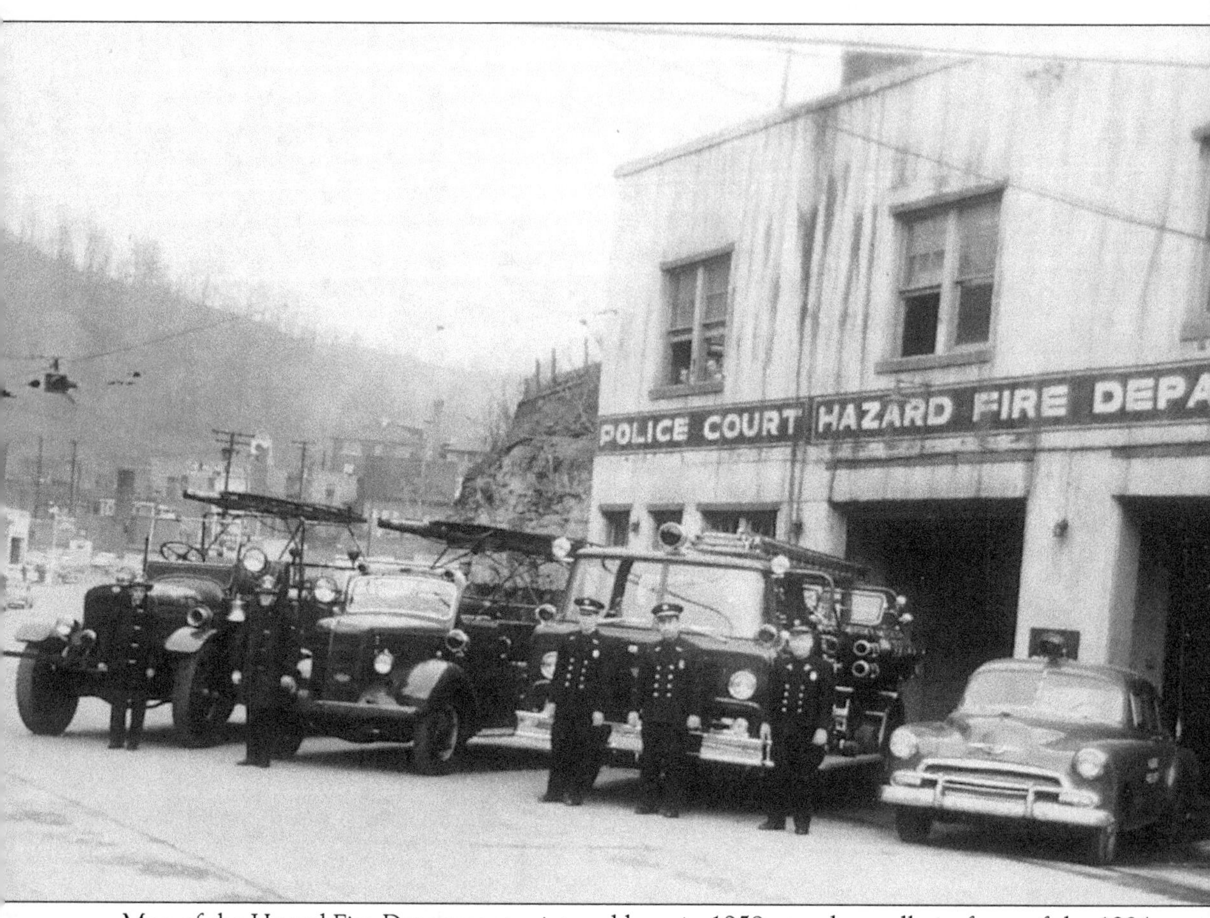

Men of the Hazard Fire Department, pictured here in 1958, stand proudly in front of the 1924 Seagrave Pumper, the 1945 Mack Pumper, the 1957 Ford Pumper, and the fire chief's car, a 1951 Chevrolet. The firefighters are Eugene Grey, Edgar "Bucky" Reynolds, unknown, George Peters, and Lawrence "Shorty" Sizemore.

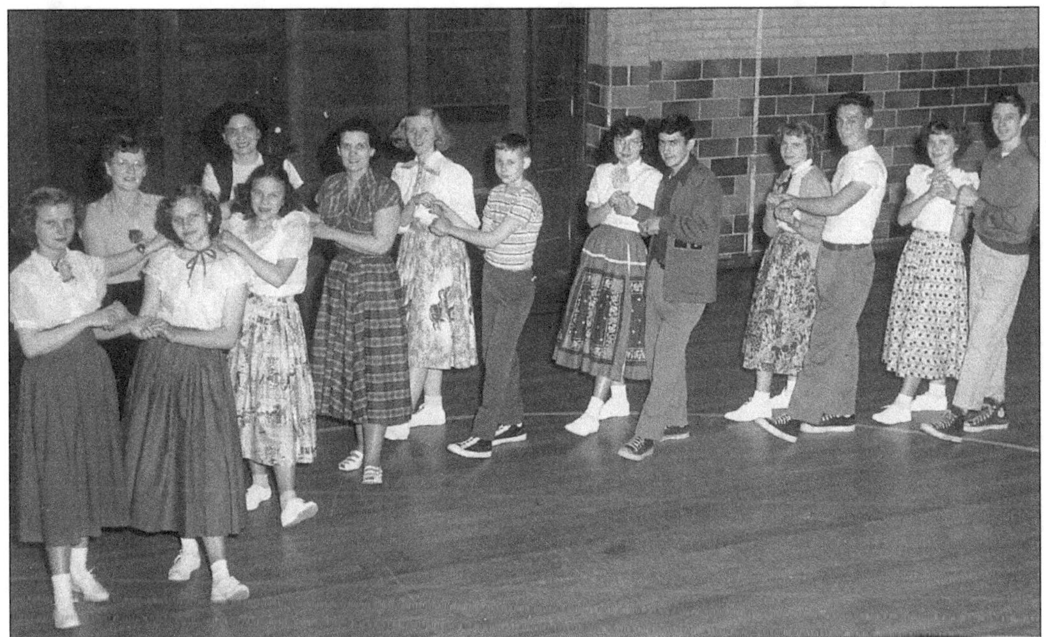

In 1949, the Lothair School Folk Dancing Club went to the Berea Folk Dance Festival. They appeared with 250 representatives, from seven states. The dancers are Mary Margaret Collins, Delores Combs, Betty Nichols, Patricia Jewell, Cynthia Ellen Bowling, Roberta Stidham, Jane Nichols, Jimmy Hall, Mary Katherine Cole, Dickie Campbell, Patsy Sue Hall, Jimmy Sinor, Ada Pearl Jones, and Delmar Combs.

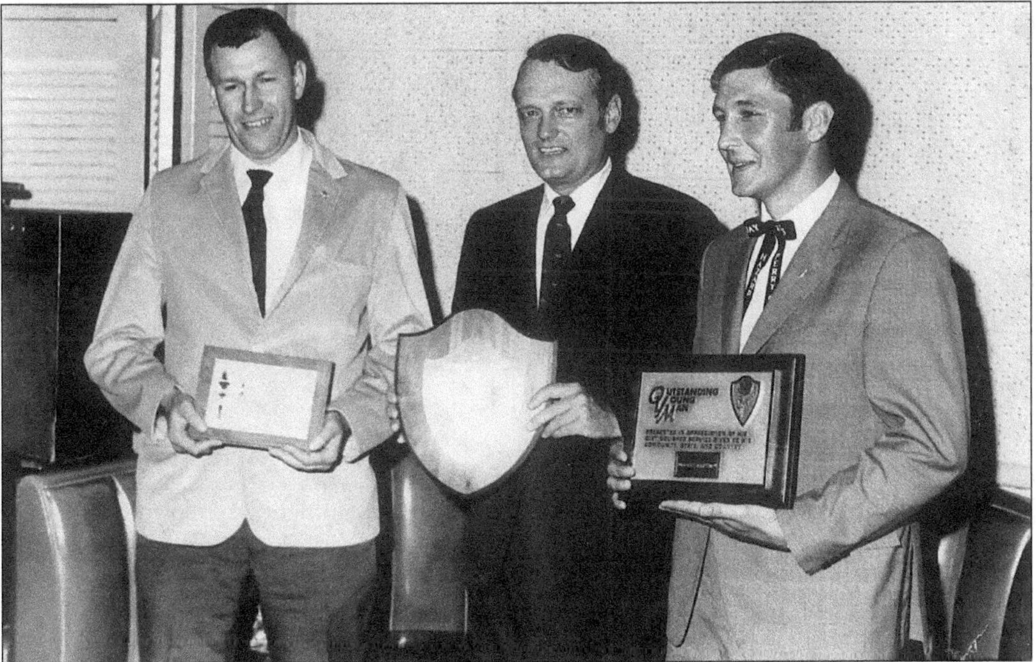

At Civic Night, April 23, 1970, local civic organizations recognized Willard Ashworth, Bill Morton, and Danny Martin for their community work. The following year women were honored at Civic Night for the first time. The first Civic Night was held in 1953.

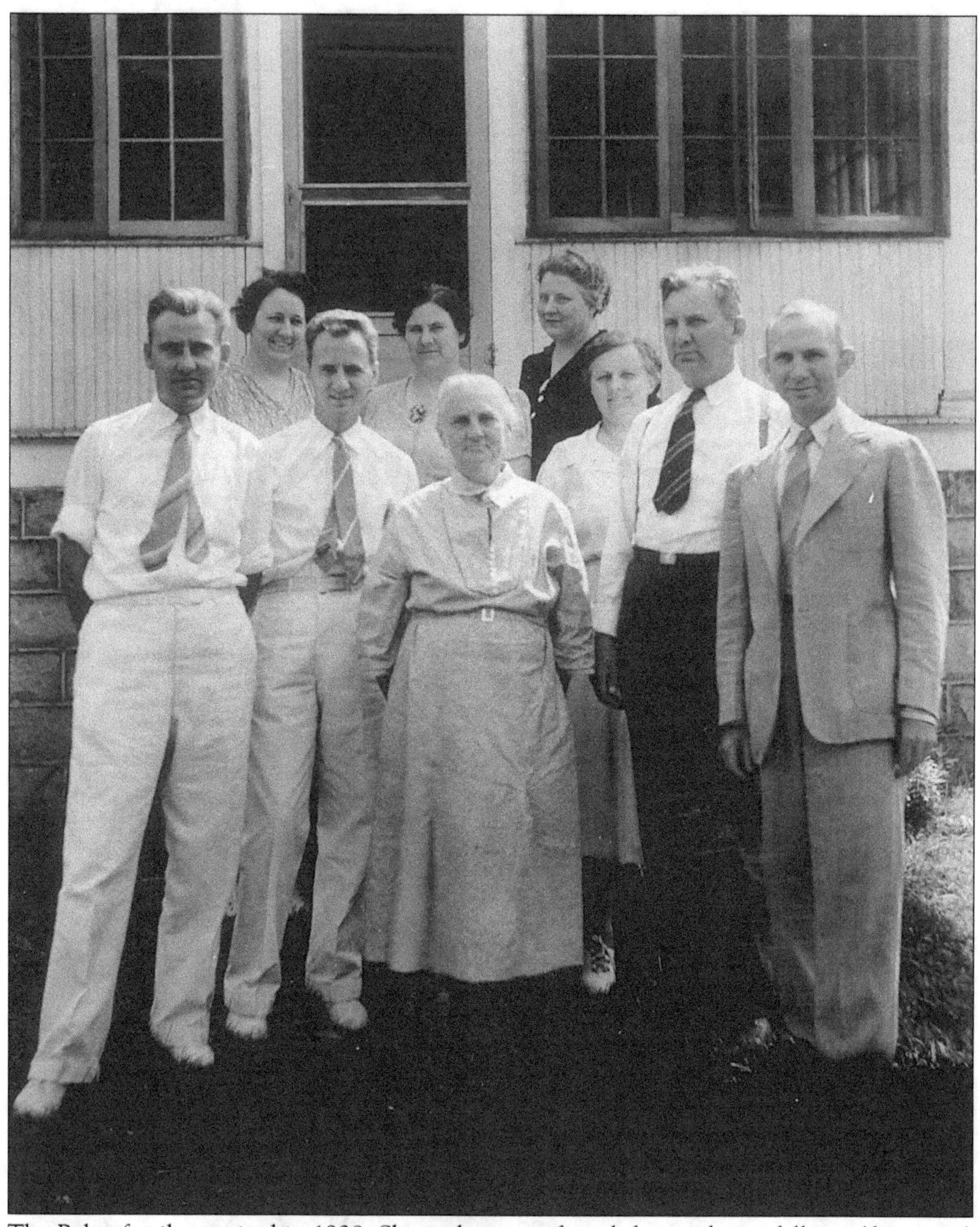

The Baker family reunited in 1938. Shown here are, from left to right, as follows: (front row) Ted, Prent, Kate DeHart, Barney, and Floyd; (back row) Bell, Mary, Lize, and Clydia.

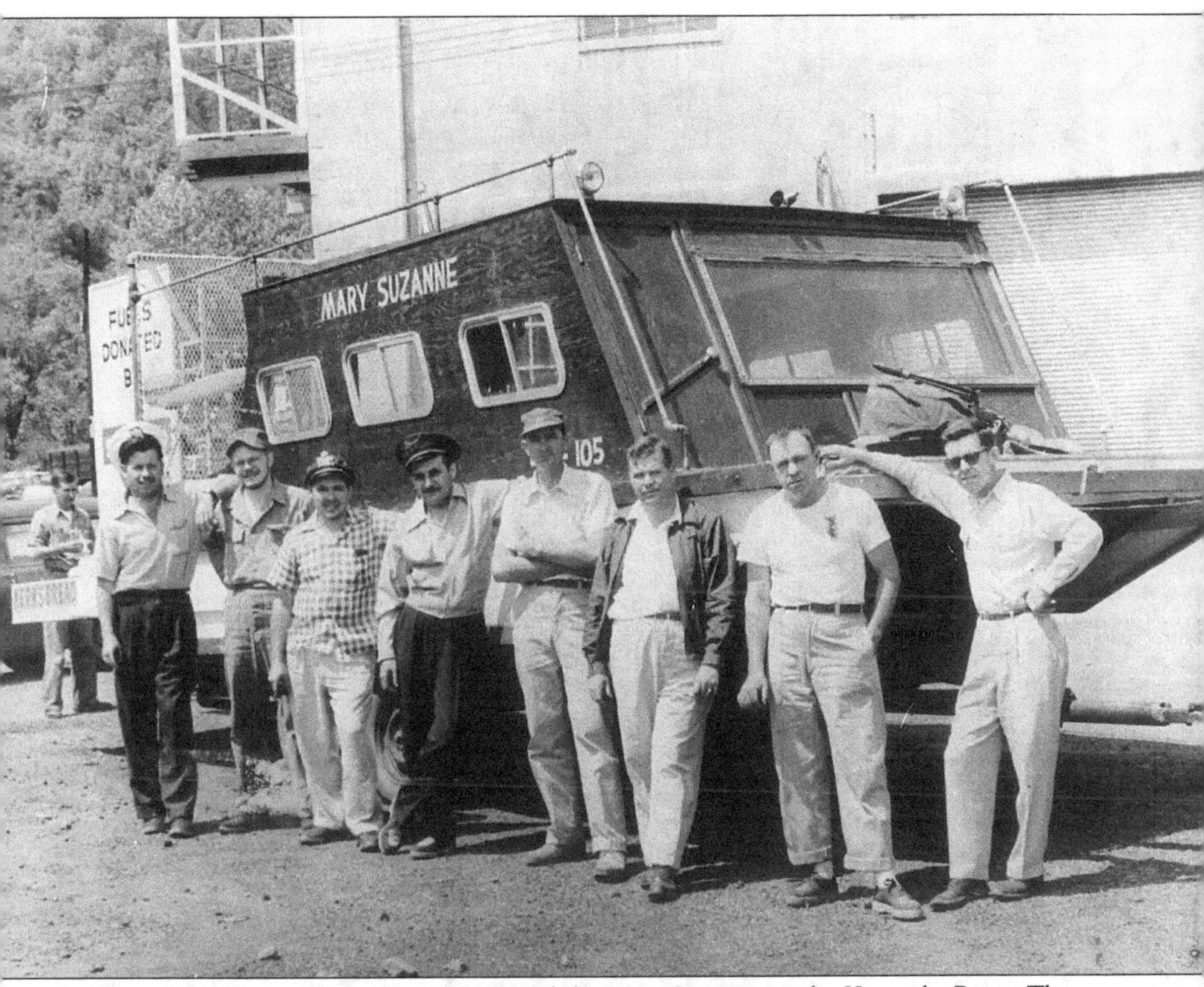

In the early 1950s, nine men bravely manned the *Mary Suzanne* on the Kentucky River. They traveled from Hazard to Frankfort to call attention to the need for flood control. They were Bill Gorman, Billy Sparks, Charlie May, George Kawaja, Bob Marcum, Bernard Faulkner, Jack Allen, and Joe Goodlett. Rip Stevens is not pictured. Bill Gorman made this river trip on three different occasions.

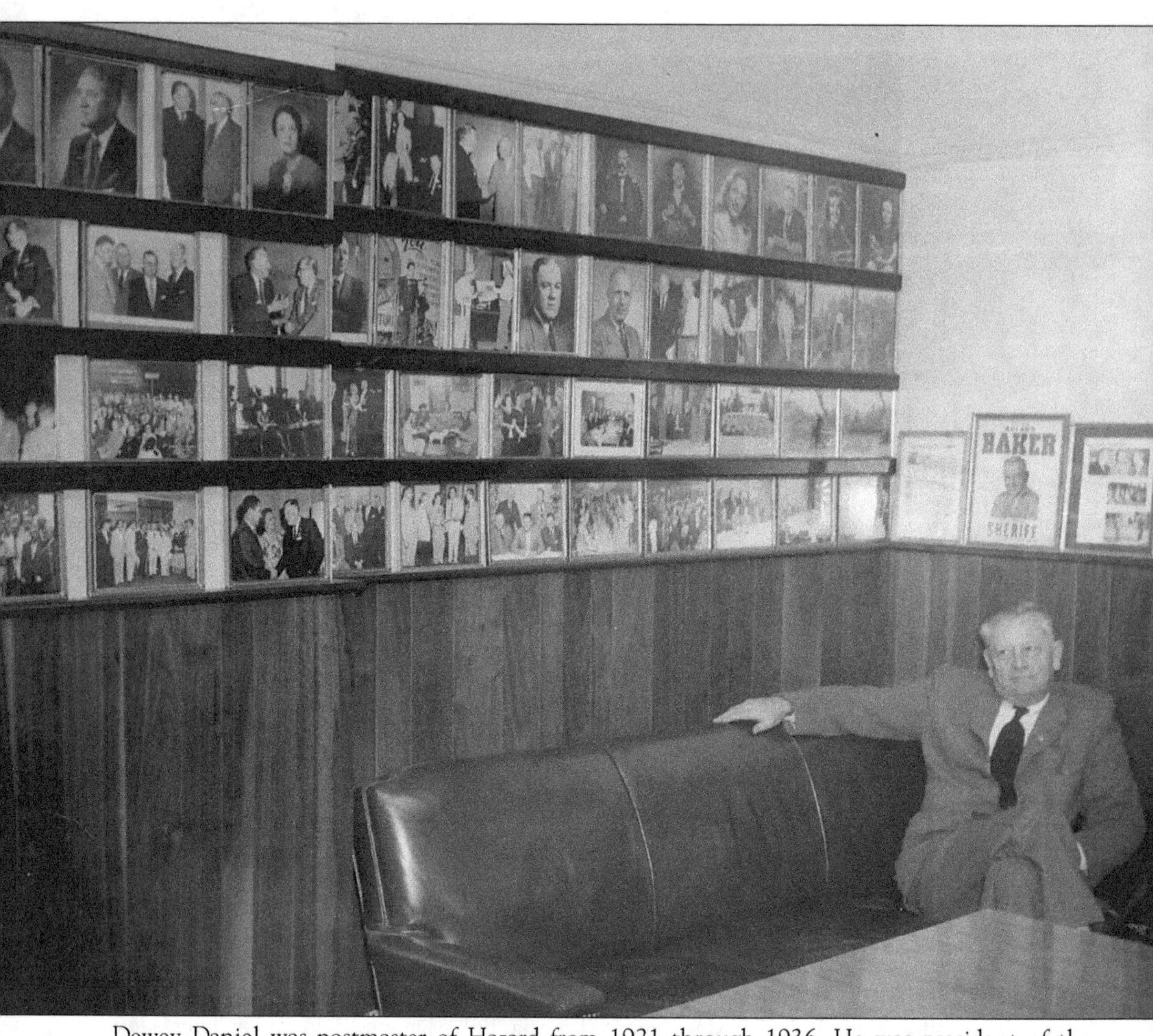

Dewey Daniel was postmaster of Hazard from 1921 through 1936. He was president of the Peoples Bank in the 1950s. Here he sits in his office at the bank next to a gallery wall covered with pictures he collected. Daniel was well known throughout Kentucky for his participation in the Republican Party. He was the chairman of the Republican State Central Committee from 1954 to 1959. He was an officer of the Hazard and the Kentucky Chambers of Commerce.

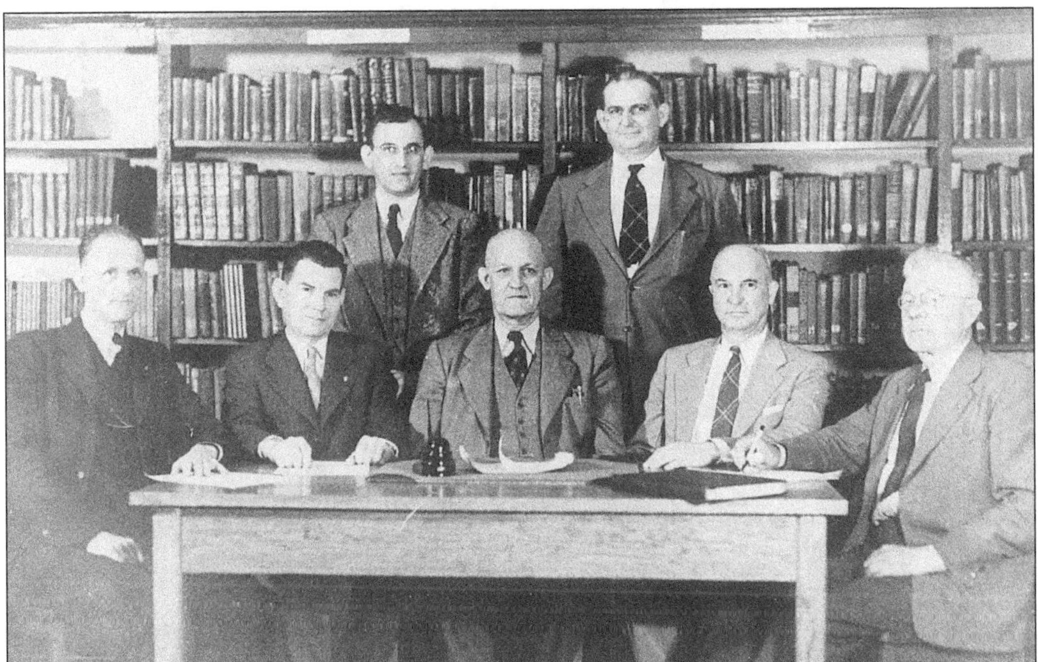

Members of the 1946 Hazard Board of Education sit for photographer Hal Cooner in the library of Hazard High School. Board members were from left to right, as follows: (front) Clyde Leveridge, J.C. Eversole, Dr. R.L. Collins, W.W. Reeves, and E.C. Wooton; (back) Roy Eversole and "Rube" Gordon.

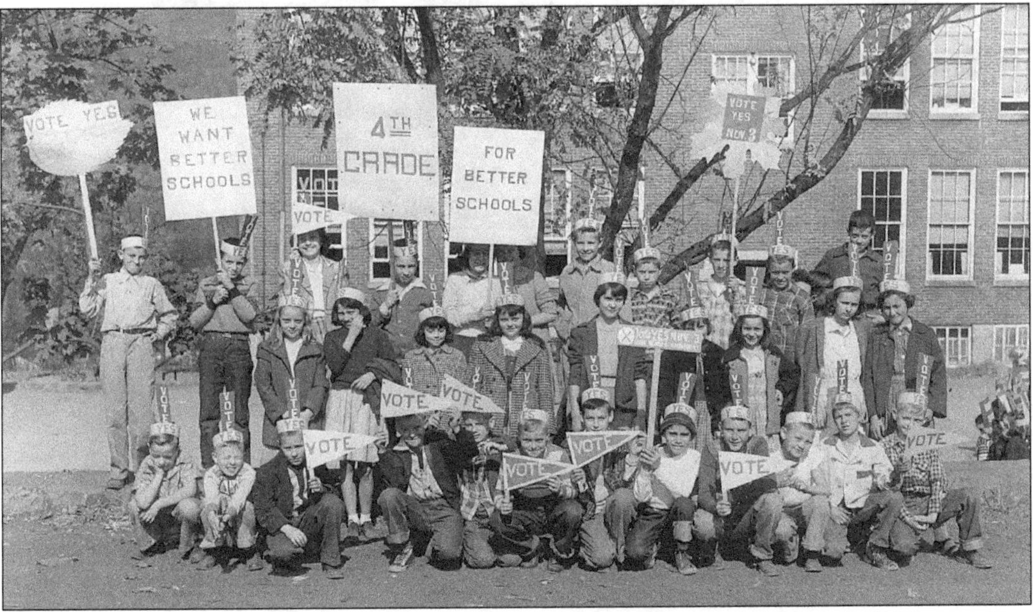

Schools throughout Kentucky joined the minimum foundation campaign in 1953 to reduce class sizes. Classrooms had as many as 50 children crowded together. Some of the children in this picture behind Lothair Elementary School include Linda Cuddy, Michael Flanery, Donnie Collins, Bobby C. Riley, Johnny Franks, Tommy Arimes, Ava Pate, James Tucker, Bonnie Tucker, Betty Patterson, and Michael Sammons.

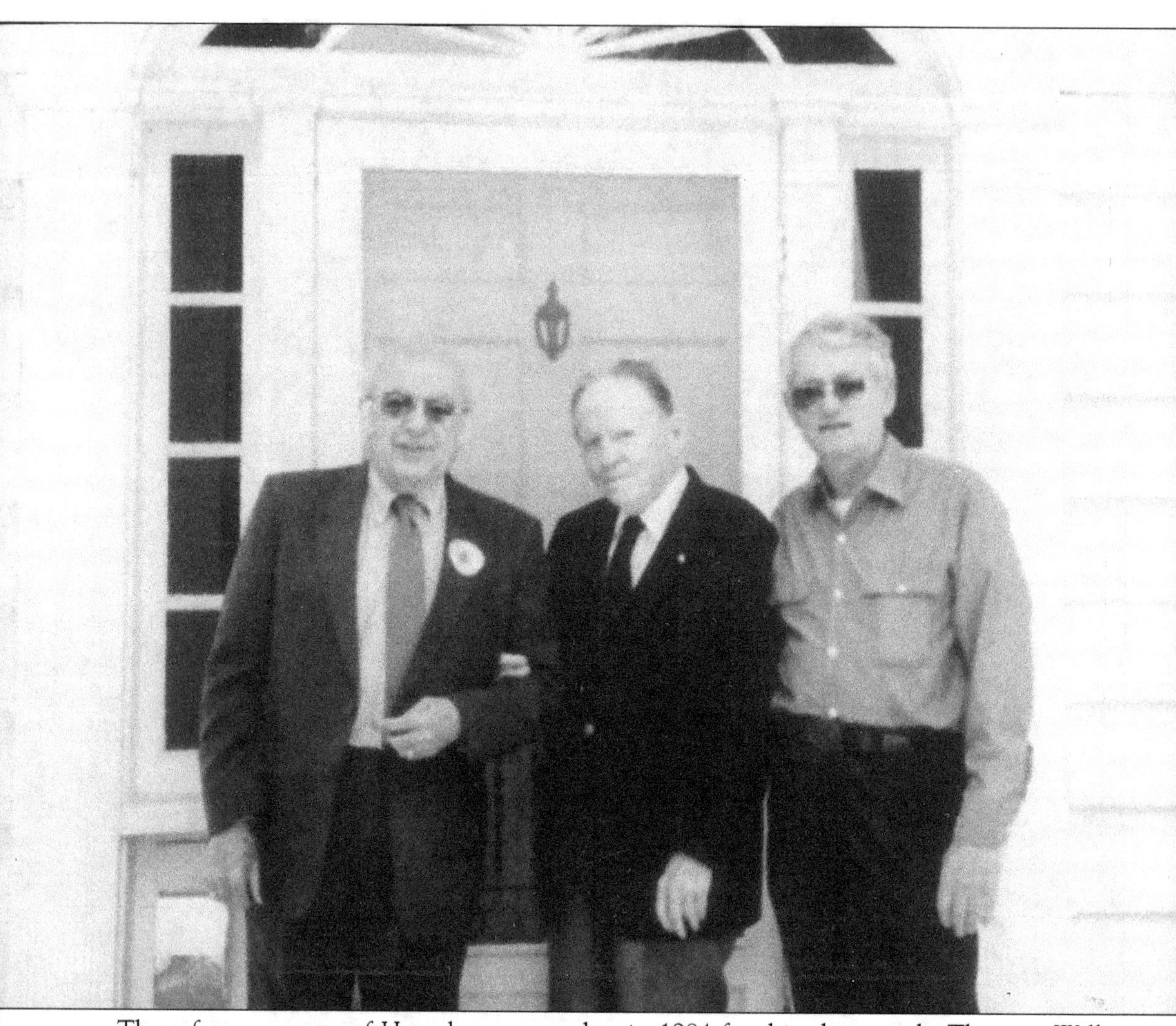

Three former mayors of Hazard came together in 1984 for this photograph. They are Willie Dawahare, mayor from 1962 through 1969, M.K. "Blondie" Eblen, mayor from 1934 to 1935 and 1950 to 1953, and Bill Morton, mayor from 1970 through 1977.

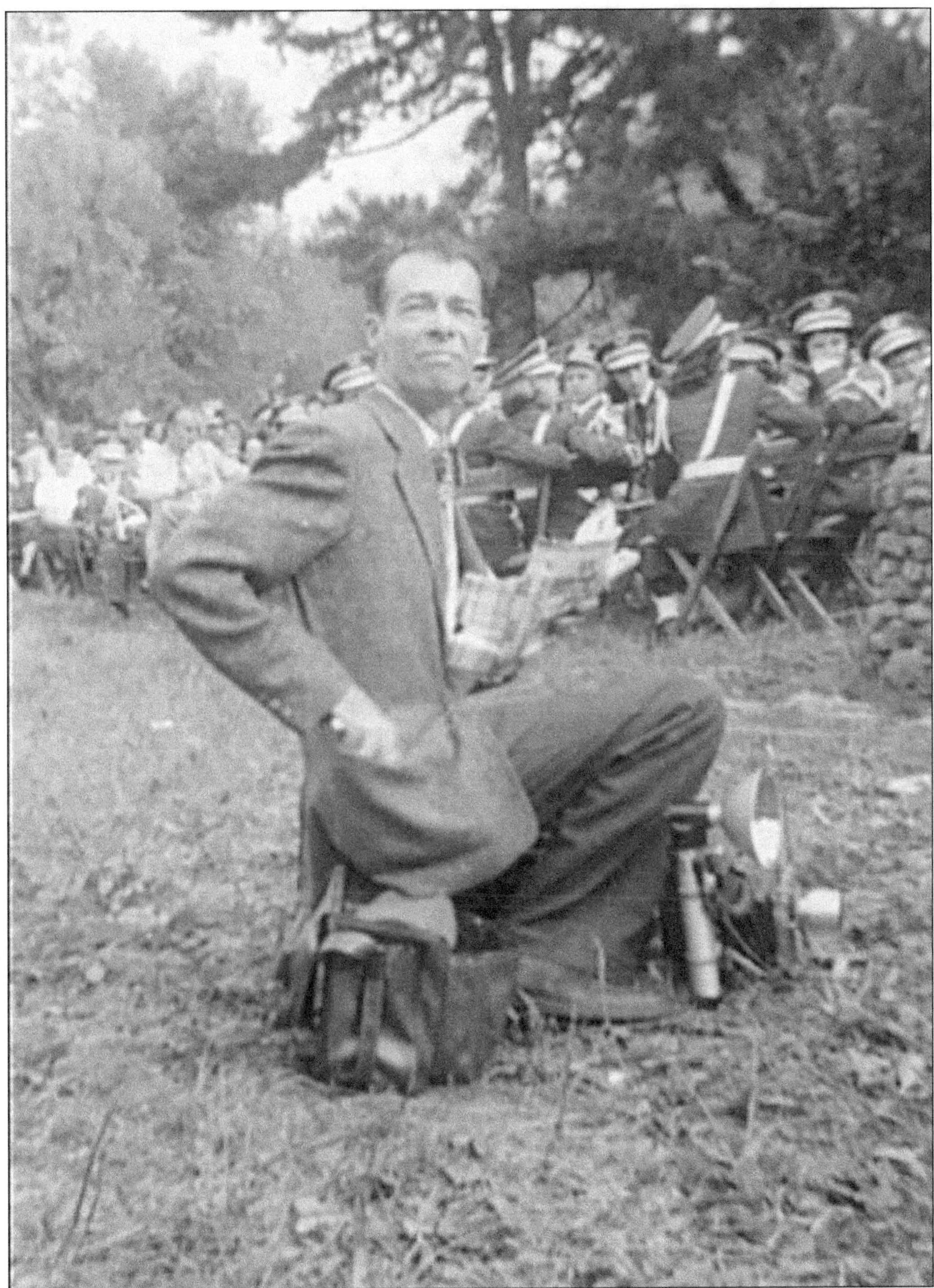

Hal Cooner prepares to take photographs of dignitaries at the Buckhorn Dam ground breaking. This rare photograph, taken by W.R. Hall, captures the man who took thousands of photos around Hazard and Perry County from 1945 to 1965.

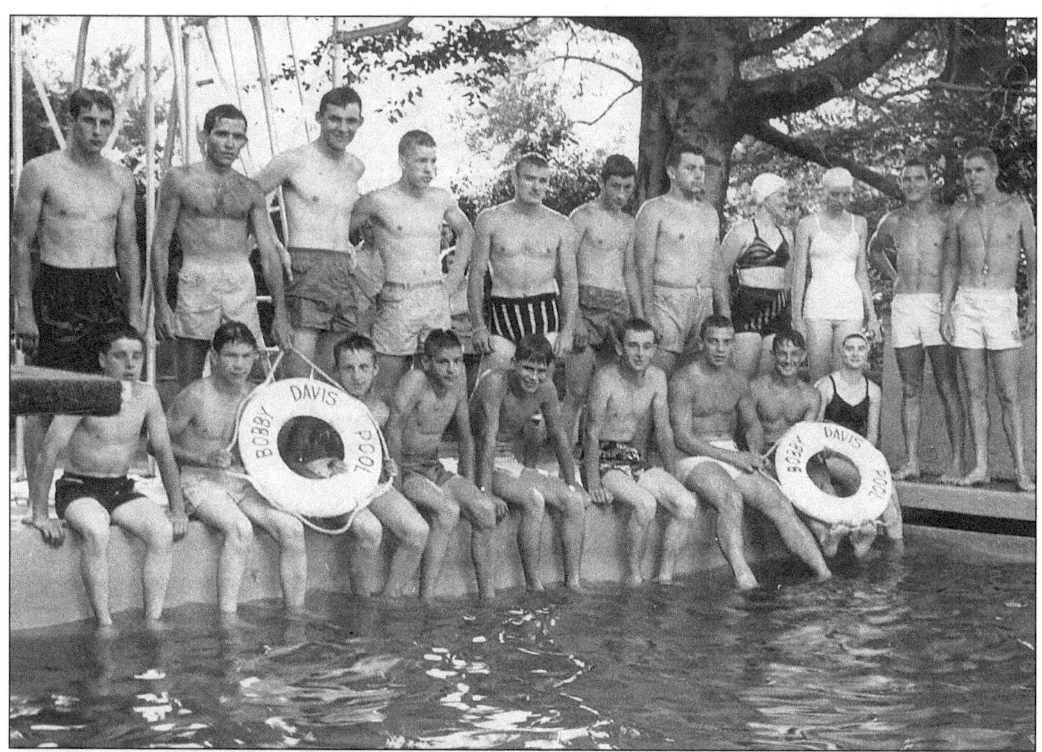

The Red Cross conducted Lifesaving Classes at the Bobby Davis Pool. This group in 1948 consisted of the following, from left to right: (front) Roland Combs, unidentified, Buddy Beetles, Sonny Gumm, John E. Bowling, Dickie Eversole, Paul Townes, unidentified, and Lillian Seamon; (back) Charles Luttrell, Ray Henry, Walter Ward, Kenny Gilbert, Arnold Gene Feltner, John "Patch" Brewer, Tom Turk, Janet Gazay, Betty Carson, Jack Gazay, and Bill Davis.

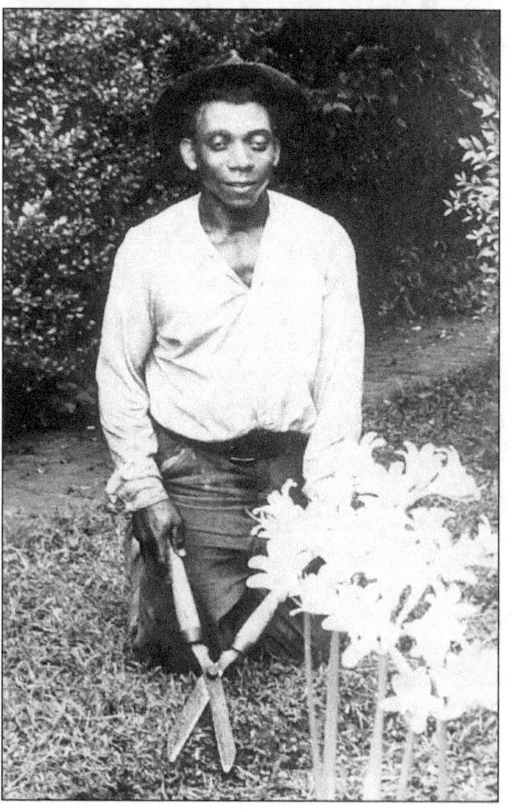

Bill Adams cared for the beautiful gardens in Bobby Davis Park. The best exhibition of his talents was the rose garden behind the library, where he tended exquisite and rare varieties of roses that drew thousands of visitors from miles around.

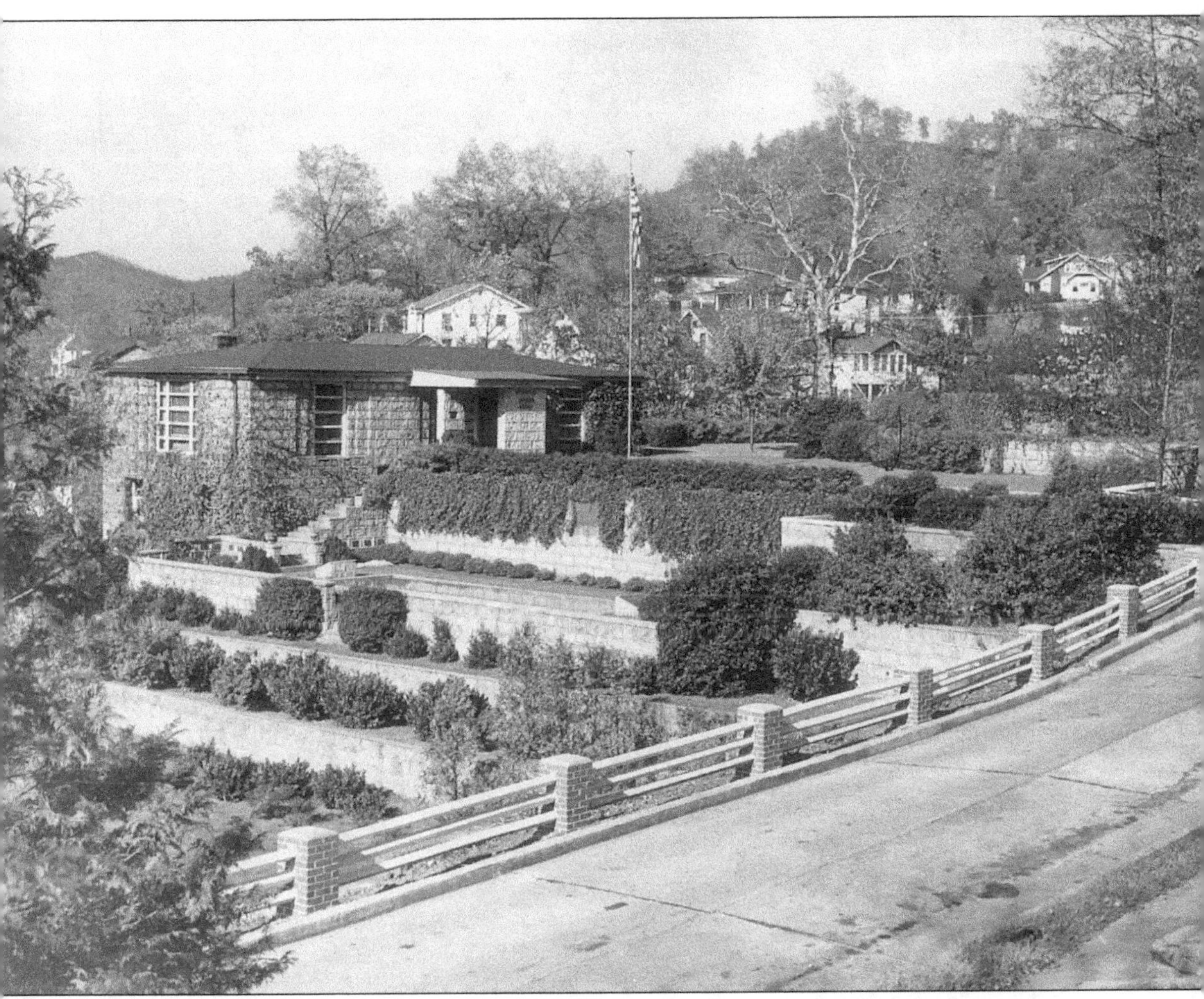

The seed of inspiration for building the Bobby Davis Memorial Park was planted soon after the death of Bobby Davis, in Europe, on July 13, 1945. He died in a train wreck on the first leg of his journey back to the United States. Bobby's father, Lawrence O. Davis, landscaped 4 acres of mountainside in the center of Hazard. He wished to commemorate his son and the other Perry County casualties of World War II. The sandstone building in the picture housed the Bobby Davis Memorial Library, which had a capacity of 22,000 books. The park, with its library, gardens, swimming pool, and picnic area, was the activity center of the town and county all during the 1950s. Its unfortunate decline began in the early 1960s. Today, the park is again an event center of Hazard. The Bobby Davis Museum is in the library building.

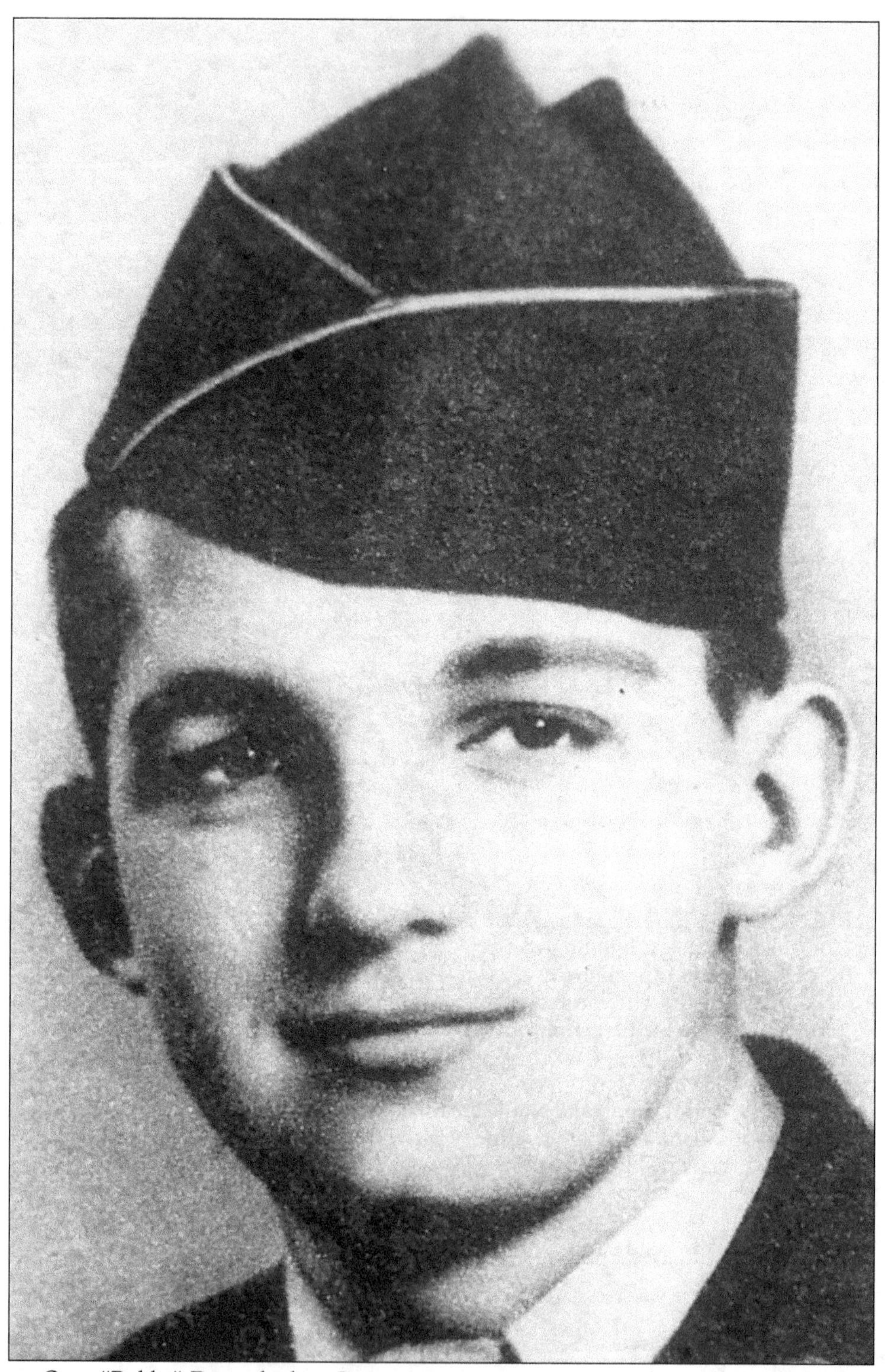

Robert Oren "Bobby" Davis died in Germany in a tragic train wreck two days before his 20th birthday. He was loved and admired by everyone who knew him.

www.ingramcontent.com/pod-product-compliance
Lightning Source LLC
LaVergne TN
LVHW081543100826
845153LV00004B/298

* 9 7 8 1 5 3 1 6 0 3 7 0 0 *